My Life as a Radical
Jewish Woman

THE MODERN JEWISH EXPERIENCE

Paula Hyman and Deborah Dash Moore, *editors*

My Life as a Radical Jewish Woman

Memoirs of a Zionist Feminist in Poland

PUAH RAKOVSKY

Edited and with an introduction by Paula E. Hyman
Translated from the Yiddish by Barbara Harshav with Paula E. Hyman

INDIANA UNIVERSITY PRESS
Bloomington and Indianapolis

Publication of this book is made possible in part with the assistance of a Challenge Grant from the National Endowment for the Humanities, a federal agency that supports research, education, and public programming in the humanities.

This book is a publication of

Indiana University Press

601 North Morton Street

Bloomington, IN 47404-3797 USA

http://iupress.indiana.edu

Telephone orders   800-842-6796

Fax orders   812-855-7931

E-mail orders   iuporder@indiana.edu

© 2002 by Paula E. Hyman

The paper used in this publication meets the minimum requirements of American National Standard for Information Sciences — Permanence of Paper for Printed Library Materials, ANSI Z39.48-1984.

Manufactured in the United States of America

Library of Congress Cataloging-in-Publication Data

Rakovska, Puʻah, 1865–1955.

[Zikhroynes fun a Yidisher revolutsyonerin. English]

My life as a radical Jewish woman : memoirs of a Zionist feminist in Poland/ Puah Rakovsky ; edited and with an introduction by Paula E. Hyman ; translated from the Yiddish by Barbara Harshav with Paula E. Hyman.

p. cm. — (Modern Jewish Experience)

ISBN 0-253-34042-X (cloth : alk. paper)

1. Rakovska, Puʻah, 1865–1955. 2. Jews — Poland — Białystok — Biography. 3. Jewish women — Poland — Białystok — Biography. 4. Zionists — Poland Białystok — Biography. I. Hyman, Paula, date   II. Title.   III. Modern Jewish experience (Bloomington, Ind.)

DS135.P63 R36713 2002

320.54′095694′092 — dc21

2001003088

1   2   3   4   5   07   06   05   04   03   02

Frontispiece: Puah Rakovsky, age 18

I will make bold to claim that, to some extent, my own personal revolution might
be an interesting manifestation of a bygone age in Jewish life. As the Bible
says, "To every thing there is a season, and a time to every purpose." [1]
What impelled me to agree to the demand of my friends,
especially my esteemed friend Rachel Katznelson, [2]
[that I write my memoirs] is the hope that
my memoirs might be instructive for
others, for the younger
generation of
Jewish women.

1. Ecclesiastes 3:1
2. (1888–1975) A leader of the working women's movement in the Land of Israel, a Hebrew writer and the wife of the third president of the State of Israel, Zalman Shazar. She wrote the introduction to Puah Rakovsky's memoirs in both the Hebrew and Yiddish versions.

CONTENTS

FOREWORD

I first came upon the Yiddish memoirs of Puah Rakovsky while I was preparing the lectures that became my book *Gender and Assimilation in Modern Jewish History*. In the course of scholarly research it is rare to find a historical source that is as compelling as a novel. Puah Rakovsky's book of memoirs, *Zikhroynes fun a yidisher revolutsionerin*,[3] was precisely that — the saga of a life filled with trauma, activism, and determination. Women's voices and experience were virtually absent in the standard histories of Jews living in east European Jewish society in the late nineteenth and early twentieth centuries, a period of rapid change and political turmoil. In her memoir Rakovsky not only offered an account of her own life as a woman who was raised in a traditional Jewish home and became a secular Zionist and Jewish educator, but she also reflected on the position of women in her own time.

Eager to incorporate material on Jewish women into my teaching as well as research, I soon decided to bring the book to my students and to a broader English-reading public as well. *My Life as a Radical Jewish Woman* is a complete translation of Rakovsky's Yiddish memoirs. A few references to now obscure individuals have been deleted, the opening paragraph was relocated from the middle of the memoir, and the numerous short chapters in the original were combined. In order to supplement Rakovsky's presentation and understanding of her own life, I incorporated into my introduction as much evidence of her life as I could find. To my delight, she had left her footprints in archival sources and in the pages of pamphlets and newspapers.

Along the way I was assisted by many individuals and institutions, whom I would like to publicly thank. Shortly before her untimely death, Joy Ungerleider, the founder and director of the Dorot Foun-

---

3. Puah Rakovsky, *Zikhroynes fun a yidisher revolutsionerin* [Memoirs of a Revolutionary Jewish Woman] (Buenos Aires: Tsentral-Farband fun Poylisher Yidn in Argentine, 1954). An abbreviated version was published in Hebrew, translated by David Kalai under the title *Lo Nikhnati* [I did not Yield] (Tel Aviv: N. Tversky, 1951).

dation, agreed to finance the translation of the memoir. The subsidy granted by the Dorot Foundation enabled me to engage Barbara Harshav to lend her considerable talents as translator to this project. As usual, my friend and colleague Deborah Dash Moore proved ready to share her ideas and editorial skills. I appreciate the relevant materials from nineteenth-century periodicals that David Assaf brought to my attention and my conversations with Shaul Stampfer, who graciously provided me with a copy of the Hebrew version of Rakovsky's memoir. Yael Olmer kindly allowed me to see the material that she had prepared on Puah Rakovsky and her family tree. At Indiana University Press, Janet Rabinowitch encouraged this project and provided useful suggestions for the shape the book would ultimately take. I would also like to acknowledge the courtesy of the staffs of the YIVO Institute for Jewish Research, the Jewish National and University Library, and the Central Zionist Archive. Finally, I am most grateful to Hemdah Allon, Puah Rakovsky's granddaughter, for sharing her memories of her grandmother with me and for responding thoughtfully to all of my questions.

Paula E. Hyman

A Note on Transliteration

Both Yiddish and Hebrew words appear in transliteration in this book. In general, I have used the transliteration formats employed by the *Encyclopedia Judaica*. Because Puah Rakovsky spoke Yiddish, when a word appears in both languages, I have employed the Yiddish transliteration. In the case of transliteration from Hebrew, I have employed the Ashkenazic pronunciation that Puah herself would have used rather than the Sephardic pronunciation that is currently in use in Israel and has become the international standard. Diacritical marks are not employed in the Hebrew transliterations.

There are some exceptions to this rule. Words that are likely to be recognized by English readers are rendered in their familiar form — i.e., Pesach rather than Peysekh. Names of Zionist political parties that frequently appear in historical literature are transliterated as they generally appear in English — i.e., Mizrachi rather than Mizrahi.

My Life as a Radical
Jewish Woman

The Jewish Pale of Settlement
Late Nineteenth Century

Introduction

Puah Rakovsky was an activist who took full advantage of living in revolutionary times. She was one of the few Jewish women of her generation who assumed a leadership role in the public arenas of education and politics within the Russian-Polish Jewish community. Her memoirs recount a life of engagement in the events of her day. She could envision no other way to live.

Puah was born in 1865 in Poland, which was then in the Russian Empire. As an adolescent and young woman, she witnessed the flourishing of a variety of radical political movements that emerged in the 1870s and gathered strength in the last decade of the nineteenth century and the first decade of the twentieth. These included Russian populism, anti-tsarist radical movements that coalesced as the Russian Social Democratic Workers' Party, Jewish socialism, and Zionism. She herself chose to agitate for Zionism among her fellow Polish Jews. She saw the pogroms of late tsarist Russia, experienced the dislocations created by World War I, and spent some time in the young Soviet Union. Among her many siblings, and later her children, she counted socialists of different stripes, anarchists, Zionists, and Communists.

When Rakovsky styles herself a revolutionary Jewish woman, as she does in the Yiddish title of her memoirs, she chooses her words carefully. With those words she refers not only to her political activities but also to the personal choices that she made as a woman. She was sympathetic not only to the Russian revolutionary movements that were most intense in the years around 1905 and 1917 but also to the Jewish revolutions of the Haskalah (Jewish Enlightenment movement), Yiddish socialism, and Zionism that transformed the lives of Jews living in Eastern Europe. Moreover, as a woman she was conscious of the marginalization of persons of her sex in the traditional Jewish community and in the modern movements of her time. Because she recognized the significance of the subordination of women in private as well as public domains, she defined as radical acts the personal decisions that she made as a woman: to break with the traditional religious culture of her childhood; to abandon her first, arranged, marriage and secure a divorce against extensive familial opposition; to have a career; and, finally, to marry a considerably younger man as her third husband. These events took their place along with her Zionist activism and innovation as a teacher and principal of a private Jewish school as essential components of her revolutionary persona. All the strands of her radicalism were meshed together in her feminism, which found its most concrete expression in her leadership role in the Jewish Women's Association in Poland during the 1920s. Feminism lay at the core of her political and cultural radicalism.

Most observers of East European Jewry were more aware of the revolutionary implications of ideological movements like Haskalah, Zionism, and Jewish socialism than of the personal choices of individual women. Indeed, most scholars who have addressed the issue of radicalism among Jewish women have focused on political radicalism. They have examined the careers and thought of women who became prominent in European socialist movements, of women who became leaders in the major Jewish socialist party, the Bund, or of women who defied their families to become pioneer settlers in the inhospitable climate of Ottoman Palestine. Thus, Rosa Luxemburg, the great socialist theorist who distanced herself from all Jewish concerns, is probably, and ironically, the best-known Jewish woman of late nineteenth-century Central Europe. More recently, the Bundist Esther Frumkin and the radical Zionist socialist Manya Wilbushevitz Shochat have attracted the attention of modern Jewish historians and journalists interested in the public roles of women, though they are hardly well known to students of women's history.[1]

---

1. On Luxemburg, see Robert Wistrich, Radical Jews from Marx to Trotsky (New York: Barnes and Noble Books, 1976), pp. 76–92; Elzbieta Ettinger, Rosa Luxemburg: A Life (Boston: Beacon Press, 1986); and Naomi Shepherd, A Price below Rubies (Cambridge, Mass.: Harvard University Press, 1993), pp. 107–36. On Esther Frumkin and Manya Shochat, see Shepherd, Price below Rubies, pp. 137–71, 172–207. On Shochat, see also Shulamit Reinharz, "Manya Wilbushewitz Shohat and the Winding Road to Sejera," in Deborah Bernstein, Pioneers and Homemakers (Albany: SUNY Press, 1992), pp. 95–118. Shepherd's work, while interesting, is marred by errors.

The definition of radicalism in strictly political terms, and in terms of male-dominated movements, has led historians of East European Jewry to ignore the lives and accomplishments of women whose radicalism and activism found expression outside the realm of partisan politics or in specifically women's settings. As Rakovsky's memoir demonstrates, we need to extend our definition of radicalism to include conscious decisions to protest against social and cultural conventions in private as well as public life. Puah Rakovsky chose to work among other women to achieve social, economic, and educational change. She defied accepted Jewish norms in teaching girls Hebrew and Jewish subjects on a high level, focused her Zionist work on organizing women, and founded a feminist organization that saw its goal as the empowerment of the most vulnerable of Jewish women. She herself became a role model, demonstrating that women could have an impact on the Jewish and general communities. And she chose to live her life as an independent woman in ways that departed from both traditional and secular bourgeois expectations for wives and mothers. She pursued her career as school principal and teacher while she was married as well as when she was a single mother.

In the Russian Empire, virtually all Jews were confined to the western provinces that comprised the Pale of Settlement, the region in which Jews were permitted to live after Russia's acquisition of a large Jewish population in the partitions of Poland at the end of the eighteenth century. Even a century later, 94 percent of the Jews were restricted to an area in which fewer than a third of the non-Jews lived.[2] The Russian Empire, and its interwar heirs — independent Poland and the USSR — contained the largest Jewish population center in the world until their physical destruction by the Nazis in the Holocaust and their cultural and religious persecution by the Soviets. During the course of the nineteenth century, the Jewish population had mushroomed from about 1.6 million in 1825 to more than five million in 1897, even though almost a half million Jews had left tsarist Russia in the last three decades of the century.

Until 1844, Jews lived in governmentally recognized communities, maintaining their own charitable, religious, and educational institutions. Jews supported their own schools, ranging from the *kheyder*, the traditional elementary school, to the yeshiva, the advanced Talmudic

---

2. Simon Kuznets, "Immigration of Russian Jews to the United States: Background and Structure," *Perspectives in American History* 9 (1975), p. 69.

academy in which talented adolescent and young men studied. Beginning in the 1840s, the government established state schools for Jews, and in 1844 it abolished the *kahal*, the official, state-recognized Jewish community, but most Jews continued to be largely segregated (and self-segregating) in their local communities. They interacted economically with the local population and an increasing number of the younger generation attended state schools. However, on a de facto basis, traditional Jewish communities, with their lay leaders and rabbis, remained in place in nineteenth-century Russia.

In the second half of the century, Jewish communities were weakened by a variety of forces. Many younger Jews left traditional religious observance behind as they acquired secular education and felt the seductive attraction of the promise of civic emancipation, social integration, and, later, the end of tsarist autocracy. As a result of the vagaries of governmental policy and the uneven development of the Russian economy, masses of Jews also suffered from increasing poverty.[3]

In the Russian Empire, Jews had played a particular economic role in the Pale's market towns, its *shtetlakh* (plural of *shtetl*). As merchants and small artisans, they marketed the peasants' produce and sold manufactured goods to them. By the 1860s, the development of the railroad and the liberation of the serfs eroded the marketing role of the Jews and their place as intermediaries between the shtetl and the city. In the villages, Jews had also run inns and exercised a virtual monopoly over the liquor trade. Governmental policy, however, increasingly restricted Jewish presence in the villages and Jewish livelihoods as well. At the end of the nineteenth century, a significant component of the more than five million Jews in Russia perceived fewer possibilities for the improvement of their economic fortunes and their legal status than had been the case two generations earlier.

Typical of her generation, on July 3, 1865 Puah was born into a traditionally observant Jewish family, unusual only in the rabbinic lineage of which it boasted. She spent her childhood in the place of her birth, Bialystok, a city in northeast Poland, then located within the Russian Empire. In the decade before her birth, Jews accounted for more than two-thirds of its population of some 14,000; as the city industrialized and grew to having a population of close to 70,000 by the end of the century, Jews maintained their proportion of the total. Al-

---

3. Michael Stanislawski, *Tsar Nicholas I and the Jews* (Philadelphia: Jewish Publication Society, 1983); John Klier, *Russia Gathers Her Jews: The Origins of the "Jewish Question" in Russia, 1772–1825* (DeKalb: Northern Illinois University Press, 1986) and *Imperial Russia's Jewish Question, 1855–1881* (New York and Cambridge: Cambridge University Press, 1995).

though the majority of the Jews were poor, Puah's family was relatively prosperous. Her father ran a successful business as a grain commission agent.

By the end of her adolescence, like many young and educated Jews, Puah had abandoned traditional religious observance for a secular self-definition. That is, she understood herself as a Jew in ethnic and cultural, rather than strictly religious, terms. But she was fully at home in traditional Jewish culture; she grew up in a religiously observant family that prided itself on its descent from a long line of rabbis. She also received a broad Jewish education. Among middle-class Jews in the Russian Empire in the last part of the nineteenth century, girls were frequently sent to government primary schools and occasionally to secondary schools. Puah was one of a small coterie of Jewish women who were also educated in Hebrew and in Bible and the non-legal aspects of rabbinic thought, generally by private tutors. By the time she completed her studies to become a teacher, she knew Russian, Polish, German, and French, in addition to Hebrew and Yiddish. How unusual Puah's accomplishments were is indicated by the fact that in the 1897 Russian census 59.9 percent of Jewish women of her age were illiterate (including in Yiddish) and 82.2 percent did not read or write Russian.[4]

Although few women were allowed in its ranks, the Haskalah — the Jewish movement for Enlightenment — had emerged in full force among intellectuals and successful businessmen by the middle of the nineteenth century. The Haskalah had prominent representatives in Bialystok; for a brief time the Haskalah poet Menahem Mendel Dolitski was Puah's private tutor. Like its predecessor in central and Western Europe, the East European Haskalah promoted the social, cultural, and economic transformation of the Jews. It sought to radically alter the educational agenda of the Jews. Math and science, literature and history, and European languages would take precedence over the traditional Jewish curriculum of Torah and especially Talmud study, to which the education of Jewish boys and young men was often limited. Jews would no longer be linguistically or culturally isolated from the peoples among whom they lived.

Not only did the Haskalah promote the acquisition by Jews of the secular culture of the educated urban classes of their countries of residence; it also aimed to remake the economic profile of the Jews so that they might become productive members of society and achieve upward social mobility. Haskalah intellectuals shared the view that productiv-

4. Kuznets, "Immigration of Russian Jews," p. 80.

ity inhered in agriculture, artisanry, and industry, but not in commerce. The majority of Jews in the Russian Empire who engaged in petty trade perpetuated a negative assessment of the entire Jewish community. They were therefore an obstacle to Jews' acquiring citizenship.

What was the place of girls and women within the vision of the Haskalah? They would benefit from an education that provided secular culture and the moral values they would need as mothers of the next generation. With western bourgeois domesticity as their model, *maskilim* [adherents of the Haskalah] stressed the importance of removing women from the coarsening environment of the marketplace, in which many Jewish women living in the Russian Pale participated out of economic necessity.

The teachers, writers, and journalists of the Haskalah provided a cadre of leaders who challenged the traditional rabbinic establishment along with the cultural segregation it had fostered. They established newspapers and schools to disseminate their ideas. Despite their relatively small numbers, they reached a significant proportion of Russian Jews, who were seeking ways to escape the socioeconomic and political restrictions that increasingly limited Jewish life in the Pale.[5]

The Haskalah was optimistic in its presumption that Jews could achieve full acceptance in Russian society by changing their economic and cultural practice and openly seeking integration with urban Russians. Despite the poverty of the Jewish masses, there was reason to hope that Jews would continue to experience a gradual improvement in their social and legal status under the liberal Tsar Alexander II. With his assassination in 1881 and the pogroms against the Jews that it unleashed, the premises of the Haskalah were undermined for many Russian Jews.

Most Jews were not ideologically motivated; they voted with their bellies and their feet, opting to improve their economic condition by emigrating westward, primarily to America. Others — a tiny group in comparison with the millions who migrated — were ideologically driven. They were drawn to the new Zionist movement, which saw in the Jewish colonization of Palestine a solution to the vulnerability of Jews in East European countries and a tool for reshaping the very identity of Jews in modern times. In the early 1880s, when Puah Rakovsky was an adolescent, the Hibbat Zion [Love of Zion] movement emerged

---

5. On the Haskalah movement, see Michael Stanislawski, *Tsar Nicholas I and For Whom Do I Toil: Judah Leib Gordon and the Crisis of Russian Jewry* (New York: Oxford University Press, 1988), and Steven J. Zipperstein, *The Jews of Odessa: A Cultural History, 1794–1881* (Stanford, Calif.: Stanford University Press, 1985).

as a response to the pogroms. Lacking a coherent organizational structure, it nonetheless began to train settlers for agricultural life in Palestine and to promote Hebrew as a secular as well as religious language.
Despite its lack of enthusiasm for women activists, Puah was involved
with the group from her young adulthood.[6] By the turn of the century,
some Russian Jews had developed a Zionism that combined Jewish nationalism with socialism, enabling revolutionary Jews like Rakovsky to
feel that they were participating in a movement that promised both to
solve the "Jewish problem" and achieve social justice for all humankind.

The "Jewish problem" (that is, the discrimination that Jews continued to experience in varying degrees in virtually every country of
Europe) engaged all politically active Jews in the Russian Empire at the
turn of the twentieth century to a greater or lesser degree. Unlike
general progressive political movements that presumed that the "Jewish problem" would be resolved automatically with the triumph of their
programs, both Zionism and Jewish socialism placed the situation of the
Jews at the center of their platforms. Socialist Zionism was a natural
amalgam for leftist Jews deeply rooted in Jewish circles and Jewish
culture, as was Rakovsky. Particularly after the conclusion of the First
World War, she became associated with the leftist Zeirei Zion [Youth of
Zion] faction of the Zionist movement.

It is no surprise that Rakovsky, like many other Jews living in the
Russian Empire, was drawn to Zionism (although most did not opt for
settlement in Palestine). In Eastern Europe, Jews perceived themselves,
and were recognized by others, as a people or nationality, one among
many in the multi-ethnic empires that existed in the region. Their
religious identity was but a single component of their culture, and the
linkage of religion and ethnicity was a feature that they shared with
their neighbors. Poles were Catholic, Russians and Ukrainians were
Orthodox (of two distinct versions), and Jews were Jewish. Like their
neighbors, who spoke Polish, Ukrainian, or Russian, Jews, too, had a
particular spoken language — Yiddish. In the 1897 Russian census, fully
97 percent of the more than five million Russian Jews as defined by
religion declared Yiddish to be their mother tongue.[7] Yet Jews, primarily
male Jews, also maintained Hebrew as the language of their religious
culture, used in prayer, study, and rabbinic correspondence. When Zionism offered the opportunity to build a cultural center for Jews in the
land hallowed in their memory and associated with ritual longing,

---

6. See David Vital, *The Origins of Zionism* (Oxford: Oxford University Press, 1975), pp. 135–86.
7. Kuznets, "Immigration of Russian Jews," p. 69.

many Jewish intellectuals embraced the dream of a place where a modern Jewish culture, based on the historic language of Hebrew, could flourish. Responding to the rise of political antisemitism throughout Europe at the end of the nineteenth century, many East European Jews recognized the validity of Theodore Herzl's political Zionism. They accepted his revolutionary idea that only a state of their own could ensure the future security of their people. Support for Zionism was widespread among the Jewish masses in tsarist Russia, although Zionist activism, as Rakovsky ruefully notes in her memoirs, was much rarer. Puah herself did not join the pioneers of the Second Aliyah, who emigrated to the land of Israel in the years 1903–1914, largely because she was too old at the time to be part of a "youth movement." There was no room for mothers of young children — her youngest child was born in 1903 — among the pioneers.

More Jewish youth became personally involved in general Russian revolutionary movements, risking their lives in illegal work that the authorities were quite eager to prosecute, than were engaged in the less dangerous (though still largely illegal) Zionist activity. As a committed Zionist, Rakovsky mourns the losses to the Jewish nationalist movement caused by the appeal of Russian socialism and anarchism, to which she herself was sympathetic. Indeed, the Communist experiment in the Soviet Union with its universalist promise of a better society continued to fascinate Rakovsky into her old age, although she was unwilling to tolerate its suppression of dissent. In the interwar years, for many idealistic persons (among them many Jews) Communism was the single most important political movement of their time: It was purportedly attempting in the Soviet Union to create a society that would eradicate all social injustice. However, Puah's commitment to the concept of the Jews as a people and to their realization of their national goals trumped her sympathy for Communism.

Puah Rakovsky was one of a small number of women who had learned Hebrew in their youth and saw themselves as modern Jewish intellectuals who chose to remain within their ethnic group even as they abandoned traditional Jewish practice and acquired general European culture.[8] Throughout her career as an educator, Rakovsky dedicated herself to institutions in which Hebrew was the language of instruction and Jewish nationalism permeated the curriculum. She began

---

8. See Iris Parush, "Readers in Cameo: Women Readers in Jewish Society in Nineteenth-Century Eastern Europe," *Prooftexts* 14 (1994), pp. 1–23, and "The Politics of Literacy: Women and Foreign Languages in Jewish Society of Nineteenth-Century Eastern Europe," *Modern Judaism* 15 (1995), pp. 183–206.

her career in a Jewish school for girls, in the provincial city of Lomza (near Warsaw), where she pioneered as a teacher of Hebrew. Within two years, she was invited by the leaders of Bnei Moshe, a cultural society within the Hibbat Zion movement, to establish a modern Jewish school for girls in Warsaw, which she would direct. According to many sources, that institution, "Yehudiah," was the first Jewish girls' school in Poland in which Hebrew — which she taught — was a substantial element of the curriculum. Within two years, she established her own gymnasium [secondary school] for Jewish girls that included Hebrew as an official component. Her gymnasium was recognized throughout Poland as a pioneering institution for Jewish girls.[9] Rakovsky was also a public personality. She contributed to the Yiddish press, wrote several pamphlets in Yiddish, and was well known as a Zionist and feminist activist. After World War I led to the demise of her school, she supplemented her earnings by translating literature, mostly from French and German, into Yiddish.[10]

Puah's was a generation on the move. While Jews in traditional communities had frequently traveled to attend yeshiva or for the purpose of marriage, by the last quarter of the nineteenth century that geographic mobility was further stimulated by the stagnation of the Jewish economy and by the lure of urban educational and employment opportunities. After receiving her teaching certificate, like many of her peers, Rakovsky moved to Warsaw, the center of Congress Poland, then a part of Russia. Her siblings, children, and cousins, subject to quotas in Russian and later Polish institutions of higher learning, went abroad — to Germany, Switzerland, and France — to study. In fact, middle-class Russian Jews seem to have had no compunctions about traveling for study, business, or vacation. After all, they could count on their kin, who were scattered about in far-flung places. None of Rakovsky's close relatives, however, was among the one-third of Russian Jewry who emigrated westward to settle permanently primarily in the New World in the years between 1881 and 1914, as a pragmatic rather than an ideological response to their restricted opportunities. Their commitment to staying in Europe may reflect the fact that they were middle class and educated; Jewish immigrants to America were drawn primarily from those with little economic or cultural stake in Russian

---

9. Esther Rosenthal-Shneiderman, *Af Vegn un Umvegn* (Tel Aviv: Hamenora Publishing House, 1974), p. 290.
10. Between 1920 and 1931, she translated thirteen books into Yiddish, from German, French, and Russian. Among them were Erich Maria Remarque's *All Quiet on the Western Front*, five novels by Magritte, and Leon Trotsky's autobiography.

society. Among radicals, those with the tsarist police at their heels often saw emigration as a preferable option to incarceration in a Russian jail.

Choosing not to emigrate, Puah suffered the disruption that World War I wreaked on the Jewish population. Living on the front, she was forced to flee from Warsaw and had to close the school in which she had invested twenty-five years of effort. In fact, the First World War of 1914–1918 was a watershed for Jews who lived in tsarist Russia's Pale of Settlement. In its wake, the Bolshevik Revolution of 1917 unleashed a bloody civil war; up to 100,000 Jews met their deaths between 1917 and 1921 in the worst pogroms ever, carried out largely by those who opposed the Revolution. With the establishment of the USSR, the Jewish population of the former Russian Empire was divided into two communities living in two states with different political systems and cultures. Members of Puah's large extended family, too, were dispersed across the Eastern European terrain.

In the new state of Poland, established as a result of the Treaty of Versailles that formally concluded the First World War, Jews confronted discrimination, restricted economic opportunities, and poverty. The successor states of the Russian and Austrian Empires, like Poland and Czechoslovakia, were forced to accept the concept of national minority rights as a condition of their establishment. According to that concept, ethnic minorities like the Jews, Ukrainians, Germans, and White Russians were permitted to use their own languages in interaction with governmental authorities and to maintain their own educational and cultural institutions with public support. The Poles chafed at these restrictions on their national sovereignty and blamed the Jews for the imposition of national minority clauses in the Treaty of Versailles. Poland's leaders did not implement the minority rights to which they had acceded under duress. In the interwar years, Polish nationalist sentiment ran high, and antisemitism became a staple of Polish politics on the right and a tolerated phenomenon even among centrists and liberals. Jews suffered from economic boycotts, discrimination in hiring, and the imposition of quotas in secondary and university education. The rise of the Nazi regime in Germany in the early 1930s strengthened Polish antisemitism and the power of the major right-wing party, and made it clear that the prospects for Jews in Poland were bleak.

The Soviet leadership banned antisemitism with great fanfare and enabled Jews to experience enormous social and educational mobility in the 1920s and early 1930s. The anticlericalism of the new regime, its crackdown on Hebrew, and its rigid state control were less apparent to casual observers than its proclaimed idealistic goals. Puah and members of her family were attracted to the élan that characterized the early years of the Soviet Union. Indeed, Rakovsky provides evidence of the competition of the USSR with Palestine as a destination for resettlement of Jews who felt that they had no future in Poland.

Puah herself chose the Land of Israel. She emigrated alone to Palestine in 1920, when she was fifty-five. Perhaps because she had few peers in Palestine, perhaps because of the Arab riots of that year, which deeply disturbed her, she returned a year later to Warsaw. She settled definitively in Palestine in 1935, when she was seventy, and lived there until her death twenty years later.

Rakovsky spent her first years in Palestine in Jerusalem and Tel Aviv, employed as a translator of Zionist information into Yiddish and involved with Zionist women's activity and with education. Her eightieth birthday received some notice, suggesting that her initial difficulties in finding employment there did not prevent her from becoming a recognized figure, at least in certain sectors of pre-state society. The Yiddish newspaper Der Shpigl published a brief human interest article about her in 1945, entitled "The Oldest Hebrew Woman Writer." Describing her daily ten A.M. walks along Rothschild Boulevard in Tel Aviv, it noted that she had led a colorful life and summarized her activities as an educator, a Zionist, a feminist, and a translator. In Tel Aviv, it added, she participated in a variety of cultural institutions.[11] When she was no longer able to be independent, she moved to her daughter Sarah's home in Haifa and lived there with her family for many years. She is remembered by her granddaughter as a difficult person, who was strongly committed to her own point of view.[12] Bedridden toward the end, she died in Haifa on May 13, 1955.

Puah wrote her memoirs between 1940 and 1942, as she indicates in the text itself.[13] Yet she brings her story to a speedy conclusion with her account of her arrival in Palestine in 1935 and her difficulty in finding work to sustain herself. Although her autobiography was not published until 1952 (in a Hebrew translation) and in Yiddish in 1954, she chose to limit her narrative to the events that she had experienced herself in Europe, rather than engaging in reflections on the destruction of the world in which she had passed most of her life and the murder of family and friends in the Holocaust. It is clear that she was aware during

---

11. *Der Shpigl*, 1945.
12. Interview with her granddaughter, Hemdah Allon, Nov. 10. 1998, Haifa. Hemdah remembered her grandmother living with the family for at least fifteen years.
13. Puah Rakovsky, *Lo Nikhnati*, and *Zikhroynes fun a yidisher revolutsionerin*.

the writing of her memoir that the situation was grim for those left behind in Europe, but she wrote before the knowledge of the dimensions of the mass murder of European Jewry had reached the Jews living in Palestine. She opted not to revise her work in the years between the completion of the manuscript and its publication. When she learned of the mass murder of the Holocaust, however, she refrained from wearing new clothes as a sign of mourning and on the day of the celebration of her eightieth birthday in Palestine met her guests with tears in her eyes.[14] The abrupt ending of her memoir suggests the rupture she felt as she considered the trajectory of her life.

Few Jewish women in Europe wrote their memoirs, and of those, fewer still can be traced in sources other than their own recollections. Glückel of Hameln (1646–1724), a merchant woman who lived on the fringes of central European court Jewish society, the society of wealthy and influential men of commerce who served local princes, was the first Jewish woman to write memoirs that survived (in manuscript form copied by one of her sons). Only at the end of the nineteenth century were they published in Judeo-German (a form of Yiddish) and then in German and later English translations.[15] Pauline Wengeroff, a prosperous woman of Minsk whose husband and sons radically assimilated, penned her two-volume *Memoirs of a Jewish Grandmother* in German in the early years of the twentieth century.[16] She aimed to present a loving description of the world of her childhood and to lament its destruction in the process of Russification and social mobility. Neither of these women's lives can be documented in much detail aside from their memoirs. Only Bella Chagall, the author of the memoir *Burning Lights*, is a known personality because of her position as the wife of the artist Marc Chagall. Her memoir, however, which was posthumously published in 1946, is organized around the Jewish calendar and has a

---

14. David Kalai, "The Anniversary of a Woman Rebel," [Heb.], *Dvar Ha-Poelet* (1945), reprinted in a collection of his essays, pp. 88–96. The essay was translated, abbreviated, and reprinted under the title "Puah Rakovsky: The Life Story of a Rebel," in *The Pioneer Woman*, no. 117 (June 1946), pp. 2–4. I wish to thank Tracy Sivitz for providing me with the English version of this essay.
15. Glückel of Hameln, *The Life of Glückel of Hameln, 1646–1724*, trans. and ed. Beth-Zion Abrahams (London: East and West Library, 1962), and the more accessible but less faithful *The Memoirs of Gluckel of Hameln*, trans. Marvin Lowenthal (New York: Schocken, 1977), reprint of 1932 edition.
16. For further information, see Shulamit Magnus, "Pauline Wengeroff and the Voice of Jewish Modernity," in *Gender and Judaism: The Transformation of Tradition*, ed. T. M. Rudavsky (New York: New York University Press, 1995), pp. 181–90. For the first translation of an abbreviated version of the memoirs, see Pauline Wengeroff, *Rememberings*, trans. Henny Wenkart (Bethesda: University Press of Maryland, 2000).

dream-like tone, similar to her husband's paintings, devoid of historical specificity.[17]

Puah Rakovsky differs from all her memoir-writing female predecessors in that she played a public role throughout much of her adult life, and she attracted the notice of others. When she was only fifteen, she appeared in the pages of the Hebrew journal *Ha-Zefira* as the translator from Russian of a story by the poet Shimon Frug.[18] More than a decade later, in 1894, signing herself Puah of the Rakovsky family, she published three pages of original pithy sayings in the Hebrew paper *Ahiasaf*, published in Warsaw.[19] Although she first became known as an educated Jewish woman who could write in Hebrew, she turned to Yiddish later in her life when she sought to disseminate her Zionist and socialist ideas to a broad popular audience. [Indeed, Yiddishists on the political left appreciated her support of the language and her reluctance to engage in the virulent attacks on Yiddish that then accompanied the Zionist movement's promotion of Hebrew.][20] In 1902, she reported on women's roles at the Minsk conference of Russian Zionists in a Yiddish newspaper devoted to women's issues. At that time she noted progress in the treatment of women. Herzlian Zionism, she thought, was more open to women than were "the first bearers of the idea of Hibbat Zion, the rabbis and pious Jews [who] did not admit women into their circles . . . " or the elitist "Bnei Moshe [which] closed its doors to women."[21]

Years later, her presence at the London meeting in 1920 that led to the founding of WIZO, the women's organization within international Zionism, testifies to her ongoing concern both for Zionism and for women's issues. Indeed, she attended Zionist congresses and, having decided on aliyah (immigration) to Palestine, served as the first secretary of the newly formed WIZO branch in the country.[22] (During her year in Palestine, she pursued her goal of empowering women through education, opening a vocational school for girls in Jerusalem.)

Only after she was compelled to give up her school in Warsaw because of the First World War did she find the time for sustained writing and translating. In 1918, she published her first pamphlet in Yiddish, *Di Yidishe froy* [The Jewish Woman], under the auspices of Bnos Tsiyon [Daughters of Zion], the Polish women's Zionist organization

---

17. Bella Chagall, *Burning Lights* (New York: Schocken Books, 1946).
18. *Ha-Zefira*, 1880.
19. *Ahiasaf* (Tarnad, 1894), pp. 166–68.
20. Rosenthal-Shneiderman, *Af Vegn un Umvegn*, p. 291.
21. Rakovsky, *Di yudishe froyenvelt* 13 (Sept. 24, 1902), pp. 1–3.
22. Minutes of London meeting, Central Zionist Archive, Jerusalem, F49 3063.

---

which she was trying to expand. Noting the importance of women in all movements for social reform, she called on Jewish women to become more active in Zionist work. She attributed the indifference of so many Jewish women to Zionism to the traditional neglect of girls' Jewish education. That was a situation that she had set out to rectify when she first became a teacher and later the director of a Jewish girls' school that taught Hebrew and Jewish culture along with secular studies. Both the Jewish question and the woman's question, she asserted, would be solved only through self-determination, and not through assimilation, that is, the abandonment of Jewish self-consciousness. Jewish women could do their part by founding a national Jewish women's organization and by pressing for the adoption of female suffrage in Jewish communal elections. Rakovsky combined her feminist message with an appeal to ethnic Jewish pride: "It is not possible that we Jews, who were the first bearers of democratic principles, should in this regard lag behind all civilized peoples and close the way for women to achievement of equal rights and to the first step in that direction — to participation in the community."[23] To achieve her own goals for women, she included in her Zionist organizing of women the establishment of vocational courses and schools for the daughters of the petite bourgeoisie, so that they might cease being dependent on their parents and husbands.[24]

Rakovsky was committed throughout her life to the concept of separate women's organizations that would place women's concerns at the center of their activity. That commitment found reflection in her work to establish Bnos Tsiyon and to serve on its national council. The leadership of the Zionist Central Board in Poland initially refrained from recognizing the women's council and, despite prior promises, refused to contribute to the payment of the council's expenses. As a result, all the female members of the Board, including Puah, resigned in protest. Puah's strategy of autonomous organizing was strikingly successful. When the women had expanded the number of branches of Bnos Tsiyon to seventy-two, they won the Central Board's recognition.[25]

It was the founding and activity of the Jewish Women's Association in Poland (Y.F.A.), a national women's organization of explicitly feminist as well as Zionist orientation for which she served as secretary, that gave Rakovsky the opportunity to present her views on women's roles in society. She was one of three co-editors of the association's short-

23. Rakovsky, Di yidishe froy (Warsaw: Bnos Tsiyon, 1918). The quotation is from p. 28.
24. Rosenthal-Shneiderman, Af Vegn un Umvegn, p. 291.
25. N. Smiatitska, "The Organization of Women Zionists," in Encyclopedia of Diasporas [Heb.], ed. Y. Grünbaum, vol. 6, pt. 2 (Jerusalem–Tel Aviv, 1959), cols. 213–18.

lived monthly journal, the *Froyen-shtim* (Women's Voice), which the association established because of its recognition that Jewish papers were not prepared to allow women to speak for themselves. The paper's mission, its editors proclaimed, was to conduct "enlightenment work among Jewish women, because the doors of the Yiddish press are for us women closed with seven locks; . . . to awaken . . . the Jewish woman to take her fate in her own hands, herself to demand and defend her rights."[26] The editorial reflected Rakovsky's message of female self-empowerment and her recognition of the need for middle-class Jewish women — "those of us who can speak" — to assume responsibility for effecting social change, as equals with men. The Jewish Women's Association worked with the poorest women and their children to prepare them for making a living in the straitened economic circumstances of interwar Poland, where antisemitism combined with the country's lack of industrial development to limit severely possibilities for Jews to be employed as artisans or to participate in petty commerce. At the age of sixty, Rakovsky was attuned to the fact that "new ways of life" were in the process of being created.[27]

Three years later, in 1928, she produced a second Yiddish pamphlet, *Di moderne froyen-bavegung* [The Modern Women's Movement], which placed the Jewish women's movement within an international context and argued that throughout the industrial world women found themselves in a similar situation. In Poland, as elsewhere, women had to organize on their own behalf to secure civic and political equality, equal right to work and equal pay, and equal opportunities for education. Within the Jewish community, they had to become leaders and not simply work under male direction.[28] As secretary of the Jewish Women's Association, Rakovsky also signed its circular letters to its members, and one, dated December 18, 1928, has survived in the YIVO Archive in New York City.[29] It called on the organization's members to become more involved in its manifold activities that addressed the social problems of Jewish women and children in Poland. The organization's programs ranged from summer camps for children and youth and the provision of vocational education to enable girls to become self-sufficient to international efforts in support of abandoned wives and courses and lectures (in Yiddish) on Jewish and Polish cultures.

When Puah immigrated to Palestine for the second time in 1935, it

---

26. *Froyen-shtim* 1 (May 1925), pp. 3–4.
27. Ibid.
28. Rakovsky, *Di moderne froyen-bavegung* (Warsaw, 1928).
29. YIVO Archive, New York. Poland-Vilna Archive, Warsaw, no. 45.

was difficult for her to sustain her public life, though she tried. She was already seventy years old, and, as she recounts in her memoirs, Zionist officials saw her age as an obstacle to her employment. Moreover, what could an old woman from a downtrodden Jewish community in the *Golah* [Exile, or Diaspora] have to say to the young, up-to-date New Jews of the Zionist Yishuv [Jewish settlement in Palestine]? Nonetheless, when Rakovsky enrolled in a seminar for working women held in 1937, she managed to get the attention of the organizers of the event. They allowed her to recount her experiences as a Zionist and feminist leader to her fellow participants on the day devoted to different manifestations of the movement for women's freedom. Her story was considered part of the "pre-history" of the women's movement in Palestine. The women's newspaper of the labor movement, *Dvar Ha-Poelet* [Working Woman's Word], then published an article based on her seminar presentation.[30] Her remarks were sufficiently compelling for the newspaper subsequently to print a piece in which she strongly articulated the need for women to organize a separate women's list in elections in the Yishuv, even though, as the newspaper was careful to note, the organized women's movement in Palestine opposed such a point of view. Never one to shun controversy, she continued to promote the position that she had long advocated, from the time that she organized women for Zionism in Poland.[31]

Puah Rakovsky's contemporaries were well aware of her unusual status as a Jewishly educated young woman from an Orthodox family who broke with tradition in so many ways. In 1893, a novella appeared in Warsaw, written in Hebrew, that was based loosely on Puah's story. The author, Ben-Avigdor, called his heroine, and his story, Rabbi Shifra, the name of one of the two midwives in the book of Exodus (the second midwife was named Puah). Like Puah Rakovsky, "Rabbi Shifra" was learned in Jewish culture but no longer an observant Jew; she was fluent in several languages; and she was a Zionist and a feminist, committed to her work. And like Puah, her love for a cousin was thwarted by her family. Clearly, Puah Rakovsky was sufficiently known among the Hebrew-reading elites of Warsaw Jewry for her to serve as the heroine of this roman à clef.[32]

In fact, she was well-known in general among Warsaw Jewry. One memoirist, Esther Rosenthal-Shneiderman, wrote of Rakovsky's popu-

30. *Dvar Ha-Poelet*, Nov. 11, 1937, pp. 154–58.
31. Ibid., Jan. 16, 1938, p. 206.
32. Ben-Avigdor, "Rabbi Shifra," in *Sifrei Agora*, vol. 1 (Warsaw, 1893).

larity and stature in 1920s Warsaw: "When Puah (then a woman already nearly 60) would go by on the 'Jewish street,' both the little people and the well known would greet her with a 'good morning,' even if they were not personally acquainted with her." Moreover, Rosenthal-Shneiderman noted that already in Puah's youth legends had sprung up about her, "like a real heroine."[33]

In addition to appearing as a fictionalized persona and in post-World War II memoirs, Rakovsky was also mentioned in the non-fiction writings of others. In M. Fried's 1939 memoir of his years in Poland, translated into Hebrew from the Yiddish, Puah is hailed as a pioneer educator of Jewish girls, "the first to open a modern girls' school in Warsaw, which she ran successfully for many years, until she was able to build a generation of Hebrew daughters in the full sense of the term, who also after they married remained faithful to the Hebrew language and literature. And these were the ones that afterward positively influenced the education of their children." Historians of modern education in Poland, he added, "sinned against history when they passed over in silence the exemplary Hebrew educator in Warsaw, Puah Rakovska."[34]

In the Zionist Yishuv in Palestine, too, Puah was viewed as a remarkable public figure, an unusual Zionist pioneer in that she had immigrated late in life and her impact had been greatest elsewhere, in the Diaspora. After noting her social contributions on her eightieth birthday in 1945, *Der Shpigl* concluded its article, in what was doubtless intended as the highest compliment one could pay to an old woman, with the comment that "the years have not left any harsh mark upon her. She is hearty, ruddy, and keeps herself young."[35] Also on the occasion of her eightieth birthday David Kalai, who later abbreviated her memoirs and translated them into Hebrew, published an extensive laudatory article in *Dvar Ha-Poelet*.[36] Narrating the story of her life, Kalai entitled his piece "The Anniversary of a Rebel." Rakovsky had made her mark on the history of Polish Jewry, he asserted, precisely through her "creative rebellion," for all her rebelliousness pointed her toward "the act of creation." Through her work as an educator, Zionist activist, and feminist, she had contributed to the renaissance of the

33. Rosenthal-Shneiderman, *Af Vegn un Umvegn*, pp. 289–90.
34. M. Fried, *Yamim v'shanim: zikhronot v'ziyurim mitkufah shel hamishim shanah* [Days and Years: Memoirs and Portraits of a Fifty-Year Period; trans. Abraham Zamir] (Tel Aviv: Dvir, 1939), p. 160. I wish to thank David Assaf for the reference.
35. *Der Shpigl*, 1945.
36. Kalai, "The 80th Anniversary of a Woman Rebel" and "Puah Rakovsky: The Life Story of a Rebel."

largest Jewish community of the time. Indeed, claimed Kalai, in the annals of Polish Jewry it was "unthinkable that a place of honor not be set for this woman . . ."[37]

When she died ten years later in Haifa, just two months shy of her ninetieth birthday, she was, in fact, honored with a front-page obituary, with a photograph, in *Davar*, the daily newspaper of the Labor Party.[38] The obituary cited her many accomplishments as an educator, organizer of women, translator of tens of books into Yiddish, and one of the first socialist-Zionists. In fact, the paper exaggerated her historical role, calling her the founder of the first Hebrew school for girls in the Diaspora and of a nationally oriented Jewish women's movement, for which there were no precedents. Focusing on her work in the Yishuv, it noted her participation during her first stay in Palestine in 1920–1921 in the struggle for women's right to vote in the elections for the Congress of Representatives. Leaving a son in Russia and a daughter in Haifa, grandchildren and great-grandchildren in Israel, she had chosen to be buried in Jerusalem.[39]

Shortly after her death, the American Yiddish poet Jacob Glatstein devoted an essay to Puah's life and work.[40] Rakovsky, he declared, was committed to emancipation, particularly of Jews and of women. In his view, she was one of the first Jewish women's rights activists on the world stage, from the time that she, still in her twenties and a mother of two young children, "went out into the broad world to seek and find the way for the Jewish woman."[41] And she remained always committed to Zionism, which for her was simply the liberation movement of the Jewish people.

Glatstein was a great admirer of Rakovsky's "highly developed Yiddish-publicist style."[42] In fact, her style reflects her position as a Jew born into a traditional community who fully confronted the culture and politics of secular modernity. Well-educated in Hebrew and in biblical and midrashic texts, she unselfconsciously included citations in Hebrew within her Yiddish narrative. Biblical and rabbinic allusion formed part of the repertoire of educated Jews of her generation, and Rakovsky's Yiddish was all the richer for its allusiveness. She clearly

---

37. Ibid., p. 88.
38. *Davar*, May 15, 1955, p. 1.
39. Despite the claims of the obituary, it is possible that her son in Russia was no longer alive.
40. Jacob Glatstein, "Zikhroynes fun a yiddisher revolutsionerin," in *Sum and Substance* (Buenos Aires, 1960), pp. 177–83. The essay is dated 1955.
41. Ibid., p. 178.
42. Ibid., p. 179.

assumed that her allusions would be familiar to her readers, for she included sources neither in the text nor in footnotes.

Puah Rakovsky was not typical of Polish Jewish women of her generation or social class. Most memoir writers are exceptional in some way, if only because they consider their lives worth writing about. Puah was exceptional in her level of education and in the varieties of political and social activism that engaged her during her long life, and perhaps in the number of contradictions that she balanced. She was a rebel who broke with the traditional religious heritage of her family yet remained profoundly connected with the fate of the Jewish people. In her own understanding, she transformed the religious heritage she had received into a culture appropriate for the twentieth century. She devoted herself to Zionism but lived most of her life in a Diaspora community in an increasingly inhospitable Poland. Puah Rakovsky was a romantic ideologue who succeeded in translating her idealism into pragmatic organizations that worked, from schools to summer camps to Zionist women's groups, to a national women's association. She was also unusual for her time in recognizing feminism as essential for improving the situation of women. Her reflections on gender issues in Jewish education and in Zionist politics speak to readers born a century after her and living in quite different social circumstances from her own.

Puah acceded to her friends' suggestion that she write her memoirs because she hoped that her experience would be instructive for others. A new generation of readers, who speak a language that she never learned and live in a place she never visited, may fulfill her expectations.

One

Bialystok — Warsaw

I was born in 1865 to a fifteen-year-old mother and a seventeen-year-old father. On my father's side, I am the descendant of thirty-six generations of rabbis, with a lineage that goes back to Rashi.[1] There is testimony about this in our family tree, published by one of our relatives in Warsaw, Haim Zakheim, a fine Jew but a *Kaptzan*, a very poor man. He carefully researched all our relatives and favored them with the pedigree of our descent. According to him, our family is very extensive, and there is hardly a city in Russia or in Russian Poland where I don't have a relative.

My mother was born in Bialystok. She didn't remember her father, because he had died when she was little. My mother's mother, Yente Sarah, whom I still remember very well, was a true "woman of valor."[2] In Soprasle, a small town not far from Bialystok, she had a large water-mill, and in Bialystok she owned a substantial flour warehouse. Bobbe Yente Sarah was famous for being a flamboyant and very clever businesswoman. Her parents married her off when she was twelve years old, and at the age of thirteen she divorced her first husband. Later, she picked her own second husband, who became my mother's father. This one was a "genius," who studied while his wife ran the business and

---

1. Acronym for Rabbi Solomon ben Yitzhak (1040–1105), the most popular Bible and Talmud commentator.
2. The first words of a biblical text (Proverbs 31:10–31) that praises the active woman who contributes to her family's support. It is traditionally recited by a man in honor of his wife at their Sabbath evening table.

supported the family. Yente Sarah's second husband was a delicate young man, as they said in those days, a serious scholar but, obviously, not much of a man. With him my grandmother had only two daughters — my mother and her older sister.

One day, my zeyde, that delicate young man, went to the flour warehouse and observed how the porters loaded sacks of flour on their shoulders and walked around with them. They were young Jews, used to hard work. But that delicate man thought this feat wasn't so hard, and bet one of the porters that he could do it too. He hoisted a sack of flour on his shoulder, but he couldn't carry it. Soon Grandfather started hemorrhaging and fell ill with a lung disease. He died while still young. Grandmother, a very beautiful young widow, continued to run her big business and maintain her large house right in the middle of Bialystok. It is interesting that although Grandmother didn't know any other language than Yiddish, she dealt with high officials, even the governor of Grodno; and she had good luck when she had to go to trials. For she had a weakness for suing, and she always won her case.

Bobbe Yente Sarah lost her older daughter, who died in childbirth with her third child, and my grandmother then brought up the three little orphans. The children's father soon remarried and for the rest of his life never took the time to care for his children. When they were grown, Bobbe got married for the third time to a man who was about her own age. Her third husband was an established merchant; but my grandmother remained the great "woman of valor," running the whole business, with her husband as her helpmeet[3] for the rest of his life. He simply assisted: She commanded and he obeyed. And if he ever made a business deal on his own, it turned out badly. With this third husband, Bobbe also had two daughters; in fact, she had seven other children with him, but they all died young. Because of this curse, Grandmother took a vow never to kiss either her children or grandchildren.

In her day, Grandmother Yente Sarah was an interesting example of a "primitive," independent woman, a stray spark of an ancient matriarchy. And if we believe in atavism and Freud's theories of inheritance, we can assert that a spark I inherited from my long-dead grandmother is hidden in me, the contemporary fighter for women's rights. I remember as if it were yesterday that, as a child of six or eight, if anyone wanted to compliment me, they said: "Bobbe Yente-Sarah's head [kop]."

Not having any sons, my Grandmother strove to compensate for that lack with extraordinary sons-in-law, and she did indeed make fine

---

3. A play on the story in Genesis, where Eve is created to be Adam's helpmeet. See Genesis 2:18.

matches for her daughters with the sons of famous rabbis and men of good family. Following the custom of that time, she gave her daughters handsome dowries, provided the sons-in-law with food and lodging in her large home, and generally kept them with her.

By the time I was eight years old, my mother had given birth to her fifth child. She would have fifteen children altogether — nursing for a year and then being pregnant for nine months. At that time, I lived on the second floor in my grandmother's house. Bobbe herself had taken over a big apartment on the ground floor. My father, a rabbi's son (Zeyde, Rabbi Leybele, was then a rabbi in Stavisk, in the Lomza district), had also received *semicha* [rabbinic ordination], and Grandmother really wanted him to practice as a rabbi. Right after they were married, my father did study with his friend Haim-Hertz Halperin, the son of the Bialystok Rabbi Lippa Halperin. But my father didn't want to be a rabbi. While he was studying Torah, he also taught himself — without the aid of tutors — Russian, German, history, natural science, and accounting. Later on, he became so adept in accounting that the directors of banks in Bialystok would ask his advice.

When my parents' family size increased and they were still were boarding at my Bobbe's home, my father set out for Kovno, where he became a commission agent. But that endeavor ended in failure, and Papa spent my mother's entire dowry. When he returned home, he looked for a way to make a living locally, switching to shipping because you didn't need any money to get into that field. Merchants would give the shipper their receipts, and in exchange the shipper would claim the merchandise. For the trouble, he was paid a certain fee. It was important for shippers to have a large volume of customers. And because my father had a very good reputation and was considered an honest and smart man, he soon attracted a large clientele. Papa quickly started earning a living, and seemed content with his new path. He often told a remarkable anecdote about his first independent earnings: in a big synagogue, he had a good friend, who greatly respected him for his good qualities. That man — I still remember his last name, but I won't mention it because he was a moneylender, a usurer — refused to lend my father some rubles he needed for a short time so that he could unload merchandise from a train for a number of customers. The moneylender listened nicely to Papa's request and finally said: "Reb Mendel, I know you're really a very fine, honest man, but where will you get money to pay me back?"

My father didn't answer, but parted from him silently and went off. Years later, when my father was a prominent merchant and one of the most distinguished Jews in Bialystok, known as the cleverest man in the whole Grodno District, people who remembered that incident would recount it as proof that a Jew shouldn't behave like that. You should trust a person! . . . And they would tell that the moneylender subsequently lost all his wealth and — may it not happen to us — died destitute.

My childhood really began at the time when my father became a shipper. It wasn't a childhood as we understand it today, with a nursery, toys, a kindergarten, and all the paraphernalia that go under the slogan "Everything for the child." Such things I didn't have. What Jews had a childhood three generations ago? And did a fifteen-year-old mother and a seventeen-year-old father know what to give their children? My father, for instance, used to tell us that when he wanted to pick me up, he would say: "Give her to me in a little kerchief." Who knew about child rearing when you had fifteen children, like my mother? Both my grandmothers had eighteen children; and one aunt, the wife of my uncle, the writer Abraham-Abba Rakowski,[4] was brought to child-bed twenty-one times. Her first seven children died young, and when the eighth was born, they went to all the rabbis, dressed him in linen until he was thirteen, and used many such remedies. But it made no difference. Three generations ago, Jewish children weren't brought up; they had no childhood, but they grew up like the trees in the forest — "man is the tree of the field."[5] They simply saw their parents' example of dignified life and grew up healthier than the "well-bred" children of the twentieth century, of all nations, including the Jews.

I grew up like all Jewish children in my day. When I was six, I attended *kheyder* [traditional Jewish elementary school] with little boys. I remember the rabbi as if I were seeing him now. A tall, handsome Jew he was, with a long, blond beard. He was named Joseph Tsigarenmakher. To this day I don't understand why he was called that, for I never saw him make any cigars in *kheyder*. He taught us as God commanded: from morning until late at night. I studied with that first teacher only for a short while. Then the rabbi came to my papa and reported: "Reb Mendel, I have no more Torah for your little girl. She needs a greater rabbi. Your boy can still stay in my *kheyder*." In addition to the *kheyder*, I also had a Yiddish teacher. In those days, he wasn't called a teacher, but a "writer" who taught a group of boys and girls to read and write Yiddish.

---

4. Writer and translator (1855–?).
5. A quotation from Deuteronomy 20:19.

After *kheyder*, at the age of seven, I was sent to a private Jewish school where the language of instruction was Russian and the curriculum was that of the public school. The teacher's name was Ezriel Kaplan, but he doesn't seem to have meant much to me. At home, a rabbi taught me *Humash* [the five books of the Torah], which was really very easy for me. I didn't have to do much homework; I would finish the written work very quickly. I was an extraordinarily diligent student. All I had to do was hear a story or a poem during the lesson and I could remember it by heart. Before I went to sleep, I would read it once, put the book under my pillow (I considered it a good luck charm), and the next morning I knew everything fluently.

Studying wasn't everything. I was very busy *all* day long. When I came home from school, I became Papa's assistant at work and gave Mama a hand with the younger children. I was the oldest girl, the oldest of all the children. Papa would send me to the railroad station if something arrived unexpectedly for one of the merchants and he had just returned from the station. In addition, I would wash and comb and feed the smaller children. No work was hard, because everything I did was dictated by my sense of duty as the oldest child in the family. So I was obliged to help. I bore that yoke only a few years — as long as my father was only a municipal shipper, that is, and as long as he dealt only with merchants from Bialystok. It wasn't long before Papa opened a shipping office, and big merchants from many cities in Russia entrusted hundreds of cars of goods to him to be shipped to Germany. The goods consisted mainly of produce that went through Grayeva-Prostken to Königsberg. At that time, no direct railroad connection existed, and every car had to be unloaded and moved from one railroad line to another. My father had won the merchants' trust, and the number of his customers increased by the day. Father employed a staff who worked very intensely all night long to satisfy the customers. My parents' situation was much improved, and we moved out of Grandmother's house into a larger place. We hired a servant so that Mama could rest from her hard work. She started devoting herself to public work, mainly to charity: creating various societies that offered free loans or provided dowries for poor girls, and such. She no longer went shopping by herself in the market, but ordered everything delivered. "Poor women should also earn something, since God has helped us," she would claim.

My mother was so pious that the wives of all the great rabbis came to learn piety from her. And I respected her because her piety was a genuinely Jewish, human goodness. It was more goodness, in fact, than piety. In such an environment of pure Jewishness did I grow up, and never in my life have I seen such love as between my father and mother, not even in any of the modern couples who married for love, as it were.

We children were, in fact, not brought up or trained, but we were never hit, either. Whenever Papa got angry at one of us and wanted to hit us, he would burst out laughing before he went over to the guilty child. And they would say of my grandfather, the rabbi, that whenever he would strike a child, he did it as fast as he could with the palm of his hand. Just a slap and nothing more.

I was very lively. In school, I showed a penchant for moving around. Very joyful by nature, with a strong personality, I would sing and dance and was always the favorite of the whole class, the life of the party. Along with all that, I was a pious girl, almost as pious as my mama: I prayed on the Sabbath, read the *Taitsch-Humash*,[6] the *Menoras Ha-Maor* [a well-known book on morals],[7] recited Psalms, and didn't comb my hair or wash with soap on the Sabbath. If I went to my girlfriend's house and found her reading a Russian book on the Sabbath, I would slam the door and leave. That's how it was until I reached the age of thirteen.

When I finished grammar school, I implored Papa to send me to high school. In Bialystok at that time, there was a four-grade pre-gymnasium, as well as a private and a public gymnasium. But I couldn't persuade Father to do that; he didn't want me to continue in those institutions because they forced you to write on the Sabbath. But my father did want me to continue my studies, and he often said: "Too bad you were born a girl and not a boy." Unfortunately, Jewish parents, even intelligent ones, felt that girls should not have the same education as boys — never mind the idea of a girl wanting to learn the Holy Tongue! That was certainly considered to be heresy, because "teaching a girl Torah is teaching her licentiousness."[8] Our nation has paid dearly for that outmoded view. If our grandfathers and fathers and our rabbis, as spiritual leaders, had not adhered to that rule; if the Torah had been taught without distinction of sex; if both Jewish girls and boys had studied our Torah, culture, and customs; then how many thousands of Jewish mothers would have been saved from assimilation and conver-

---

6. A name for the *Tsene-Rene*, a Yiddish version of the Pentateuch, interwoven with rabbinic stories. Compiled by Jacob ben Isaac Ashkenazi, it was first published at the end of the sixteenth century and was regularly read by women.

7. *Candlestick of Light*, a book of religious edification, was written by Isaac Aboab, who lived at the end of the fourteenth century, probably in Spain. It was first published in 1514 and was translated into Yiddish by the beginning of the eighteenth century.

8. A citation from the Mishnah of Sota 20a (Babylonian Talmud). An alternative translation to licentiousness (*tiflut*) is "frivolity."

sion, along with the Jewish sons we lost because of the education they received from their assimilated mothers! And hosts of Jewish sons have also been lost for our national liberation movement.

Personally, I hold no grudges against my parents for not sending me to high school because they wanted to protect me from having to write on the Sabbath. They did continue my education privately — I studied Russian and all the other subjects that were taught in the Gymnasium. I also learned German, which was then one of the languages spoken in Bialystok, because our city once was a part of Germany.

At the same time, I learned Hebrew. My first Hebrew teacher was the poet Mendel Dolitzki,[9] the son of the Bialystok ritual slaughterer. A former *yeshiva*[10] student who fell away, Mendel Dalitski was both a Hebrew teacher and a great heretic. I wasn't fated to study with him for long because once, as we were studying the Book of Job, my father happened to hear him interpreting the chapter: "Yet in my flesh shall I see God"[11] as "yet in my flesh I shall see nothing." That interpretation was enough for Father to fire the teacher, because he was afraid that Dolitzki would have a bad influence on me, God forbid. Afterwards, Father hired a new teacher for me and my brother, who was scarcely two years younger than I. That teacher, Asher Khaves, had come from Krinek as a young man, but by then he had a wife and two little children. He was a typical maskil[12] of those days, a former yeshiva student, self-taught. He knew Russian and German, and was a teacher by the grace of God. But he had nothing to do with the nihilist educated people who were called "Bread and Light" heretics. He was not a heretic out of spite, but one who considered that the masses had to be enlightened, taught, and educated. My teacher Asher Khaves was a good family man, an idealistic teacher. Every Sabbath and holiday, we children would go to his home. He conversed with us and later, when we were older, he told us what to read. I studied with him until it was considered time for me to get married. My brother had less desire to study; he preferred to be with my father in the office. But the teacher couldn't bear that this boy didn't want to study and one day he announced to my father: "Reb Mendel, I will not teach your boy anymore. It's a waste of your money and my work. I'd rather devote the time to your daughter. I won't take any money from you." Incidentally — that

---

9. Hebrew and Yiddish poet and author (1856–1931), born in Bialystok.
10. A school for advanced Talmud study in which adolescent boys and young men studied.
11. Job 19:26.
12. A follower of the Haskalah [Enlightenment movement], which promoted the acquisition of a secular education and acculturation to the larger society.

Asher Khaves was far from rich and for many years, he remained my friend, or as he called it, "my spiritual father."

It will certainly sound strange if I say that just as I had no child-hood, neither did I have a youth. Educated at home, I sat for days, as they say, over Torah and work. From my earliest years, I devoted all my senses to studying.

Fifty or sixty years ago, Jewish girls from pious houses didn't know anything about flirting, didn't sit in coffee houses with suitors, didn't go to dance classes. When I was young, boys didn't even cross the thresh-old of a respectable Jewish house to spend time with the grown girls. A girl was only allowed to talk with boys who were close relatives, and even then they could converse only in the presence of her parents. Whoever heard of it — a chatterbox, going out, God forbid, for a stroll with a boy. That was unheard of. Such things as a silent love affair might develop between the children of relatives; and each one knew, but yearned in silence, without the courage to show the feeling openly. In those days, we didn't know about Jewish cultural organizations, polit-ical movements, or sports federations. Jewish boys sat in study houses or in yeshivas and studied. It wasn't until years later that secret cultural work began in the big yeshivas, of all places, where young men would covertly read a Russian or a Hebrew book, hidden behind the Talmud. Those heretics became many of our famous cultural activists, poets, scholars, professors, doctors, political activists, and revolutionaries who joined both the Russian Revolutionary parties and the Zionist move-ment. Some of those enlightened young men also rejected the un-wanted patrons of Jewry at that time, who espoused the obsolete slogan that "all Jews are responsible for each other."[13] The bold ones burst out of the readymade Jewish ghetto and made their way to programs of general education, to enlightenment. They even ripped apart the tight bonds to their families and the old traditions.

But it was different with the women. Even though many of them were already caught by the winds of enlightenment, they remained in the dark. They bowed obediently to Papa's orders and later, after they were married, became subject to the rule that "he [the husband] shall rule over you."[14] Jewish girls weren't bold enough to break out of the fence of unbending customs that actually kept them enslaved. A girl didn't even have the nerve to oppose the match her father made for her.

---

13. The slogan of the Alliance Israélite Universelle, an international Jewish defense organization founded in France in 1860. The slogan comes from Babylonian Talmud, Shevuot, 39.
14. The curse imposed on Eve, found in Genesis 3:16.

In many cases, the bride didn't know her groom until their wedding. What Jewish girl would have dared consider a love match, when, ever since her childhood, she had been told that her match had been made in Heaven even before she was born?

As for me, my youth began very early. At the age of ten, I was already a grownup, a *Polner mentsh*, as the Jews said. Besides my diligent studies, back then I was a "God-seeker." I felt confined, and something was raging in me; I wanted something more than study. At the age of thirteen, every Sabbath day I would gather all the serving maids of the courtyard and read them a portion of the *Taitsch-Humash*, choosing chapters from *Menoras HaMaor*, of Psalms, and the Bible. On the Days of Awe, I went to the women's *shul*, where I was accepted as a *firzogerin* [a prayer leader] for the women who couldn't read by themselves. At that time, when I was thirteen, an absurd idea suddenly was born in me: is there a God or not? That was what I wanted to find out, no more and no less. I remember it as if it were now: I wouldn't have told anyone, for the very idea terrified me. But the idea didn't leave me alone. For perhaps a half year I couldn't sleep at night, as I considered and considered and at long last came to the conclusion that there is no God. If that is so, I said to myself, you don't have to be pious. And I stopped praying three times a day; I started combing my hair, washing myself with soap, and reading books (on the Sabbath); and I often took to expressing my thoughts. That aggravated the relations between my parents and me. Mother was especially annoyed with me. At that time, I didn't care so much that I myself was no longer pious, but I did want to attract attention. I stirred up the younger children in the house, my girlfriends, and anyone who would talk with me, listen to me. When my mother preached morals to me, I would always say: "Mama, how come I understand that you can't be like me, but you won't understand that I can't be like you?"

Along with my spiritual maturity, at the age of thirteen or fourteen, I was also physically well developed, and my parents started considering finding a match for me. Naturally they thought that a match was the only way to save me from my strong yearning to study and from my heretical thoughts. There was an even more potent factor: my child-love for my father's youngest brother.

From my earliest childhood, my bobbe—the wife of the rabbi of Plock—had loved me very much. She herself was "of beautiful form and fair to look on."[15] I remember that when she came to visit us in

---

15. Esther 2:7.

Bialystok and I went walking with her in the street, people stood still and looked at her. And it *was* plausible that my grandmother's youngest child was only a year older than I, that grandmother had given birth to her youngest son a year before I was born. When I was a child, my father would often take me along on visits to Zeyde, usually making such trips when his sisters or brothers got married. My bobbe would simply take me by the hand and would say to my father: "You know, Mendel, your Puah will be my youngest daughter-in-law. My Jacob-Moshe and your Puah are a suitable couple. He is only a year older than she is, and, with God's help, she will be his bride."

Thus they persuaded us, from childhood on, that we were bride and groom. And in truth, even as children we would write long letters, and often even brief notes, to each other. My young uncle became a rather handsome young man, dressed like a rabbinical student in a long caftan, but also a bit elegantly: he was always clean, with polished boots. He was also a capable youth; he liked to study and was preparing to be a rabbi. But that did not prevent him from being a lively, smart fellow, or, as they put it — as smart as he was pious. My father agreed to the match and even hinted that he would take Jacob-Moshe in and let him study law. But when I was fourteen and my young uncle was fifteen, my grandmother suddenly contracted typhus and died young. Our romance dragged on a while after Bobbe's death, but it was destined to be interrupted; more precisely, our love was destroyed in a strange way.

My father's oldest sister, who lived in a small town not far from Bialystok, had a daughter too. She was a few years older than my so-called bridegroom. She was far from a beauty, but was a proper Jewish girl from small-town, rich people, and she had a good lineage. They were trying to make a match for her, but it was hard to find the right match that was made in heaven. Shortly after Bobbe's death, my aunt wrote a letter to Zeyde in Plock, saying: "Puah is still a child, and she will get another bridegroom. I am giving my Bashke a dowry of two thousand rubles, I will release Moshe-Yankele (as she called Jacob-Moshe) from the army, and I will board the children forever and take from you, dear Father, the entire burden."

Zeyde forwarded the letter to my father, asking him if he would give up the match for his older sister's daughter or if he insisted on having his youngest brother as a bridegroom for his Puah. As if it were today, I remember Father calling me into his office, reading me both letters (the one from Grandfather and the one from my aunt), until he finally said to me: "Leave the bridegroom for Bashke. You'll get another bridegroom."

The truth is I practically didn't react to the whole thing, because at that time it looked to me like I was playing a children's game. My mind was taken up with quite different things, with studying and reading books. When I was fifteen, I published a translation of Frug's[16] story "Sponge" in *Ha-Zefira*.[17] I just wasn't interested in being a bride and getting married. Certainly, at the time, I didn't yet understand what they really wanted from me. So my father soon answered Zeyde that he had nothing against Moshe-Jacob marrying Bashke. When Zeyde got my father's answer, he agreed with his oldest daughter — naturally, the bride and groom practically didn't know each other — and the match was concluded. As we were about to go to the wedding of his youngest daughter (her name was Puah as well), it was agreed that at a propitious moment at the father-in-law's estate near Bialystok, all the children would meet beforehand at the house of my uncle, Abraham-Abba Rakovsky in Zembrowa, where the engagement contract between Bashke and Moshe-Jacob was to be written. It wasn't long until the entire extended family, myself included, gathered in Zembrowa. They always took me to family weddings. I met Zeyde, Aunt Puah, and my "former" bridegroom earlier at the Tshizhev station. They had taken the train from Warsaw and I came with Papa from Bialystok. On the way, in the train, my young uncle, my former bridegroom, told me in deepest secrecy that his match was not going to take place. His bride, he told me, wasn't Bashke, but *me*. My feelings for that fellow at the time are really hard for me to describe now. As I understand it, there really were no feelings; it was just a children's game.

In the evening, when we were all in Zembrowa at my uncle Abba's house, Aunt Sheynke, her husband, and her daughter Bashke, the bride, arrived. They came by horse cart from the small town of Sokolow, and it didn't take long for them to sit down and write the engagement contract. Meanwhile, the bride took a nap. They had to wake her up to sign the engagement contract. To this day, I don't know if she really saw the bridegroom, but I do remember one fact. The relatives started joking about who should get the matchmaker's fee. I boldly answered: "Zeyde, nobody but me should get the matchmaker's fee, because I let Bashke have the bridegroom." They all liked my answer and broke plates for luck. In the morning, we all went in a wagon to the farm in Stavick for my Aunt Puah's wedding.

During the week of the wedding celebrations — which was then the

16. A Jewish poet (1860–1916), who wrote in Russian and later in Yiddish as well.
17. A Hebrew newspaper, published from 1862 to 1931.

custom — my young uncle followed me around. He maintained that even though they had an engagement contract, he would never marry Bashke. Aunt Sheynke saw him following me around and went to tell Zeyde, who gave the fellow a good scolding; they threatened to let the army get him if he didn't agree to the match.

The young man was obviously not in an enviable situation. After a year, the time between the engagement contract and the wedding had run out. Meanwhile, he had done everything he could in such circumstances: he didn't write to the bride. Then he sent an anonymous letter to her parents, telling them to give up the match because no good would come of it. My father got similar letters, telling him not to make three people miserable because he, the bridegroom, Jacob-Moshe, would not marry anyone except the other Puah, his daughter. But nothing helped. They did marry him off to Bashke. And, understand, that I also went to the wedding in Sokolow, wearing a violet silk dress made especially for me for the occasion. In the *shtetl* [small town], people later stated that when the bridegroom came to lift Bashke's veil, he looked at me. You should know that the entire town of Sokolow was as big as a yawn. The bride's family were among the leading people, and everybody knew all about the "tragedy." I must add that for a while after the wedding, my young uncle still fought with his oldest sister, his mother-in-law, and even with her daughter, his wife; but the other side was stronger. In the end they conquered him. But he didn't give up easily.

About two months after his wedding, he came to see us in Bialystok. That is, he was suffering from a disease of the throat and the local doctor sent him to a specialist in Bialystok. He stayed at our house for a few days, and allegedly went to the specialist, but secretly he sought an opportunity to confess to me that it wasn't to a doctor that he came, but to me. He yearned for me. Under no circumstances would he stay with Bashke. He would work it out until she'd agree to accept a divorce from him.

My father immediately figured out that his illness was only a pretext. He told my uncle to get out of his home and never darken his doorstep again. As soon as he got home, my aunt (that is, his mother-in-law) came to us and told my Papa what trouble she had with the young man. My father shouted that they should let them get divorced. She advised my Papa that since he was so much in love with me, I should marry him right after the divorce. "I am a sister to him," my aunt claimed — "not a mother-in-law." My father got angry at my aunt and said furiously that if he wanted to marry me off to Jacob-Moshe, he would have done it earlier . . . He apparently told her to do all she could to stave off a divorce. Papa went with his sister to Sokolow and came back happy that he had made peace between the youngsters.

And then my real troubles started. My Aunt Sheynke was not altogether at peace with her son-in-law, and she kept pestering my father to marry me off as soon as possible. "As long as your Puah isn't married," she constantly argued, "he won't calm down. He'll always be thinking of Puah." And to keep the altar free of tears from the divorce of such a happy first union, they started seeking a match for me. My grandfather the rabbi naturally knew about the whole mess and it was very important for him to find a solution, so he too sought a match for the "old maid" of fifteen.

After my grandmother's death, and after having married off all his children, Zeyde married Bobbe's younger sister, a divorcee. He left Plock and obtained a rabbinical position in Mestislava, in the Smolensk District. In Yiddish, Zeyde's town was called Amtsislava. Grandfather had been the rabbi of Plock for seventeen years, although all that time he had wanted to leave.

My grandfather Leybele Plotzker was a great *Misnagid*.[18] He detested the *Hasidim* [followers of Hasidism], who therefore gave him horrible troubles. For example, in Stavisk, where Zeyde had been the rabbi as a young man, they had on one Friday put nails with their points sticking up into his bath. By chance, one of Zeyde's children happened to be sick in the house, so he didn't leave home to go to the bath house that day. When the water was later poured out, the nails were found in the bottom of the tub. After that episode, Zeyde left for Plock, where, too, there was a large community of Hasidim. There was constantly an open battle between the Misnagdim, who were the rabbi's adherents, and the Hasidim who turned out to be clear-out opponents of his.

My grandfather was known to be an honest man. Whenever he had something to say, he didn't mince words. No matter if it was one of the dignitaries of the city, no matter if it was one of his adherents or an opponent — he still said what he had to say. So the Hasidim persecuted him. I must tell of one such case. It happened one Yom Kippur [the Day of Atonement] before *Ne'ila*, the closing prayer. Grandfather was delivering his sermon. (Incidentally, he was an extraordinary speaker and would really hypnotize his audience.) All of a sudden, in the middle of

---

18. An opponent of Hasidism, the pietistic, mystical movement that developed at the end of the eighteenth century.

the sermon, he noticed on the *Bimah* [the raised dais] a Gentile woman holding a child. She approached the rabbi and asked him for food *for his child*. Grandfather controlled himself and said very calmly to the woman: "If this is my child, then you know where I live. Come to me at home." And with the same inner calm and with his previous fervor, he finished his sermon.

Later, they said in town that the Gentile woman was really a disguised man who was frightened of the rabbi's majestic bearing. Subsequently, the man gave my grandfather the names of the Hasidim who had sent this person to "negotiate." Years later, my grandfather's adherents claimed that all the people involved came to a bitter end. Zeyde didn't want to stay in such a town any longer. Right after the fast [of Yom Kippur], he left. But his adherents pursued him, unhitched the horse, hitched him to the carriage, and brought the rabbi back with a big parade.

After that incident, Zeyde didn't stay long in Plock. As I said, he moved to Amtsislava. And it was there, in Amtsislava, that they started looking for a bridegroom for me. But they didn't find one. My grandmother, Zeyde's second wife, a very energetic and clever woman, didn't want to damage our lineage and chose a bridegroom for me from a truly distinguished family. He was a relative from Karlin, a great-grandson of Rabbi Yankele Karliner. She spotted him and didn't doubt for a minute that he was my true mate, declared by Heaven on the day I was born.[19]

My parents were very pleased with the match and the bridegroom's side also consented immediately. I was the only one who didn't even know about the deal. I didn't find out about it until one day, when I was informed that the bridegroom's grandmother was coming to see me that evening. The father-in-law's mother was a daughter of Rabbi Yankele Karliner; at that time, she knew French very well, and was not some shriveled up daughter of a rabbi. I passed the examination with the grandmother with high marks, and she immediately wrote to her son in Pinsk that she found no defects in the bride. But Jewish Torah scholars had to engage in *pilpul* [casuistry], interpreting her words and asking, if she didn't find any defects in the bride, did that mean she didn't find any virtues either? The grandmother therefore immediately got up, went back to Pinsk, and asked my father to come to see the bridegroom. Papa didn't stay long. A few days later he sent a telegram in German from Pinsk: *Waare prima* [first-class commodity]. Right after that, he

---

19. From the midrash, rabbinic interpretation, Genesis Rabba, Parasha 68.

wrote a detailed letter, asking Mama to come with me to Brisk where an engagement contract would be written. It was summertime, actually the first days of Tammuz.[20] We children were then in the summer house in the big forest near Bialystok. People would travel there from the city in a *Kankes*, a horse-drawn trolley. On Friday afternoon, Mama returned to us with the glad tidings that tomorrow, right after the Havadalah service,[21] God willing, we were going to Brisk, where the engagement contract would be written. To this day I remember what I said to my mother: "Mama, what do you want from me? I don't want any bridegroom and no engagement contract. Leave me alone. I still have time. I have to study first." Then I wept bitterly and kept on crying all through the next day.

Weeping and lamenting didn't help me. Mama started coaxing me to go because Papa was already there, waiting with the bridegroom and the in-laws. You can't disgrace people. They certainly have invited friends and relatives to the betrothal. What can I lose by going? She softened me up. If I didn't like the bridegroom, she wouldn't force me. Thus, Mother got me to go to Brisk. I didn't meet the bridegroom until the engagement contract ceremony. On Sunday evening I was taken to a big hotel room where a lot of people were sitting at covered tables; the in-laws were sitting at the head of the table and the bridegroom was between them. From the distance, I saw a young man with a little yellow beard and a Homburg hat. He was ten years older than I, so his parents said. Seeing me as Mama led me to the mother-in-law, he cast shameful looks at me, knowing that everything was already prepared. The engagement contract was soon written and plates were broken. At the crash of the plates, I wept, and the mother-in-law asked my mother: "Why is the bride weeping? Doesn't she want the bridegroom?"

I pretended not to hear and didn't answer. But I did hear what the mother-in-law said to my Mama about the bridegroom's virtues. She considered him a delicate boy, and with God's help, right after the wedding she would give money so that the two of us could go "to the baths." Soon, the day after the engagement contract, the bridegroom and his parents left before anyone else. It's hard to describe how miserable I was. The only person I could weep out my bitter heart to after I came back from the engagement contract ceremony was my Hebrew teacher Asher Khaves. A few days later, when he came to congratulate my parents, he didn't restrain himself and in my presence said

---

20. Hebrew month, generally falling in July.
21. The ritual ending the Sabbath, literally "the division" between the sacred and the profane.

to my father: "I would have been happier to congratulate you five years later."

And then a new plague began for me: the correspondence with the bridegroom. Can there be anything more painful than writing love letters to a stranger? And since people had said I was a great Hebraist, who had even written in *Ha-Zefira*, my correspondence had to be in the Holy Tongue so that the bridegroom and the in-laws could show the letter around to friends and relatives and say: Look what a clever bride Shimon has got!

But writing letters wasn't all. The engagement contract had been written in early summer and at Sukes [Sukkot],[22] the bridegroom was "sent for" as a guest. When Papa took him to the big prayer house to pray on the holiday, one of his friends said to him: "Reb Mendel, we don't know which of you is the son-in-law and which is the father-in-law — he looks older than you!"

But it was decided. A few months later, they started preparing for the wedding. For those times, I was a rich bride. The bridegroom got a thousand rubles as a dowry and my papa gave me two thousand rubles as a dowry; he also supplied two years of board. My father was a big merchant of herring, salt, and petroleum. At that time, the merchandise was brought from Germany by the carload. Quite often Papa went to Königsberg, Memel, or Danzig for merchandise. Once, before my wedding, he took me with him to Königsberg, where he bought me a complete trousseau. I gladly went, since I wanted to see another country, but I had almost no interest in the purchases. With the money I got from the bridegroom's side as a bridal gift, I felt even then that it was more important to buy books than jewelry. My teacher Khaves, seeing that everything was lost, and that they would marry me off against my will, nevertheless wanted to prepare me for my life's profession. So he bought me all the books of Dr. Klenke: *The Woman as Wife, The Woman as Mother, The Mother as Educator of Her Sons and Daughters, The Sick Child,* etc.

If I were to describe now how I felt a year before I got married, I would I would say that I was in a state of lethargy. I wasn't involved in anything, and I reacted to everything as if it had nothing to do with me, but with somebody else. I was an automaton, a creature full of resignation. The closer the wedding approached, the stronger my apathy became. I responded to everything with "leave me alone," "do what you

---

22. The festival of Tabernacles, which takes place in the autumn, five days after Yom Kippur, and lasts for a week.

---

want," "it's none of my business." That was my emotional state when a special seamstress came to our house to sew the beautiful trousseau, even when she measured me for the white silk bridal gown with a long train that impressed the people in the house.

The wedding was set for the first of Tammuz. But the celebration started a whole week earlier. Our close relatives and distant relations gathered from many cities and towns. For an entire week they cooked meals for poor people, and the whole city talked about it. It was no secret that I didn't want the bridegroom. On the wedding day, people even said I would probably run away from the *khupe* [bridal canopy].

On the morning of the wedding ceremony, they made me a big wig so that not a single strand of my own hair should be seen, God forbid. In general, they did what was considered correct and necessary, as befitting a proper Jewish girl from a pious family. I was still apathetic, didn't reply to anything. All my feelings were atrophied.

That was the saddest time of my life. To this day, I cannot understand what paralyzed the stormy spirit that I had definitely been born with. Whether it was because of my youth — I was almost a child — or because the atavism of generations of enslaved Jewish women had an effect on me, I was harnessed and yoked.

My parents had promised two years of board and lodging, and had rented an apartment for us in the same courtyard where they lived. The apartment was already furnished, and we ate at my parents' house. After the honeymoon, they started talking about setting up a business. Before long we opened a shop for window panes and glass, located in the same courtyard. A big glass factory sent us whole shipments of glass sheets packed in crates, and we sold it to municipal glaziers by the crate in the nearby towns.

My parents' son-in-law — as I said — was a delicate young man; in winter he sat at home and I became the real "woman of valor," the complete merchant. But the business didn't last. "For one who wants to lose his money, deals in glass!"[23] Part of the dowry was invested in the trade, and was lost. Meanwhile, at the age of seventeen, I was nine months pregnant and gave birth to a son. [We named him Yehuda-Dov and called him Yud-Ber].[24] My parents immediately started looking for a new business. Since Bialystok was a city of big cloth factories, they decided that the son-in-law should become a commission agent. For a

---

23. In Hebrew in the text. A paraphrase of a Talmudic story, found in Baba Metzia 29.
24. The diminutive is formed from the condensation of his first name, Yehuda, and the translation of his second name, Dov (bear) which is Ber in Yiddish.

while, he went to Pinsk to be with his parents, and several Pinsk merchants promised to come to Bialystok to buy merchandise through us from the factories there. Of course, for such mediation, you earn a percentage from both the manufacturer and the buyer. In those years, that wasn't a bad livelihood to have in Bialystok. And the customers began to discover that it wasn't *he* who was the commission agent, but *I*.

It didn't take me long to wake up from my apathy. I started feeling that I couldn't remain the way I was any longer, and I experienced an internal struggle. But only when I was twenty and gave birth to a second child, a girl, whom we named Sheyna and affectionately called Sheyndl, did I go through the necessary crisis. The dormant revolutionary spirit in me woke up and I decided to end my unbearable situation. My life with a husband had given me incessant physical and moral pain. However, to be fair to him, I must say that it wasn't his fault that I was thrown at him. It wouldn't have mattered whom they had married me off to at the age of sixteen; I would no doubt have run away at the age of twenty. And if that same young man had married one of my younger sisters, they would have lived happily ever after. But I couldn't. It is enough to say that, in spite of the course of my tragic, brief family life, when I worked either selling window panes or as a cloth commission agent bringing up two children by myself, I nevertheless managed not to let myself grow dull. Like a pious Jew who takes care to pray every morning, I studied the Bible every day, learned Midrash, and attended a whole course of *"Ein Yaakov"*[25] with Haim-Jacob Kremer. I read a lot and became interested in the Hibbat Zion [Love of Zion] movement.[26] My husband complained about my activities and shouted: "May you vomit up everything you have learned!"

He was convinced that all his troubles derived from my learning, my so-called education. I concluded that I finally had to break my shackles and begin to realize my plan. I knew very well that my parents would surely not help (on the contrary, they would probably hinder me). As soon as I came up with my idea, I suddenly ceased being interested in the business and violated that law that "a proper woman does the will of her husband."[27] We began to have furious quarrels. He gave me terrible troubles and complained about me to my parents, who always took his

---

25. A collection of legends from the Talmud. Its compiler was Jacob ben Solomon Ibn Habib (1445?–1515/6), a Spanish rabbi and scholar, who also added a commentary to the sources. It has been published in more than one hundred editions.
26. A widespread Zionist movement among the masses of Russian Jews in the last two decades before the rise of political Zionism. It promoted settlement of the Land of Israel.
27. Tana Debe Eliyahu Rabba, 9.

side. He was stingy by nature, and business was very bad, so I constantly lacked money for expenses. He didn't want to give me any money and I used this as a pretext to save myself. When my parents constantly preached to me that I wasn't treating my husband right — and I couldn't reveal my internal suffering to them because they wouldn't understand me — I grew brave and argued that he was horribly stingy, that I couldn't stand him. But in order to live in peace with him, and not have to ask him for money for my expenses, I decided to learn a profession. This made an impact. I took advantage of the situation first of all to become independent. It was a means to a further goal, but things at home became unbearable.

Our conflicts grew more intense, and the business declined altogether. My husband had to liquidate it. At that time, my husband's cousin, a rich young man, went to Odessa where he engaged in large-scale commerce. The two cousins corresponded, and that cousin in Odessa offered my husband a job. That was my moment to act. I decided to go to Petersburg to enroll in a course for midwives and to give Hebrew lessons in the homes of rich Jews there. I received a certificate stating that I was a seamstress from a large tailor shop; the certificate gave me the right of residence outside the Pale of Settlement. The paper was signed by the Bialystok tailors' guild, and all I needed was an affidavit from my husband confirming that he allowed me to study. I wanted to get this before he left, and that's when the real tumult erupted. At first I spoke nicely to him — as with my parents. I implored, "You see that all attempts at commerce were unsuccessful, I have to have a profession so I can earn money. And you'll have a job with your cousin. I also want to stand on my own two feet . . ."

When he heard my arguments, he started a noisy brawl: "What! You'll study to be a midwife? Well then, go and convert instead — as far as I'm concerned, it's the same thing!" My parents took his side. I postponed persuading them until later. My main objective was to get his signature. Moreover, at that time, I was still a minor, not yet twenty-one years old. When he absolutely refused his permission, I went to the pharmacy, brought a vial of drugs, and told him: "Either you go with me to a notary or I'll throw this right in your eyes." That worked. He understood that he could drive me to take such a step, and he went with me to a notary and signed the permission paper.

With all the necessary papers in hand — and he saw that I was serious — he started preparing to go to Odessa. My first problem was getting money to travel to Petersburg. My parents would not hear of it; they simply laughed the plan off because they knew I couldn't go there against their will. I would have to leave my two children with them while I was gone. I owned a little gold watch that was the size of a Russian kopeck, and I went to sell it to a watchmaker, who agreed to give me sixty rubles for it. I told my husband, and he himself bought the little watch from me for sixty rubles.

So now I had travel expenses. But it was, of course, impossible to study and take care of two small children. My parents told me categorically: "If you do that, we'll disown you and your children. You'll study to be a midwife and you'll blacken our name. We still have to find husbands for six girls. Who will marry them if the oldest daughter is a midwife? Take your children and go wherever you want!"

In the meantime, I had to liquidate not only the business, but also the apartment; and my husband had left for Odessa. I tried to imagine staying with my parents with both children, and I saw no way out except to drown myself. Planning to burst forth into the world, and to move to Petersburg, a plan that I had delayed until now — and first your hands are tied! I waited a while, and started talking nicely to my parents: "You must understand now that I can't remain like this. I have to learn a profession and earn money. Since you don't want me to be a midwife, let me take an examination to become a teacher and open a school in Bialystok." I talked and conversed, and they agreed.

At that time, I had two aunts in Warsaw, Mother's sisters, and I asked my parents to let me go to one of them. There I would study, take an examination, and get a teacher's certificate so that I could open my own school. Even though they liked the plan, they absolutely refused to let me go to such a big city as Warsaw, although it was only a four-hour train ride from Bialystok. Their excuse was that I was too young and pretty — and I was not pious and wouldn't say that I had a husband; so, they wouldn't let me go anywhere. Moreover, they were sure that the son-in-law would do well in Odessa and would bring me and the children there. Then I would get rid of all my crazy fantasies. It didn't occur to them at the time that I didn't want to be the wife of their chosen son-in-law anymore; this was because I hadn't told them the truth. I assured them only that as soon as I could earn my own living, everything would be fine.

Here I recall an episode that made me experience another tragedy. When I was suffering torments in my so-called family life, my brother, who was a year and nine months younger, got married. That match had also been made by my grandmother, my grandfather's second wife. Once again she didn't let the lineage divert from the family; she chose a bride for my brother from Samara, deep in Russia, who was also a relative. The bride's father was one Wolf Frenkel. From Slutzk, he was a maskil, even a bit of a freethinker, who had settled in Samara where he was a distinguished merchant. He had three sons and an only daughter. Their mother, a pious woman, saw that the sons were following in their father's footsteps: They studied in the gymnasium, and the oldest one was already at the university. She wanted to save her only daughter and to marry her off to a boy from a pious Jewish home. So she wrote to her two closest relatives and the match was concluded, sight unseen. My grandfather, Rabbi Leybele, as I've mentioned, was rabbi in Amtsistlava, in the Smolensk District, at that time. Grandmother wrote to Samara that she had a bridegroom for their daughter—a relative—and they immediately sent a photograph of my brother to Samara and soon got a picture of the bride from there. Thus, bride and groom were pleased with each other and it was decided that the families would meet in Smolensk to discuss the engagement contract. And if the bride and groom liked each other in person, they would not only write the engagement contract, but would also hold the wedding right then and there. And that's what happened. My grandfather and grandmother, my parents, and the groom and the bride along with her father and mother gathered in Smolensk and a wedding was indeed held. My parents returned to Bialystok, the in-laws went back to Samara, Grandfather and Grandmother went to Amtsislava, and the young wife stayed with her husband. That couple lived happily ever after and had nine children—may the same be said of all Jews.

My brother came to Bialystok with his young wife and boarded with my parents. They stayed in our house until they opened a branch of Father's business in Malkin (four railroad stations from Bialystok). My sister-in-law, who came to be with us, became very dear to me. I was close to her all my life, and it is certainly not her fault that I had a sad experience. When they stayed with us, my sister-in-law constantly told me about her brother Moshe, a chemistry student at the university in Riga. One time she said to me: "If my brother Moysei [the Russian version of Moshe] saw you, he'd fall in love with you on the spot!"

Her words made me shudder; they really scared me. She immediately wanted to show me his photograph. I told her I didn't want to see it and I ran away; I wouldn't read his letters to her even when she insisted. As I later learned, all this didn't keep her from constantly writing to her brother about me. This went on until my brother and his wife stopped boarding with us and moved to Malkin.

Meanwhile, I was waiting for my parents to agree to my trip to Warsaw. Once, in summer, my father had to go to Warsaw on business, and he asked me to accompany him. At home they saw how cheerful I was. "Bring the children," Father told me. "You'll leave them in Malkin with Yente (my sister-in-law), and you'll go to Warsaw with me."

Even before we set out, my sister-in-law had written me, inviting me to visit her with the children for the summer. Why sit in the heat in Bialystok, when you can be in such a nice summer place as Malkin? Moreover, she wrote, you will have interesting company here. My brother is *coming here from Riga for vacation*. And that was precisely what made me not want to go. I was scared when I thought about that encounter. But I did want the children to enjoy fresh air while I, meanwhile, might succeed in getting Father to let me stay with one of my aunts in Warsaw to prepare for the examination. I took the children and left.

My sister-in-law was waiting for us at the train in Malkin. She took the children home with her and I traveled to Warsaw with my father. Father stayed only a few days, and I stayed a few days more with my older Aunt Berman. But I promised Papa that I would go to Malkin for the summer. I stayed about a week in Warsaw, and was pondering whether to go to my sister-in-law, who was pelting me with letters asking why I was spending the summer in suffocating Warsaw. But I was afraid to go because of that encounter, and for a long time I didn't. At last, I made myself do it. When I came to Malkin at midnight, nobody in my brother's house was asleep; they were all sitting at the table, including Moysei, my sister-in-law's brother from Riga. As soon as I saw him, I knew that not for nothing had I feared that encounter. Later he also told me his experience, that his sister's letters had made him fall in love with me — from a distance. He could hardly wait for the day when he would arrive. He felt that he would meet a person he was destined to wait years for, for a chance to bring us together.

Before long a genuine, pure love emerged in us — not a physical love, not a banal love, but a spiritual, platonic love that can be born only in a time of romanticism. We were together at my brother's during the vacation, about ten weeks, and never again in our life did we meet. When we parted, we thought the separation was only temporary, that it couldn't destroy our happiness. He was in his third year at the university, and had almost three more years until he finished his studies; while I now had to start a life-and-death struggle for a divorce. For me this effort was accompanied by a sense of exaltation so holy I wouldn't confide it to anyone, not even to my sister-in-law. But when I returned to Bialystok, I had to confide in my Hebrew teacher Khaves so I could get letters at his address. But there was one thing I didn't tell him — that

Moysei was a Cohen.[28] Neither of us had considered that to be a problem. He had so little concern for Jewish laws that he even laughed at
them; as for me, with my heretical world view, I said to myself: If I get
the divorce, we'll go to another country. His last name is Frenkel, not
Cohen, we'll get married without a rabbi.

Obviously, that event reinforced my desire to become independent
immediately. Once again, I initiated very serious discussions with my
parents, explaining to them that I had to take an examination, become
a teacher, and open a school. At long last, my father found a way. My
grandfather was leaving Amtsislava to become the rabbi in Mariompol,
in the Suwalki district. He was seventy years old and wanted to spend
his old age in the city where he had been a rabbi — without pay — back
when he was a young man. As we know, my grandparents were well off.
In Mariompol was the estate of Zolshup which my grandfather had
owned in his youth, when he had been engaged in agriculture. Indeed,
my grandfather was called Leybele Zolshuper. The grave of his mother
Puah, the Suwalki rabbi's wife after whom I was named, was also in
Mariompol. When my papa was convinced that he couldn't do anything
with me, for I was determined to go and study, he said to me on one fine
day, "If you want to go study, I have some advice: Go to your grandfather
in Mariompol. There is a boy's gymnasium there. In Grandfather's
house, you can study to your heart's content and take the examination in
the gymnasium." "What are you talking about?" I said, frightened. "How
can I go to Grandfather's, since I'm not so pious? And will Zeyde allow
me to study?" "That's my business," answered Papa. "Tomorrow I am
going to Mariompol and will bring you a letter from Grandfather saying
that you should come and study for the examination."

And that's what happened. Papa went and brought me a letter from
Grandfather. Zeyde warmly invited me to come to him: He wouldn't
prevent me from studying and taking the necessary examination. It
wasn't long before I set out. My sister-in-law took my three-year-old
daughter. My five-year-old son had already started kheyder. By the age of
seven, he was learning seven pages of Talmud a week and my father was
sure that he would grow up to be a great rabbi. There was only one
obstacle: when I fell into "depravity," I threw away the big wig that had
been put on me after I was married. How could I go to Grandfather, the
rabbi, with my own hair? I finally came up with the idea of ordering a
little artificial pompadour, as it was called in those days. It was worn
more on the forehead than on the head. People would make them from

---

28. According to Jewish law, a Cohen (of the priestly line) could not marry a divorcee.

their own hair. My hairdresser was experienced in making one, and in April 1888, under a good star, I left for Mariompol.

Studying along with me in Zeyde's house was his grandson from a daughter who had died at the age of thirty-seven. The orphan was almost the same age as I. He was preparing to be ordained as a rabbi. My arrival was a real surprise for the small town. Two little boys made a bet: One said that he knew for sure that I was a wife with two children; the other claimed that he knew from a reliable source that I was a maiden. They stopped the rabbi's servant in the street and questioned her. It turned out that the truth naturally made one of them lose the bet. Meanwhile, I was corresponding with my sister-in-law's brother, Moysei Frenkel. I received the correspondence in general delivery and everything remained strictly secret.

When I started studying, I had to have a tutor, a gymnasium student from the sixth class. Grandfather agreed on condition that the teacher be a Christian. "Why a Christian?" I wondered. "Understand, my child," Grandfather explained to me. "A Christian will come, give you your lesson and go away. But a Jew will get into various conversations with you. You're not pious; it's not the same." "Zeyde," I retorted. "Never in my life have I studied with a Christian and you certainly don't know that I detest *goyim* [Gentiles]." "Good," Grandfather agreed. "There are two brothers, gymnasium students, named Burak; the older one is in the eighth class and the younger is in the seventh. I'll make a deal with the younger one. He is a pious boy. I meet him every morning going to pray before he goes to the gymnasium."

I didn't try to tell Zeyde that I needed the older one more because I had to master the course of the eighth class. But out of politeness to Grandfather, I let it go. I studied with the younger Burak for only a few months because his eyes became diseased — he had to go to Königsberg for an operation — and his older brother took his place. I studied for the examination for eight whole months. The entire time, I spoke and corresponded in Yiddish. I spoke Russian without errors, but not fluently. I wrote better than my tutor, the gymnasium student. Quite often he used my written compositions on themes that students in the eighth class had to write. I really did study diligently, day and night. Grandmother would often find my untouched dinner from the day before. In summer, when it was very hot, I studied in the cellar. Grandmother was very sad that I was destroying my health.

She wasn't a great beauty, that grandmother, but she was a clever woman. Not only did she love me — she also understood me. We all called her Aunt Sonya, and in a certain sense she had experienced a tragedy like mine. She had been married off very young, as was the custom in those days. She didn't love her husband and demanded a divorce from him, but he absolutely refused. She had only one daughter with him. With a small child in her arms, she left him while still young, ran a business by herself, raised the daughter all by herself, and married her off to a "genius," who later became a rabbi in Odessa. For years Aunt Sonya was an *agunah*, a grass widow, waiting for a divorce.[29] But that wasn't all. During her shattered life, she liked a relative and he liked her, too; but he was a Cohen. Even if she got a divorce from her husband, both that pious woman and her relative couldn't get married. This was a powerful experience for both of them. Naturally, my grandfather knew the story of Aunt Sonya, who had wasted her youth on a man who was a semi-idiot. After Bobbe's death, Grandfather's children began to be very interested in Aunt Sonya's fate and — as she would later tell — after so many years, she miraculously managed to get the divorce, and shortly thereafter married my grandfather, the rabbi.

Why I studied so diligently was obvious: My whole life now depended on my examination, my self-liberation from the shackles that fettered me. My own future and the future of my children depended on it. I hadn't corresponded with their father from the moment he left for Odessa. He was living with the Odessa rabbi, Aunt Sonya's son-in-law (one was tied and bound, all around us were relatives from the same line). My parents often got letters from him, and would send me his regards. It never occurred to my parents that I didn't want to be his wife anymore. To achieve my goal, over the eight months I didn't think about anything except studying. The only indulgence I allowed myself was writing letters to Frenkel, which gave me the courage and energy to prepare for my goal.

Fate decreed that my first written examination should fall on Yom Kippur. Seven other young people — all Christians — were examined along with me. I was the only woman and the granddaughter of a rabbi. At Grandfather's request, one of his friends went to the director, told him who I was, and arranged for me to take the examination after Yom Kippur. Even now I remember what happened: Grandfather gave me his blessing for the examination. As he saw it, his blessing — along with my strenuous studying — was what did the trick. For the first examination, I had to sketch my autobiography. I was a sensation for the whole faculty, mainly because I was the granddaughter of a rabbi. The exam-

29. In Jewish law a husband alone has the power of divorce. If he refuses to grant his wife a divorce, she cannot remarry.

ination lasted a few days; and I passed it with high marks, doing much better than all seven young men.

After the examinations, I had to teach some "sample lessons" from the material I had selected for my specialty. Most chose mathematics for their specialty, but I took the German language. First of all, from child-hood on, I had loved *languages* and not *arithmetic;* second, at that time, back in Bialystok, there were no authorized German language teachers in the Russian schools and gymnasia. I gave my test lessons in the second class in the gymnasium. The teachers, the director, and the inspectors were all present. Incidentally, this was the first class I had ever taught in my life. Afterwards, the director shook my hand and said approvingly that I would be a good teacher. Unfortunately, my joy at that time was overshadowed by great sorrow. Shortly before the exam-ination, Aunt Sonya entrusted me with the painful secret that Grand-father was suffering from a tumor on his chest, and that the tumor was growing. He had to have an operation, and so I spent a few weeks in Mariompol after the examination.

I came back to Bialystok at Sukes. My parents and everyone at home congratulated me on achieving my goal; and Father addressed these words to me: "Well, my child, now you have achieved what you wanted, and you are independent. Shimon [my husband] has a good job in Odessa with his cousin. You will go to Odessa to open a school, and with God's help, you will live happily."

This time, I replied on the spot. I wasn't seventeen years old any-more, as at my wedding, but twenty-three. Very calmly, but firmly, I told my father that I didn't want to be Shimon's wife anymore. I had been taken to the engagement contract at Brisk by force; I would not be taken to Odessa by force; and I wouldn't go until the train from Bialy-stok to Odessa ran underground. "How can that be?" my father argued. "You yourself said that you simply wanted to be able to earn money yourself, and everything would be fine. Does that mean you fooled us all? And whoever heard of a wife who doesn't want to live with her husband, especially when you have two children with him — because you don't love him? A strange motive: Yashka and Stashke love each other, but Jews? . . .You get married, you have children, and you live." "Papa," I answered, "for my children I am willing to do anything in the world, except for one thing: I will not be their father's wife anymore! All I have to do now is make him give me a divorce."

It's hard to imagine the turmoil my harsh complaint evoked in my whole family, as well as the family on the other side. My husband's father immediately came from Pinsk. He had a very serious discussion with me: first nicely and then nastily. First he promised to give his son a second dowry to replace the three thousand rubles he had lost in business. I answered him:

"Even if he drove me in golden carriages, I still wouldn't want to be your son's wife. If you see him as a devoted father, let him release me because I am as great a misfortune for him as he is for me." "Never in your life will you get a divorce!" the father-in-law shouted angrily. But I said calmly: "*He* needs the divorce, not me. For me, the world is now open even without a divorce."

Since my parents were against me, the two sides carried on negotiations. My father winked to the father-in-law: "Let her go. Now she's simply crazy. The craziness will pass; she will come to her senses and everything will be fine." After the father, my husband's younger brother came from Minsk. He stayed with us for a few days, had long discussions with me, convinced he would persuade me to take the children and go to Odessa as soon as possible. Seeing that he was powerless to do anything, he concluded his talks with me and said grimly: "You know, Puah, that you will get a divorce from Shimon only over my dead body . . ."

After all the wrangling, it was impossible for me to stay with my parents. I rented an apartment and started seeking pupils for lessons in Russian, German, and Hebrew. Before long, I had several female students and started earning money. Meanwhile, I started preparing documents to send to Grodno so that the school inspector would allow me to open a four-grade pre-gymnasium in Bialystok. But they turned me down. According to them, I had no right to run any school in the Vilna educational district — to which Bialystok belonged — because I had taken my examinations in Mariompol, in the Warsaw district, so I was allowed to open a school only in a city within the Warsaw district. I was upset, went to Grodno, and set up a howl, which naturally had no effect. Then I went to Vilna and protested to the head of the educational district. But it was like talking to the wall. If you want to run a school in the area of the Vilna educational district, you have to be examined again in the Vilna district. I didn't calm down and I appealed to the educational ministry in Petersburg. That ministry demanded all the written work I had submitted for the examination in the Warsaw teachers' circle; as their response showed, my teacher's certificate was confirmed by the ministry. The ministry was aware that such an absurd law existed, but the outcome was the same: if you don't want a school in the Warsaw educational district, you have to take the examination again. That sad episode certainly affected my life. In Bialystok, I already had several pupils who were simply waiting for me to open the school. I loved my hometown. In general, in those years, Bialystok was a city of Torah and learning, of maskilim and Jewish intellectuals. Even then Bialystok was a cradle of Hibbat Zion, under the influence of Rabbi Shmuel Mohilewer[30] and his secretary Rabbi Yitzhak Nissenbaum.[31] When political Zionism emerged, Bialystok was distinguished for its Zionist activists; even then, they diligently studied Hebrew. Even girls were allowed to study the Holy Tongue — in the most pious houses.

The harsh decree to leave my hometown, my relatives, and my loved ones, was very difficult for me. It was painful to move suddenly to another world, in Russian-Poland, where even the Jews were foreign to me; in the forty-six years I later lived there I remained the Litvak [the rationalist Lithuanian Jew] — I was absolutely unable to assimilate with my Polish brothers and sisters. But there was no choice. I received permission to open a school in Lomza and there I had to go. And in my first school, more than a half century ago, I started teaching my students Hebrew. At that time, we didn't yet know about teaching "Hebrew in Hebrew." The official language of instruction in the schools was Russian, so I taught Hebrew in Russian translation. I left my six-year-old son with my parents temporarily, and soon took my four-year-old daughter with me. Later, I was joined by one of my younger sisters who was preparing for the entrance examination to dental school. She studied and helped me in the school at the same time. In Lomza, I ran the school for only two years, and then I moved to Warsaw.

In Lomza, I came across one of my father's former friends, one Tikotshinski. First, he brought his children to my school, and soon he and his family became very close to me. A clever man, Tikotshinski could have studied, but he was "caught up in action." He was quite a heretic. As a director of businesses, he often made trips to Warsaw and various cities in Russia. I don't know how it happened, but I confided all my secrets to Tikotshinski, even about my romance with my sister-in-law's brother, the Cohen, who was about to complete his studies. Incidentally, our correspondence intensified during the two years I spent in Lomza; I often got letters from him and woodcarvings that he himself made. We had the patience to wait — he for his diploma and I for my divorce. But my husband wouldn't consider a divorce, and my parents didn't want to hear about it either. All we could do was wait. My only interests were my school, further study, and bringing up my little girl.

---

30. A member of Hibbat Zion and one of the founders of religious Zionism (1824–1898).
31. A Hebrew writer and religious Zionist (1868–1942).

My first real, platonic but genuine love warmed me, and was once again destroyed by my parents. This is how it happened.

Before my parents knew about my love, my Lomza friend Tikotshinski came to tell me that he was going to Odessa on business, and wanted to take that opportunity to meet with my husband to try to persuade him to release me. I liked the idea and gave him my husband's address, but asked Tikotshinski not to tell him forbidden things about me: that I had become a terrible heretic, had thrown away my wig, had a non-kosher kitchen. My parents washed their hands of me and thought I might ultimately marry a *goy* [non-Jew]. Tikotshinski followed my good advice, but nothing came of the meeting. My husband answered him, "She is a heretic; I believe that, but as a wife she is very decent and she will not get remarried; neither to a *goy* nor to a Jew, if she doesn't have a divorce." And a divorce he would never give me. My parents learned by themselves, from my sister-in-law's parents, about my romance with their oldest son, and it's easy to imagine what happened. A dreadful tragedy! Can there be anything more terrible than an affair of a Cohen and a divorcee? My father immediately came to Lomza, sat with me for three days in a row, and demanded only one small thing: a letter stating that I gave up Moysei. I began explaining nicely to Papa that Moysei didn't know about anything, and second, I asked him not to ruin my young life again. Since my arguments didn't help, I declared calmly: "Papa, even if you cut me up into twelve pieces,[32] every individual piece will tell you: 'I will not give up Moysei, unless you make him give me up.'"

My father left with nothing, and a few days later my brother arrived. I hid from him because I was told that he would pour a liquid on me that would make my face ugly, and then his brother-in-law wouldn't have me. My brother stayed in Lomza a few days, didn't see me the whole time, and went back.

And what was happening in the meantime with the Cohen? He graduated before my parents found out that he loved me. Before his examinations, he started asking me in his letters to let him come see me before he went home to Samara. "For three years I have loved air, and I can't hold out anymore. I won't come to you at home, but to a hotel. I know you live in a small town, and as an educator you have a position in society. I simply want to see you, that's all." I didn't agree and wrote firmly that until I had the divorce, I didn't want to see him at all. I couldn't disgrace my children and didn't want them to condemn me when they grew up. Since he had no choice, he went straight home to

---

32. Reference to an incident in Judges 19.

Samara from Riga where, in his parents' home, he first learned what obstacles lay on the path to our happiness. When his mother tried to persuade him, he took out my photograph, showed it to her, and said: "This is the picture of my bride." His mother knew me very well (she once visited her daughter and had often met me), and answered: "For that person, I am willing to give my soul, but she has a husband!" He countered: "She will get a divorce, Mama!" Only then did they explain to him that, even after a divorce, he was not allowed to marry me because he was a Cohen. That surprised him so much that he immediately wrote to me about it, ending the letter with the assertion that no law in the world could shatter our happiness. He thought I shouldn't wait for a divorce, but should come immediately with the children to Samara; or — if I wanted — we would go to America.

Stubbornly adhering to my decision to wait for a divorce, I wrote back to him that I couldn't take such a step at present. Aware of the danger to my family with its lineage of thirty-six generations of rabbis, my parents used all means possible to prevent me from getting a divorce. Meanwhile, they proceeded to the second family, that is, the Cohen's. When Moysei didn't give in, they went after his mother. His father, the heretic, naturally informed my parents that he scoffed at the superstition that a Cohen may not [marry a divorcee] . . . My parents wrote to the mother to prevail upon her son to extricate himself from the outrage. And if she wouldn't help, they would send the daughter and her three children back to Samara; that is, her husband, my brother, would divorce his wife. In this atmosphere, it was hard for Moysei to stay home so he went to take a job with a chemist in the village of Bagotia. In despair, he didn't want to see how all this would end.

When his mother saw that he was preparing to leave, she urged him to promise her that he wouldn't marry me without her consent. She pestered him until he finally gave her his promise. Then he left. I got a letter from him in Bagotia almost every day, telling me about the family of the elderly chemist, who was bringing up his orphaned brothers and sisters after his father's death; one of them was a grown-up girl. His landlord soon regarded him as a match for his sister . . . That can be assumed because he wanted to know whom Frenkel was constantly writing to. He replied that he was corresponding with a friend, but the elderly chemist immediately noted that the letters were written in a woman's handwriting. Strange, he'd say, is this how a man writes? And when Frenkel argued that a man could also write like that, knowing jokes started. But the fact is that that correspondence lasted only four or five months and suddenly broke off. I waited a few days and cabled:

"What happened?" Anything can happen to a person. But no answer came. Of course, my parents in Bialystok already knew about the happy occasion, and my father wrote to tell me that Moysei was engaged to marry his boss's sister. "Now, daughter"—Father urged—"you don't need a divorce anymore, right?" I answered short and sharp: Even if he had told me that Moysei had already got married, I would still demand the divorce. And now he didn't have to be afraid anymore and should tell Shimon to divorce me. Jews who can study Talmud can also split hairs. My father explained that the story of Moysei's engagement contract was only a trick to get the divorce and really to be able to marry me. What! For me that was no fiction. I packed up all the letters that I had gotten from him over the past three years, along with his woodcarvings, and threw them into the fire. With that I also burned my first real, pure love, and wrenched it out of my heart. In reality, before long I learned that Moysei had gotten married.

Despite my difficult experience, one fact is enough to show how cheerful I was at that time: Three or four months after Moysei's engagement, my little daughter, my father, my younger sister, and I went from Lomza to Kutne to the wedding of my cousin, the one who had studied for ordination while I was also studying in Grandfather's house. When I came to Warsaw, where my father and sister were waiting for me to continue on to Kutne, my sister told me about Moysei's wedding. I simply said: "May they be happy." We traveled all night long and the next day, at my cousin's wedding, I danced all night, and none of the guests would believe that I was the mother of the four-year-old girl.

At the same time, I thought that after his wedding, it might be easier for me to get the divorce. But the trouble was that my father still believed the marriage was a fiction. Now I seemed to have the hope of leaving the provinces immediately and going to teach in Warsaw. My father's friend, Tikotshinski, stayed in Warsaw on business, where he lived with a good friend of his, Eliezer Kaplan, who was an agent for the big Tshereshevski tobacco factory in Grodno. Eliezer Kaplan was a Zionist who belonged to Bnei Moshe [an elite Zionist group] and was a member of the recently founded publishing house *Ahiasaf*. I often wrote to Tikotshinski in Hebrew about my personal life, and he would read my letters to Kaplan to show him how a woman could write Hebrew. Kaplan started asking about me and soon realized that he knew who I was. His wife happened to be from Bialystok and knew my family. When he heard that I ran a school in Lomza, Kaplan rejoiced and asked Tikotshinski to invite me to teach in a *kheyder* for girls that Bnei Moshe had established in Warsaw. They had been looking for a licensed teacher who knew Hebrew, but couldn't find one in all Russian-Poland. The members of that founding committee included Shefer-Rabinovitch, Nahum Sokolow,[33] A. S. Friedberg, M. M. Pruss, Ze'ev Gluskin, Eliezer Kaplan, and Attorney Stavski.

I received an invitation to come to Warsaw from that committee a few days before Pesach [Passover], and as soon as I closed my school for the Pesach holiday, I set out; and during the week of Pesach, they were already having discussions with me. The committee members went into everything: Yes, you are a good teacher for all subjects, even foreign languages, since you are licensed, but how can we be sure that you can teach Hebrew? It was a fair question, and I suggested we carry out some test lessons together in Hebrew, which we did. Throughout the Passover week, they called a group of women students from a class, and in the presence of Shefer, Friedberg, Pruss, and Nahum Sokolow, I took my Hebrew examination. Obviously, they liked me as a Hebrew teacher, and offered me a salary of thirty rubles a month for six hours a day. We agreed that right after Passover, I would come to work. I promised to go back and close my school.

But things didn't go smoothly. As the saying goes, bad luck goes before me. The writer M. M. Pruss was a classmate of my husband, and knew my whole story. He told the school committee that they couldn't have anything to do with me because he knew for a fact that my husband would immediately drag me away by force, right from the start. His argument was effective. They called me to another meeting and told me that we couldn't proceed with the deal until I got a divorce from my husband. I saw that arguments wouldn't help and I was ambitious; I stated only that this was my personal affair and nobody else's business, and I went back to Lomza.

Needless to say, this turn of events upset me very much. Both my parents and his didn't care that I was considered separated, and not permitted a divorce — they didn't let me move freely, didn't let me live as I wanted, on my own. To say that this was dreadful for me is an understatement. My brain went to work and I finally came up with a daring invention: A month before Rosh Hashonoh, I wrote three letters, deliberately in Hebrew. One letter to my grandfather the Mariompol rabbi (after the operation, he lived three more years), one to my father in Bialystok, and one to my husband in Odessa. The letter said: "If you won't release me and send me a divorce immediately, I will convert with both of the children." That letter had the proper effect.

---

33. Nahum Sokolow (1859–1936), Hebrew writer, journalist, and prominent Zionist leader.

Neither my parents, my husband's parents, nor my husband himself understood how far I was from such a step. They knew only that I wasn't pious; therefore, they assumed that *such a thing* could also be believed. The first one to respond to my letter was my grandfather. He wrote to my father that they should give me a divorce, and his letter was tough, and really a command. Then the in-laws discussed it among themselves and with my husband, and the divorce decree was sent to the Lomza rabbi. But that did not yet bring my salvation. The rabbi found a defect in the divorce decree and wanted to send it back, but I wouldn't let him. I had become friendly with the daughter of the rabbinical authority in Lomza at that time, and he helped me. I urged him to show me the law that said that the divorce decree was defective, and I told him that if they refused me my divorce, that would be the end of me. My husband was very pious, and if the divorce decree came back to Odessa, he would see it as the finger of God, would never give me a divorce, and my life would be ruined. Without telling the rabbi, the rabbinical authority assured me that the divorce decree was not defective according to the law. I stood firm against the rabbi, didn't let him send the divorce decree back, and won the battle. Eventually, the rabbi delivered the divorce decree to me, and I felt released. I immediately wrote to the school committee in Warsaw that the only obstacle had been cleared — I had received a divorce and could come to take the job right after Sukes.

That's exactly what happened in September 1891: I became principal of the *kheyder* for girls in Warsaw.

Two

A *Kheyder* for Girls

I was twenty-six years old in 1891 when I came to Warsaw to teach Hebrew and Russian at the girls' *kheyder* of Bnei Moshe in Poland. I left my eight-year-old son with my parents in Bialystok. My father wanted to educate him to be a rabbi because the boy had a good mind, and at the age of seven had learned seven whole pages of Talmud a week. I took my six-year-old daughter with me. Even though I was very happy to get my teaching job — the work was intellectually gratifying — I was even more satisfied by my economic independence.

I felt that I was a teacher by the grace of God and even then I realized that, like an artist or a writer, a teacher had to be born; yet, I also felt that I had to study more, and not be satisfied simply with a teacher's diploma. I thought that I needed to go abroad to study pedagogy. I knew I could earn enough teaching Hebrew in Switzerland, for example, to be able to live modestly and study at the same time. With that goal in mind, I settled in Warsaw that first year, finding room and board for myself and my little daughter in a boarding house at Karmelicka 27, in a home run by a former principal of a Polish school, a very assimilated Polish Jewish widow with two sons. She herself had lost her right to run a school because the Russian school inspector caught her teaching Polish in one of her classes. I lived frugally so that I could save enough from my income that year to be able to travel abroad to study.

But one thing bothered me very much: Should I take both children with me or leave the boy to be educated by my father? I was afraid that such an education would separate my own child from me since my father and I were far apart spiritually, and that distance was liable to open a chasm between me and my son. I was torn apart: It was bad enough that I had taken my child's father away, but should he also be robbed of his mother? The idea often hurt me — who knows if, years later, my children wouldn't condemn me for my fateful step of leaving their father!

This internal struggle lasted almost a whole year and ended with the triumph of maternal love. I decided I could complete my studies at a university in Warsaw, where instruction would be in Russian. I wrote my parents to bring my son to me, rented a small apartment in a poor neighborhood, and made do on my salary. Since I couldn't keep house, I asked my mother, may-she-rest-in-peace, at my request, to send me her maid Rachel, a widow with a child, who had previously worked for my parents and now was willing to work for me. I agreed to let her and her child live in our house; I put everything in her hands and could go on working. That pleased my mother because she was sure that Rachel would keep a kosher Jewish kitchen in my house. Naturally, I let her.

Living my independent life, along with my teaching, I didn't forget my inner obligation to fight for the freedom of women, especially Jewish women, always the most enslaved of all by self-appointed guardians who burdened them and apparently wanted to save their souls. I saw the economic independence of women as the main factor behind their personal and social liberation, and I set myself the goal of working with all my might for the their liberation. I wanted to spread that idea among the various classes of Jewish women. Today's youth who have cast off the solution of "Torah and work" cannot even imagine how we Jews regarded work and crafts more than fifty years ago. The greatest disgrace in a family was to have a relative who worked as a craftsman; families of high status boasted with the greatest pride that they had no such stain. Today, who even talks about teaching a girl to work? But back then, you didn't dare say such a thing. The words of the folksong we sang in those days sound typical:

The nursery rhyme who will sew?
Sarahke the seamstress, lower than low! . . .

Jewish girls had to sit and wait for their intended bridegrooms, for a match, which was determined by Heaven for every single one of them forty days before they were born. Go study a profession? God forbid!

Uprooting that crippled notion, cleaning the mold off the psychology of generations, was not easy. Enlightenment-work like that went on for decades. Even in our national and historical home, where we have come to reeducate ourselves emotionally and economically so that we can rebuild ourselves; even in the Land of Israel, we have dragged our Exile-notions. Strange as it may sound, I can boast that I was one of the pioneers of the movement in Poland to make the Jewish masses productive. Intuition led me to start that work among individual Jews.

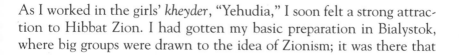

Our family was large and very extensive. I had relatives in almost every city and town of Russian-Poland at that time, and my example reverberated among the members of my family. As soon as I moved to Warsaw, I started getting letters from female cousins and other relatives who were coming to Warsaw to study some profession. They asked me to help them get settled and I gladly agreed. My little apartment at Pokorna 6 soon became a gathering spot for all the candidates. It was a good time because various industries in Warsaw were operating at a fast pace; Russia was an enormous market that gobbled up all kinds of merchandise. There was a shortage of labor in the production of women's clothing, scarves, millinery, straw hats, etc. There weren't enough hours in the day: People worked three or four shifts — during the day, and at night they took work home.

I had no lack of acquaintance with merchants because the only school in Warsaw where girls learned the Holy Tongue was very popular; therefore, I could get work for all the girls who needed my help. Incidentally, there was also a small workshop in my home: Two of my cousins worked on scarves and a third studied hatmaking. From eight o'clock in the morning, my two children and I were at school, and my empty room was turned into a workshop. My two cousins, from Plock, were orphans from my father's sister; the third was a young woman who was stuck in a bad marriage and whose husband wouldn't give her a divorce. We all lived together. At night we set up beds. The main thing was that everyone was cheerful, lively, and energetic. My two children attended my school; I found a *melamed* [tutor] who taught my son Talmud, and I studied alongside him.

What an interesting and rich life, especially since we struggled so hard for it!

Als I worked in the girls' *kheyder*, "Yehudia," I soon felt a strong attraction to Hibbat Zion. I had gotten my basic preparation in Bialystok, where big groups were drawn to the idea of Zionism; it was there that leaders like Reb Shmuel Mohilewer and A. S. Herschberg emerged.[1] It's hard for me to say when and how I became a Zionist. I often think I was a Zionist from my earliest childhood because of my education, the *kheyder*, the Bible, and later, perhaps, because of the pogroms against the Jews. One fact from my childhood has remained deep in my memory: My mother's mother owned a big mill not far from Bialystok, in the town of Soprasle, a picturesque area with a large forest on one side and green lawns on the other, along with splendid farms and low mountains in the background. The Soprasle brook flowed through the town. In summer, we children would go to a *dacha* in Soprasle. When I was eight years old, on one summer Saturday afternoon when the grown-up world was sleeping, I crossed the bridge and went off to the mountains, believing I would find the Land of Israel beyond them. When the servants noticed that I was gone, they went looking for me and when they finally found me, they asked me where I had gone so far. I innocently answered that I had gone to the Land of Israel. Thus, the Land of Israel later came to me both in dream and in reality.

In 1891, when I arrived in Warsaw, I heard that a Fräulein Leah Levin-Epstein had recently returned from the Land of Israel where she had spent a whole year with her brother, the founder and administrator of Rehovot. I got her address from a member of the school board of Yehudia, the distinguished Zionist leader, Ze'ev Gluskin.[2] I went over to her home and purely and simply told her: "I heard you were in the Land of Israel, I have come to see you, and I want to be your friend." That was the Land of Israel for me at the age of twenty-six. From that moment on, I became friends with Leah Proshansky — née Levin-Epstein — a friendship that has lasted fifty years. Not only did we feel a close personal bond, but we were also connected by the common ideal of working in our liberation movement.

Right after we met, Leah became very interested in the Yehudia *kheyder* and its financial situation. She was curious about the financial bases of the first *kheyder* for girls in Hebrew. The budget of Yehudia had to be covered by: 1) tuition; and 2) the school board that collected dues from members. The chairman of the budget committee was Ze'ev Gluskin. Tuition was two rubles a month for children of wealthy parents; a certain discount was given to those who were less well-to-do; and a

---

1. A member of Hibbat Zion, a textile manufacturer, and a Hebrew scholar and writer (1858–1943).
2. An early Zionist (1859–1949), in 1905 he immigrated to Palestine where he was among the founders of the publishing house Ahiasaf and of the Zionist settlement of Rehovot.

number of poor children were completely exempt from tuition. Naturally, there was a big deficit each month.

At that time, in Jewish schools, as in khadorim [pl. of kheyder],
pupils were accepted not for an entire school year but for a semester:
from Pesach to Sukes and from Sukes to Pesach. There were no vacations. Jewish children mustn't rest; Jewish children must study day
and night, summer and winter, without any interruption. Vacations,
dachas — they were for others, for Christians. For years, the faculty itself
hadn't allowed vacations at khadorim and schools. And there was no
school year, no yearly tuition. If a child dropped out of school because
he was sick, God forbid, you didn't have to pay any tuition for him. This
was also the case in Yehudia, where even tuition for richer children
wasn't paid on time, and people didn't take into consideration the
difficult financial situation of the educational institution. Even fathers
who were drawn to Zionism didn't appreciate the importance of Hebrew for their daughters, and pious Jews strictly maintained the rule
that "everyone who teaches his daughter Torah, it's as if he teaches her
licentiousness." More progressive fathers gladly taught their daughters
other languages, but the Jewish fathers argued that Hebrew — the Holy
Tongue — was for boys. Therefore, Yehudia, a Hebrew school for girls,
had a hard time. Ze'ev Gluskin was the business manager for the famous
Trackenheim Company on Nowlecki Street. As principal of the school,
I had each month to get the budget from him to pay the faculty, rent,
and so on. Each time, I waited hours until Ze'ev Gluskin gave me the
necessary sum. It was hard, and my friend Leah Proshansky helped a
great deal to cover expenses. She formed a women's committee to
expand the membership that paid monthly fees, and women who were
on the committee also paid dues. The women worked so well that I was
able to introduce evening courses for poor children. For fifty kopeks a
month, they could study in Hebrew for four hours a day.

This was a major undertaking, but I was not completely satisfied
with either the *kheyder* or the evening classes. Many of the girls were
desirable students who studied in my school for a year or two and then
went off to larger schools. And Hebrew didn't suit everyone, not even
the parents with Zionist tendencies, who ultimately regarded their children's education more practically.

Things reached such a pass that I began to think of changing my
kheyder into a two-grade primary school. I had no trouble getting permission for this from the school authorities, because Russian was the
language of instruction in the school. The change worked. The school
was extended to three years, and the expanded curriculum made for

greater success, even with the study of Hebrew. The school's financial situation also improved.

But all this still wasn't enough for me. Hebrew is a difficult language, I said to myself; and Torah needs to be taught. It's not used at home or on the street. Our fathers and brothers study for years in *khadorim* and yeshivas to master the language. So what was the value of a single Hebrew school for girls in big Jewish Warsaw? A whole system of Hebrew schools had to be created to instill Hebrew into their hearts. I thought about this constantly and finally decided to act.

One day I presented a proposal to my school board: I am the principal of the girls' school Yehudia, which is already rather popular, and I request permission of the school board to open a seven-grade girls' school with Russian as the language of instruction and Hebrew as a subject that would be taught more than three times a week in every grade. I want to open a school on my own. My proposal evoked disputes among the members of the school board. Some considered it revolutionary, almost treason. But others, including Attorney Boris Stavsky, defended my proposal. May we have many more such revolutions, said Stavsky, when individual teachers want to open Jewish schools with a broad Hebrew curriculum. His side triumphed and shortly thereafter I implemented my plan. I remained the principal of Yehudia until I received permission for a seven-grade school, which I opened in the central Jewish area. Yehudia was moved to a wealthier neighborhood, where it became a gymnasium that offered Hebrew as a language of instruction.

My life wasn't bad, even though my material conditions weren't easy, as was the case for all Jewish teachers. Although many children were in the school—and most of the students in "the first Hebrew school of Puah Rakovsky" were middle-class girls—I experienced several difficulties. The Jewish struggle to revive our ancient national language was patient and obstinate, and if you taught Hebrew to Jewish children, didn't you have to connect with our past and with the Land of Israel? And when I taught my students a poem about the Land of Israel, the girls would say to one another: "The teacher will soon start crying." Yes, I must admit that I couldn't talk about the Land of Israel without tears in my eyes. I devoted all my strength to the school. I hired the best teachers, and all of us worked six hours a day. Despite the material struggles, I loved it.

My independence upset my parents' house. My sisters and brothers considered my example and they too became boundary breakers.

We were seven sisters and four brothers, all capable, and my father hadn't prevented us from studying. He himself also studied languages, bookkeeping, and natural science, and read all the books his children read. You could do anything except attend gymnasium, where they wrote on the Sabbath.

But time had an impact, and before long two of my sisters came to Warsaw to study dentistry, with Dr. Shimanski from Odessa. You didn't need a high-school diploma to get into his course; you just had to read and write Russian. Many middle-class Jewish youngsters, mainly girls, were enrolled in the three-year program. When you finished, you had to take a special professional examination in one of Russia's cities, and most people went to Odessa or Kiev to take it. A diploma from that course also gave a Jew the right to live outside the Pale of Settlement. There were so many students that a certain Dr. Trop immediately opened another dental school and it was soon overcrowded, too. When my sisters came to me, I was living in a two-room apartment near the school. In their free time, they both helped me in my work. Father sent them only their tuition; they were responsible for earning the rest by themselves.

My school grew and so did my fame, so that my house became a kind of community center for scholars. This was in the early nineties, during the "famous" Moscow expulsion, when a tsarist decree deprived masses of Russian Jews of the right to live outside the Pale of Settlement. Within a short time, hordes of Jewish refugees arrived in the larger Polish cities, especially Warsaw. They included well-known merchants, manufacturers, and professionals, along with writers, editors and staffs of Yiddish and Yiddish-Russian newspapers, as well as Jewish jacks-of-all-trades, activists of Hibbat Zion, and Zionist pioneers. Those Russian and Lithuanian Jews brought Zionism to Poland. Even our great leader, Nahum Sokolow, of blessed memory, joined the Zionist movement only years later.

There was a considerable group of Jewish youngsters, *maskilim*, most of them former Yeshiva students and later external students [who did not enroll in schools but studied independently]. Many of them were devoted to preparing for the revolution in Russia. After the expulsion from Moscow, they felt badly disappointed and a great many of them returned to the Jewish national movement. Later they became some of the most dedicated Zionist activists. This was still the time of Hibbat Zion, but political Zionism was already hovering in the air.

Zionism as a movement was illegal—the slightest Zionist agitation could bring the harshest punishment—and yet there were Zionist activists. Since Jewish cultural work was all that was permitted, organizations of Lovers of the Hebrew Language were founded, setting up modern *khadorim* and evening courses for young people, especially for boys from Hasidic circles. These courses were offered at the existing Jewish schools and were tuition-free so that they could attract students. At night, my school was the center of that cultural and educational activity. The teachers were frequent visitors in my house and were my friends. And what warm friendship and idealism there was in those years! We shared a little bit of bread, and gave away the pillows off our beds. This was a "going to the people" of *our* educated youth.[3]

When I recall that era, I remember the first time I met Jacob Lestschinsky.[4] One fine afternoon, the door to the corridor opened—my door was never locked—and a young man with lots of brown hair and high boots appeared. He introduced himself in Hebrew, and told me that he had come from Russia a few days before. He wanted to meet me, he said, to see the school where girls learned Hebrew, and from a woman and not a man. His simple behavior and his whole appearance impressed me favorably; and like many others, he soon became a frequent visitor to my home. Even then, Jacob Lestschinsky was a loyal Zionist who spoke only Hebrew and devoted himself to Zionist work. Shortly after he came to Warsaw, the two of us established the first young women's federation, Ha-Tikvah, which was naturally an illegal organization. The members of Ha-Tikvah were students in the upper classes of my school; and they were later joined by girls from other schools. We held each meeting in a different private house. The laws at that time prohibited teachers from belonging to any organization, so I knew what was in store for me if we were caught in this illegal work. But at the age of thirty, could I give up the substance of my whole life?

After one of those secret meetings (at Novolipie 7), Jacob Lestchinsky accompanied me home. On the way, I remember that I suddenly asked him: "Tell me, Jacob, what will people like us do if, God forbid, Zionism can't be realized?" "What will we do?" he answered simply. "We'll jump into the water." Many years later, we met in Vienna, at the Fourteenth Zionist Congress [1925]. By then, Lestchin-

---

3. In the early years of the Russian revolutionary movement, educated Russian youths attracted to Populism "went out to the people," the peasants, to foment revolution.
4. A pioneer in the sociology, economics, and demography of Jewish life (1876–1966).

sky had accomplished a great deal: studied, graduated from the university, got married, deviated from Zionism — but I stayed with what we had been. I was a good Zionist, was always ideologically left of the General Zionists and even went as far as the Zeirei Zion.[5] I didn't become rigid and went over to socialist Zionism. When we met in Vienna, I reminded Jacob Lestchinsky of our conversation back then in the street. In 1933, when I was working for the second time in the Palestine office in Warsaw, Jacob Lestschinsky came for a certificate to go to the Land of Israel. This time we met again as old and good friends and comrades. He got the certificate; but he didn't go to the Land of Israel because his wife fell ill. He went instead to America.

Even though I was enthusiastically involved in social activities, my personal fate was tragically muddled. When I moved to Warsaw with my two children, I wanted to prepare my studious and capable son for the fourth grade of gymnasium, and I looked for suitable teachers for him. One of my close friends, Michael Halperin, recommended as a teacher a young man named Abraham Krislavin, whose family's origins were in the Russian town of Krislovke. He was one of those who were expelled from Moscow. An intelligent man who was attracted to Zionism, he wanted to study agronomy abroad and then settle in the Land of Israel, but he had no money. In addition, he had to support his household. His father taught Talmud and his three sisters were compelled to do laundry at home for various businesses.

As soon as he started teaching my son, he became a frequent visitor in my home. I didn't notice at first that he had become interested in me, but when I became aware of it, I wasn't surprised. I had the good, or perhaps bad, luck to be appealing. If I had written my memoirs when I was young, I might not have been so frank as I am now when I am past seventy-five. Whether or not my readers (especially my women readers) believe me when I dare to say that, even though I was 26 or 27 years old and mingled with men, my demeanor kept everyone at a necessary distance. Yes, I was successful, but everyone thought that Puah Rakovsky was a serious person with high principles. Moreover, my profession, my Zionist obligations, and my burden as a mother kept me so busy that I had no time or possibility to think about my personal happiness. I was busy until four in the afternoon at school, in the evening at the Zionist clubs, and until late at night at meetings.

Coincidentally, the family of my son's teacher, the Krislavins, lived right across from my apartment. So Abraham Krislavin often started

5. Zeirei Zion, a Zionist and moderate socialist labor movement, founded about 1903.

coming to see me after his lessons with my son. Later on, he brought his younger sister to meet me. Things reached such a state that he invited me to their home because his mother wanted to see me. She was a weak woman, with a bad heart, and didn't go out of the house. I agreed and one Sabbath afternoon, I went to see her. After my visit, Krislavin's sisters started coming to my house and became my close friends. The young man showed his fondness for me, but I hadn't yet recovered from my previous "family happiness," and even the idea of getting married again frightened me. Krislavin had no such thoughts. He was seriously in love and it was a question of life and death for him. In time, his sincere love evoked a response in me and my fear of being committed to a man subsided.

The romance with Krislavin lasted almost a year. One day he came to me to announce his decision to go to Berlin to study agronomy at the agricultural college in a three-year program. He ultimately wanted us to go to the Land of Israel: "You as a Hebrew teacher and I as an agronomist, we will be useful citizens for the Land." "Good," I answered. "An excellent plan. I am willing to wait for you for three years. We're both young enough to wait." "No," he declared. "I demand only one thing from you: Let's get married and leave the same day." Naturally I agreed, but asked for a little time to consider it. He prepared for the trip, we set the wedding date, and my parents came from Bialystok. At four in the afternoon, we were married by a rabbi and at ten that night, my husband left for Berlin.

Understandably, I became very close to the Krislavins, and immediately hired one of my husband's sisters to work in my school. The oldest sister got married soon after he left and the third one was preparing to take a teacher's examination. Close to my husband's family, I lived in an expectation of the happiness that should have been in store for me had my fate not been doomed to be so bitter.

Krislavin attended the Berlin agronomic college for only one year, studying with the agronomist Soskin (Long life to him!). He came to Warsaw for vacation and didn't go back to Berlin. Right after he came, I rented a room in Mokotow Street in Warsaw, and after I finished my classes, we would take a tram to spend the rest of the day in the fresh air. My school was open all summer. Krislavin started working with me in the school and planned to take a year off from his studies to collect a little money so that he could continue. Both of us were young, willing to work, and full of energy. But fate decided otherwise. At the end of the summer, my husband said that for a few weeks, he had felt a pain in his side. As usual, I calmed him down, although I was scared. We went to a doctor who examined him and said gravely: "You're a student at the Berlin college? You have to drop out of school and go to a sanatorium immediately to get rid of your neglected pleurisy." He ordered him to stay in bed a few days and then come back to him.

When he got out of bed a few days later, he felt better, but still wanted to see his friend Dr. Rappel, a specialist in lung diseases who had cured him of typhus soon after he had come from Moscow. The typhus had left him with pleurisy as a complication, which had kept him longer in the hospital. He must have left the hospital too soon, because he hadn't felt well for a long time. Dr. Rappel cheered him up, examined him and ordered him to drop out of school for a while, to work only three or four hours a day, and not to overdo his activities. In the spring he could return to school in Berlin. We were relieved and followed the doctor's orders, but there wasn't much improvement.

In fact, things got worse. In December, when it started getting cold, in the middle of the night his throat suddenly began to hemorrhage, and in the morning he called me to the bed and asked for paper on which he wrote — he wasn't allowed to speak — that he didn't want to make me unhappy, and so he asked me to accept a divorce from him. "You have already suffered enough in your life," he wrote; "I have not yet been able to give you anything good. So I have no right to demand great sacrifices from you." Naturally, I took pains to calm him and consoled him — you will soon again be well, I said — and asked him to stop thinking nonsense.

My parents learned of my misfortune and my father rushed to Warsaw and insisted that I get a divorce. "You aren't even his wife. You don't have a child with him. God Forbid, you'll have to be released from the marriage through *halitzah!*"[6] my father pleaded with me. "If I have to, I will," I answered. But he couldn't make me leave my husband and shorten his life.

My father, of blessed memory, accomplished nothing and later I did have to be released through *halitzah*.

I kept Krislavin alive for almost six whole years, the longest time such an unfortunate illness can last in a person who was attacked by it at the dangerous age of thirty. And I didn't provide for him like a poor teacher: In the winter, I kept him in the most modern sanatorium, in the summer in Otwock; and after his death I was left with a debt of two

---

6. When a woman in a childless marriage was widowed, the brother or closest male relative of her husband had to marry her (to provide an heir for his deceased brother) or perform a ceremony, *halitzah*, to release her so that she could marry outside the family. See Genesis 38 and Ruth 4:5–8.

thousand rubles. Through my work I paid off the debts little by little, and my conscience was clean. I did all I could and accepted my fate.

❖

Now all I had was my work, and it brought me consolation. I also had more obligations because my children were growing up and I had to think about preparing them for life. Our liberation movement also assumed larger dimensions. The unforgettable figure of Dr. Theodore Herzl appeared on the Jewish horizon.[7] Zionism was approaching the important phase of turning into a legal national movement. Through his writing and speaking, Dr. Herzl agitated intensively to assemble an international Zionist Congress. The question of creating legal Zionist federations was on the agenda. The first federation, Bnei Zion, emerged in Warsaw, founded by Abraham Padlishevski, David Berkman, and me.

The first Zionist federations included both men and women. In the earliest years of our liberation movement, Jewish women, even in countries that had dense masses of Jews such as Poland and Lithuania, had nothing to do with Zionism. Intelligent young Jewish women devoted themselves to the revolutionary movements of other peoples; they gave their knowledge, their excitement, and even their lives for Gentiles. But Jewish middle-class girls had no interest in their own national revival. The first bearers of the idea of Hibbat Zion, rabbis and pious Jews, didn't accept women into their ranks. The Land of Israel had to be colonized, and to their way of thinking, that was men's work. Only after everything was ready would women be brought to the Holy Land, where they would fulfill their function — as in the six days of creation — to bring generations of Jews into the world. Even the so-called order of Bnei Moshe, that emerged much later and included the entire Jewish intelligentsia of that time, was also closed to women.

Dr. Herzl was the first to appreciate the role and significance of women for the people's liberation movement. At the first Zionist Congress, he granted Jewish women equal rights to elect and to be elected to the Zionist Congress. Unfortunately, I did not take part in the first Congress.[8]

I might have been elected as a delegate, and I could always have

---

7. The prominent leader of political Zionism (1860–1904), he put Zionism on the international map.
8. Taking place in Basel, Switzerland, in 1897.

gone as a journalist; but I simply didn't have the money for such a luxury. In the early years of our movement, there were no professional activists and no paid officials; all the work was done by volunteers.

For the Fourth Congress in London [1900], I managed to save a whole ten pounds from my various budgets. A friend of my father's lived in London, a Jew from Bialystok named Suvalski, who had once owned a bookshop in Warsaw. I arranged to spend the night at his house. Naturally, he accepted me as a good guest. A considerable number of delegates had come from Russian-Poland and from Russia itself. The trip itself was extremely interesting. The population in the European countries we passed through looked fat, calm, and satisfied. It was before the First World Slaughter, and the capitalist countries were flourishing. The moneybags could display generosity and toss crumbs from their rich tables to the real creators of their wealth — the proletariat.

I was particularly impressed at that time by Holland with her flourishing agriculture. The entire area had once been under water, like the Jordan Valley before the collapse of Sodom and Gomorrah.[9] It was not only admiration I felt, but also my constant envy of all peoples who live in safe, solid places was kindled at that moment. I was continuously persecuted by the thought of whether we "dreamers and fighters" — as we were called in those days — would ever realize our two-thousand-year-old dream of rebuilding our ancient home.

The city of London, with its nine million inhabitants, was not fascinating for its beauty, but for its extraordinary pomp and its enormous size. The Fourth Zionist Congress, which took place in 1900 in one of the largest halls in the capital of the British Empire, made an extraordinary impression on all those who attended. I myself was really enchanted and electrified by it.

I had a place in the journalists' section right across from the speakers' stand on the stage. I didn't sit among the delegates — simply because no women were elected as speakers and leaders of the first Congresses. I went as a correspondent from a Yiddish newspaper in Bialystok. From where I sat, I could not only hear the speakers perfectly, but I could also see them and could study their facial expressions. Of course, I was mainly interested in the unusual and unique Dr. Herzl, who was especially impressive. The second great figure, Max Nordau[10] — a more realistic type than Dr. Herzl — reminded me of my grandfather the rabbi.

---

9. See Genesis 18 and 19.
10. Prominent European writer (1849–1923), he was a co-founder of the World Zionist Organization.

His description of the horrible situation of Jewry at that time seemed to come from our ancient prophets. I was so captured by everything around me in the Congress hall that I felt outside of time and space.

Here, I want to tell something about our unforgettable Dr. Herzl. If our teacher Moses is described as the most modest person — "for the man Moses was the most modest of men"[11] — if in place of his modesty you find his greatness — I will allow myself to emphasize that Dr. Herzl possessed that wonderful character trait — an extraordinary modesty. A fancy garden party took place in London's Hyde Park, where the enormous audience accorded great ovations to the leaders. All this seemed hard and painful for Herzl, who simply escaped and hid. At that moment, I accidentally caught sight of his face, and to this day, his expression has remained engraved in my memory.

The Fourth Congress was not only big and substantive, but was also very stormy. The sharpest debate revolved around the question of how to take Jewish culture out of the control of the rabbis.

By 1901, I was the mother of grown children. My son was then eighteen years old and my daughter was sixteen. My educational plan for my children had been more or less successfully followed. Until the fourth grade, my daughter had studied in my school and my son prepared privately for the examination for the fourth class in the gymnasium, and also studied Hebrew and Talmud. Although I was the principal of a seven-grade school considered to be one of the best at that time even by the tsarist school authorities, I could not get my son admitted into the fourth class at a government gymnasium in Warsaw, but had to send him as far as Siedlice. The famous *numerus clausus* was in effect, so for every Jew there had to be ten Gentiles.[12] And even though the Gentiles had no trouble getting accepted, they didn't really want to go to school.

Sending a fourteen-year-old boy abroad was no easy task. First, he was still under my influence, and second, there was the material aspect. In the fourteen years since I had left their father, the children had seen him only twice. Even though he had not remarried, he had not provided anything for the children, and had never bothered to do anything to gain their love. I never said a bad word about him to them, but was careful to tell them that we simply didn't get along. As they grew older, they themselves became convinced of that. They often told me that they had no filial feelings for him. To them, he was a complete stranger.

11. Numbers 12:3.
12. A law of 1887 that imposed strict quotas on Jewish students in higher education.

After a difficult internal struggle, I decided to go to Siedlice with my son for the examination. He was accepted to the fourth class of the gymnasium. I moved him into a boarding house and went back home to my work. My son attended school in Siedlice for only two years. When he was in the sixth class, I sent him from Siedlice to Plock, where he lived with my uncle and cousins. Materially, that was easier for me because my fourteen-year-old daughter went to Plock with him, to attend the fourth class of the governmental gymnasium. The private Jewish gymnasia didn't give students the right to attend higher institutions of learning. The children had their own room in my uncle's house, could study quietly, and felt at home.

When my son went to Plock to present his request for a transfer from the Siedlice gymnasium, he had naturally submitted his school certificate. When the principal saw his perfect record, he was amazed. Papierni, the gymnasium teacher of religion and Jewish history, a Zionist Jew who knew my grandfather the Plock rabbi, may he rest in peace, introduced my son to the principal and told him who the young candidate was and what kind of background and family he came from.

But being alone without the children was too hard for me. I couldn't bear it for more than a year. I had a lot of trouble, but finally managed to transfer my daughter from Plock to the fifth class of a government gymnasium in Warsaw. My joy was boundless.

Over the forty-four years I lived in Warsaw, my house was always a meeting place for intellectuals. However, during that time, the atmosphere went through several phases. In the first ten years, when my children were small, it had a traditional Zionist character, and, even though I was an avowed heretic, I was deeply rooted in Jewish tradition. I raised my children in that spirit. At Passover, for example, I did not make a Seder, but I did send the children to my friend, the Mizrachi leader, Rabbi Levi Levin-Epstein, so they could attend a Jewish Seder. On the Days of Awe, I was the only one who did not go to *shul*; my son would go to pray with Rabbi Levin of blessed memory. And on Simhas Toyre,[13] my daughter also went with them to the Torah processions. If all my visitors were not members of Zionist organizations, they were all Zionist sympathizers. I had almost nothing to do with the materialistic, bourgeois circles we would meet at assemblies (because in the early years, the Zionist movement in general was bourgeois). Most of my visitors were teachers, journalists, writers, poets, and just plain intellectuals.

In the nineties, there were two major Jewish publishers in Warsaw:

---

13. Simhas Toyre, the day of the Rejoicing of the Law, the conclusion to the Sukes festival.

Ahiasaf, whose director was Ahad Ha-Am,[14] who was succeeded by Dr. Yosef Klausner;[15] and Tushia — later named *Central* — with Ben-Avigdor Shalkovitch[16] as literary director. The provincial literary forces, the so-called *Yunge* [young ones], soon came to Warsaw: Nomberg, A. L. Yakovovitch, Aharon Loybashitski, Sholem Asch,[17] and others.

At the beginning of our century, an interesting young man came to Warsaw from Odessa, one Alexander Segal, who had graduated from the vocational school "Trud" in Odessa. He was one of the best translators from Hebrew, and was soon employed by Tushia publishers. Loybashitski brought him to my house and I hired him to teach my daughter Hebrew. She was a diligent student and her teacher often praised her lavishly. For a whole summer, I saw only a teacher-student relationship. And one fine day, Mr. Segal came to me to talk about a personal matter. "What would you think," he asked excitedly, "if I told you I love your daughter?"

I could imagine anything except that that very smart and interesting twenty-five-year old man had seriously fallen in love with my fifteen-year-old gymnasium student. I answered him with the following question: "Did you come to talk with me first, or does my daughter know about it before me?" "Do you take me for a Yeshiva student, that you ask me such a question?" he answered, offended. "Mr. Segal," I answered him very seriously, "I have nothing against you personally. I like you very much as a smart and respectable young man. But I must say that, in this case, you have not behaved correctly. Don't you think any fifteen-year-old girl would respond favorably to a declaration of love from such a young man as you? And do you think the feelings of a fifteen-year-old girl are the expression of a serious love? For example, I won't guarantee that my fifteen-year-old daughter, who now responds to your love, won't love someone else in twenty-five years. And, besides that, how can I marry off my fifteen-year-old daughter? I would agree if it had happened at least five years later."

Segal listened to me carefully and said: "Yes, I know I don't impress you as a future husband for your daughter. But I am willing to wait for

14. Pen name of Asher Ginsberg. He was the leader of the Hibbat Zion movement and the primary spokesman for cultural Zionism.
15. A literary critic, historian, and Zionist (1874–1958), best known for his multi-volume history of modern Hebrew literature.
16. A Hebrew author and pioneer of modern Hebrew publishing (1867–1921), his pen name was Ben-Avigdor. He is the author of the thinly disguised novella about Puah, entitled *Rabbi Shifra*.
17. Hirsch Nomberg (1876–1927), Yiddish and Hebrew writer; Sholem Asch (1880–1957), Yiddish, and later English novelist and dramatist. Born in Poland and beginning his literary career there, he lived in the United States during World War I and from 1938 until his death.

her as long as I have to. I am willing, in short, to go abroad to study. I just want your agreement that she will wait for me." Thus our first conversation ended. I told him it is never too late to study, that a young Jewish writer should definitely also have a European education and that what he planned was quite correct. The Hebrew lessons didn't stop. My relation to him remained the same; I didn't pay attention to their relations, and left things to time. But a bad premonition was worrying me.

The vacation ended, my daughter went into the sixth class, and in early October, Segal went to Vienna to study. They had an enthusiastic correspondence. The girl blossomed and glowed with joy. A beautiful, cheerful, joyous girl, who lived alone. She was also gifted with an exquisite voice and dramatic ability. People were constantly urging me to give up everything and have her trained as an actress. But my daughter replied that that was not a serious profession. She preferred to be a teacher, especially since there was as yet no Hebrew theater.

My bad premonition was soon confirmed. At the age of fifteen and a half, my successful daughter experienced a terrible tragedy. Segal attended a Viennese university for only three months and then contracted typhus and never returned. Even now, decades later, it is hard for me to convey what we went through. My daughter fell ill with a bad nervous cough and had to drop out of the gymnasium in the middle of the school year. It took a lot of time and effort until she recovered and took the examination for the seventh class.

With that tragedy, which took place in 1901, the first decade of my life in Warsaw came to an end.

Three

Daughters of Zion

The transition from the nineteenth to the twentieth century was the beginning of the so-called "Sturm und Drang" period. The rise of the revolutionary movement seized almost all students, not only in Russia, but also in other lands. Everyone fell under the influence of the Zeitgeist. Even if they remained loyal to Zionism, young people were still imbued with the ideas of revolution and socialism. Other groups of Jewish youth, who didn't recognize Zionism, joined the emerging Jewish revolutionary and socialist movement of Russia, Poland, and Lithuania — the Bund. Up to then, *Ha-Tikvah* [the anthem of the Zionist movement] ruled supreme, but now one started hearing the Bundist *Shevua* [Oath] and other revolutionary songs. The labor organizations, Poalei Zion and the socialist Zionists, arose, along with the so-called "Territorialists."[1] The leaders of the *Yunge* and the *Freethinkers*, led by Chaim Weizmann,[2] an avowed "evolutionist" both in science and in politics, were also "infected" with the Zeitgeist to a certain extent. At the Fifth Zionist Congress in 1901, they created a revolution in the movement. The failure they suffered at the Fourth Congress in London had simply encouraged them to try regrouping again.

In the spring of 1901, a small committee of members of that group met in Munich. The participants included Dr. Cahan-Bernstein, a for-

---

1. Jewish nationalists who sought to establish a Jewish state or collective settlement elsewhere than the land of Israel.
2. A distinguished chemist and Zionist activist (1874–1952), he was the first president of the State of Israel.

mer social-revolutionary who came to the Fourth Congress directly from exile in Siberia. He got into an argument with Weizmann, who told him: "Your red shirt shows through your black suit."

Chaim Weizmann made the greatest speech at that meeting. And in response to a rabbinical gathering in Lodz, the Munich committee decided to summon a special meeting with the goal "to defend democratic and progressive principles within Zionism." To realize that plan, they had selected a small committee led by Leo Motzkin,[3] Weizmann, and Dr. Cahan-Bernstein. The meeting was held in Basel a few days before the Fifth Congress, and forty delegates from Russia, Germany, Austria, France, and Switzerland took part in that "Conference of Academic Youth."

Aside from the new democratic faction, the Fifth Congress achieved something much greater — the establishment of "Keren Kayemet," the Jewish National Fund.[4] The mood of the Fifth Congress encouraged the creation of the "National Fund." The speeches and decisions of the democratic faction clearly expressed the idea that the Zionist movement must absolutely begin colonizing the Land of Israel; colonization was one of the most important political factors for the final realization of our main objective. The new Zionist institution, the Keren Kayemet le'Israel, evoked great interest not only among Zionist circles themselves, but also among the masses. Those who were indifferent and remote began to see that the Zionist movement was not just a dream, but that it assumed a concrete form and was ready to do real, practical work.

When the delegates from Russian-Poland returned home, they worked to explain the report of the meetings and to popularize the significance of the National Fund for the building of the Land of Israel. A few months later, a national meeting of organizational representatives and Zionist activists was held in Warsaw, where the status and plan of action for the future Keren Kayemet's work was accepted. Aside from raising money, they also adopted a campaign to collect objects, and every organization was to create a special Keren Kayemet committee not only for demonstrations and propaganda, but also for practical work for the National Fund. That first Keren Kayemet meeting excited not only active Zionists, but also the large audience of sympathizers and visitors. The campaign to collect objects started right on the spot, when the meeting concluded. It was decades ago, but I remember it as if it were yesterday. On the podium sat Rabbi Zlotnik from Plonsk, who was

---

3. A Zionist leader and defender of Jews throughout Europe (1867–1933).
4. The land purchase and development fund of the Zionist Organization.

the first to take off his gold watch and chain. And the table was soon full of all kinds of objects: rings, brooches, earrings, and so on. In praise of the Jewish woman, I must emphasize that there were many more female donors than male.

Although rabbinic interpretation of the story of the Golden Calf[5] condemns women, I observed their positive side, and took full advantage of that mood. As the National Fund emerged, I came up with the idea that this was the best time to create a special Zionist women's organization. The Keren Kayemet had opened a broad field of activity for Jewish women. Their practical work for our ideal would also give them spiritual satisfaction, and what started out fortuitously would become full-fledged involvement over time, and would imbue the women with the idealistic aspect of our liberation movement. But when I expressed that idea to one of the leaders, he told me with the familiar dismissal: "Comrade Rakovsky, you will not create any Zionist women's movement." "Maybe I will," I answered and broke off the conversation immediately.

That brief conversation naturally annoyed me, but I wasn't discouraged. I soon summoned a group of more or less active women members and suggested creating a special women's committee to work for Keren Kayemet. It was high time, I said, to stop being elegant girls with our male companions. In fact, we do more practical work than the men, I said, but our comrades take credit for our work. We demand no thanks because it is our duty. But if we bear the same duties, we should demand equal rights, and we will achieve them only when we create a special women's commission for the National Fund, the first step to a Zionist women's federation in Russian-Poland. My proposal was favorably received. After a long discussion, it was unanimously accepted, and a woman's commission was selected.

How did the members of the Bnei Zion organization react to that revolutionary step of the women members? The older ones considered it simply as an attack on the biblical verse: "and he shall rule over you."[6] The young ones, on the other hand, argued that it was against the "principle of democracy," which did not recognize any special women's organizations. But neither side initiated a protest campaign, and the women's commission performed its work just as successfully as its male counterpart. Indeed, that active women's group eventually led to the establishment of a Zionist women's union in Poland, Bnos Tsiyon [Daughters of Zion].

---

5. Exodus 32.
6. Genesis 3:16.

The women's commission for Keren Kayemet was created in 1902 in Warsaw, and later became Bnos Tsiyon. Its most active members are now in Israel, among them my friend Leah Proshansky. One day, Leah and her husband proposed to the commission that Keren Kayemet should not be supported by random contributions at weddings, engagement parties, bar mitzvahs, and so on, but that its members should agree to pay regular monthly dues. For that purpose, they ordered small boxes in the shape of an album, with the words "Keren Kayemet Le-Israel" on a blue band with white letters. To avoid any suspicion of theft, instead of issuing a receipt, the dues collector pasted Keren Kayemet stamps in the amount of the sum paid into an album kept by the donor. At the time, it was fashionable to display large books on a table with a tablecloth, and that album always had the place of honor, serving as a means for propaganda to spread the idea of Keren Kayemet among broad circles. The fine example of Warsaw was soon imitated in various provincial cities.

Leah Proshansky also had the idea of embellishing that album artistically with pictures of the Land of Israel, etc., and appealed to the famous Zionist activist Mr. Leon Levita. She intended to send her plan to the Minsk meeting, but she suddenly fell ill and nothing came of it.

In 1901, when my son was eighteen years old and going into the eighth class of the gymnasium of Plock, he gave me a very unpleasant surprise in the middle of the school year. One fine day, I got a letter from him saying that he had decided to leave the gymnasium. He would — he wrote — give trial lessons, get a teaching certificate, and come to Warsaw to work in my school. What impelled him to do that? First, he could no longer submit to any student discipline; second, he could no longer restrain himself, but had to immediately start teaching as he felt that this was his calling. His letter excited me so much that, at first, I didn't know how to react to his plan — whether to accept or resist it. Without my consent, he couldn't do anything because the gymnasium had demanded his mother's permission. I immediately went to Plock, explained to him that I had nothing against his becoming a teacher if he felt a penchant — even a calling — for that, but it wouldn't hurt, I told him, if he first completed the eighth class of gymnasium and postponed his decision for half a year. Why should he ruin his chances for higher education even in the area of pedagogy? Since all my objections fell on deaf ears, I explained to the principal that I needed my son as a teacher in my school and asked him to allow my son to give trial lessons and award him the appropriate teacher's certificate.

When he came home, he threw himself into teaching with youthful ardor. The children loved him very much because he really was a born teacher. A hundred-percent Zionist at that time, he joined the group of volunteer teachers and counselors in the evening courses for young people. One of the teachers at that time was Mordechai Lederer, a former Yeshiva student from leading Hasidic circles, who fell into "bad company" and became an enthusiastic Zionist. The teachers and counselors soon became very close to my son, and they worked together very energetically.

Another person who volunteered to teach evening courses was Mordechai Birnbaum, from the small town of Szereszew (in the Grodno district). That young autodidact, who never received a formal education, was an exponent of the Haskalah, was adept at Hebrew and Talmud, expert in Jewish knowledge, and familiar with Russian scholarship and literature. He also made quite an impression: He was very tall — a rare phenomenon among Diaspora Jews of that time — and though his face was not handsome, it was very interesting. He looked a lot like Maxim Gorky,[7] but healthier. As he and my son got to know each other better, he made such a good impression on the boy that one day, my son said: "Comrade Birnbaum, would you like to meet an interesting woman? Come to our house and I'll introduce you to my mother."

One evening, after classes, all three of them came: my son, Mordechai Lederer, and Mordechai Birnbaum. At that time, the younger of my two sisters who became dentists was living with me. The older one, Dina, was practicing in Bialystok; and the younger one, Zilla, worked in an office on Dzieka Street in Warsaw. She was an active Bundist, and to cover her traces in the underground, she was living in my house. My daughter came with some of her girlfriends, gymnasium students from the seventh class, along with my two boarders, young relatives of my friend Leah Proshansky who were preparing for examinations in the sixth class of the government gymnasium — their parents were pleased that their sons were living in a respectable Zionist house. Friends and acquaintances started coming in their free time to spend a few hours in our house, since, in those years, it wasn't the fashion to meet in coffeehouses, as it is today. People felt freer in a small group of friends or acquaintances, with a homey glass of tea. In my house, everyone received a warm welcome, and the door was never closed to anyone. Nevertheless, we worked just as hard and created just as much as today. We talked less and split fewer hairs.

---

7. A famous writer of fiction who bridged the generation of Chekhov and Tolstoy and later Soviet writers (1868–1936).

Birnbaum impressed everyone as a very interesting young man, and as he left, he asked if I would let him come more often. Naturally, I had nothing against that. That was how I met my third husband, a match made for me by my eighteen-year-old son.

The second visit followed the first, and before long Birnbaum became one of my closest friends.

One day, he told me the story of his life and the reasons behind his present situation in Warsaw. His father was a distinguished, wealthy Jew, the owner of a big beer brewery in the town of Szereszew. His mother, who died when he was young, had been an extraordinarily pious and good woman. There were three brothers. The oldest, a merchant, was married and had a three-year-old daughter. He was then divorcing his wife because he had been married off against his will. And the youngest, a very pious boy, had attended several yeshivas, went off to the Land of Israel as a very young man, studied in a yeshiva there, and is now one of the most distinguished Jews in Petah Tikvah.

Mordechai himself had studied Talmud and law with great rabbis, but lost his faith and went into secular studies. Naturally, he didn't get a systematic education, but had learned and read a great deal. In Warsaw, he had an aunt, his mother's younger sister, whose husband managed several buildings; they had no children and were very rich. He got frustrated with living in a small remote town, and decided to go to Warsaw to give Hebrew lessons, but it turned out that he could teach only in a *kheyder* because he didn't have a teacher's certificate. That work didn't really satisfy him, but he had to make a living: Since he lived in his aunt's house, his salary was sufficient. But there were a lot of libraries, reading rooms, and cultural events in Warsaw, which was why he had moved there.

When I heard his confession, I made him the following offer:

"Listen, Comrade Birnbaum, in my school, you can give Hebrew lessons without a certificate. I will register you with the authorities as a teacher of religion and you can teach Hebrew and Bible, all Jewish studies in Russian translation, because the language of instruction in my school is Russian. And it seems to me that you will do well in the classroom, and will no doubt become a good teacher. It's my special weakness to make anyone I know into a teacher, but so far I have done this only with women because I think that education should be in the hands of women, as in North America where 90 percent of the teachers are women. But I am willing to make an exception in your case. I'll let you teach a few hours of advanced Bible studies, and I hope the experiment will be successful on both sides. I'm offering you the Bible class first, because teaching an advanced class is easier; and second, because I won't let anyone else but me teach the beginners. That is really the hardest, and therefore the most gratifying work for a teacher; and it is the basis for the whole school. Moreover, I specialized in that and have concluded that the best teacher must take the beginning class." Naturally, Birnbaum gladly accepted my offer. I took care of the formalities with the school authorities and he started teaching Bible in the fifth class.

As an experienced school principal, I was convinced that the best judges of a teacher are always the children themselves. Whenever I hired a new teacher, I always listened to the opinions of my pupils after the first lessons. The children intuitively know who is a good and capable teacher and who isn't. I wasn't wrong this time, either: The students were thrilled with his lessons and were fond of him. Years later, he became one of the most popular Hebrew and Yiddish teachers in Warsaw and the author of many Yiddish and Hebrew textbooks. After teaching in my school for a while, Birnbaum thanked me for revealing his calling. Every lesson, he said, gave him extraordinary spiritual satisfaction. He felt like a newborn and had finally found his right path.

Working together, meeting every day, and exchanging thoughts during the breaks in the teachers' room also affected our personal relationship. My children liked him very much and he became my close and devoted friend. At first it didn't occur to me that he felt anything other than simple friendship for me. First of all, he was ten years younger than I. Second, he paid the same attention to me as he did to my younger sister and my sixteen-year-old daughter. Furthermore, to some extent, I hadn't yet recovered from the tragic experience with Krislavin. Deeply wounded, I was simply terrified even to consider taking such a serious step again.

At that time, my friend from Lomza, Deborah Natanson, was teaching Polish in my school. Not only was she a good teacher, but she was also a well-educated woman and a special person. My children loved her like a mother. She herself had no children and was unusually close to me. It was she who first indicated to me that Birnbaum was not indifferent to me. For a while, I didn't react at all to what she was saying; I simply had no time for such things. The day was always too short: from eight in the morning until four in the afternoon at school. Studying with the staff the whole time. And keep in mind that in those days, children danced less in school and studied more. The old rule that "Torah needs to be taught" was observed. My evenings were devoted to Zionist and social welfare work. And there was no lack of financial cares either. To cover the monthly budget of the school and have some money left over for family expenses was not easy, even for an energetic person. Yes, life was not easy, but the awareness of being a free person, not dependent on anyone and living from the "toil of one's own hands,"[8] was sweet. My school was private and I really was the owner — the idea of a cooperative institution was brand new at that time — but in fact, for my six lessons, along with the administrative work, I got the same salary as every other teacher. My staff knew that I did not exploit them.

Because I took life seriously, an atmosphere of learning and work reigned in my house. My family and friends had a correct appreciation of the value of time, knew that "the day is short and the task is long,"[9] and none of us had time to waste on trivialities. Birnbaum noticed that, too, and to have an excuse to come every day after school, he proposed that we read Marx together. I accepted his offer and tried to find time for it. Naturally — in this time of world-shaking events — it sounds romantic that only forty years ago, there were men who wooed a woman with such an approach.

When Birnbaum became a daily visitor in our house, my family and all our close friends understood that he felt more than just friendship for me. It was hard for an ardent young man of twenty-six to control his feelings, and one fine day, he frankly declared that he had fallen in love with me soon after his first visit. And he thought I would respond to his serious and honorable feelings and would agree to marry him. To tell the truth, that declaration was not a surprise to me, but I did feel an internal conflict. At the time, I was not indifferent to Birnbaum, because he awoke feelings in me that had been paralyzed for years. I also wondered, though, how my grown children would react to the situation. The fact that Birnbaum was a full ten years younger than I was also, to a certain extent, a big minus.

My vacillation and conflicts lasted a while. But I couldn't resist the experiment, and one fine day, I went into a jeweler's shop, bought a wedding ring, and engraved on the inside: "25 Shevat, the first year of the opening of the national treasure" — that was thirty-nine years ago.[10] That evening, we went to one of my close friends, Luria, a merchant, one of the Moscow refugees, who was an active Zionist and very popular

---

8. Variants of this term (e.g., my hands, your hands) are found in Genesis 31:42; Haggai 1:1; Psalms 128:2; and Job 10:3.
9. Ethics of the Fathers, 2:15.
10. A reference to the Keren Kayemet, the Jewish National Fund, founded in December 1901.

among the youth in Warsaw. He had invited two employees from his office, and in the presence of three witnesses, we performed the marriage ceremony "according to the religion of Moses and Israel"[11] and went home. Obviously, the affair caused somewhat of a sensation among my friends, but I made little of it. One of my closest friends, however, Chaim Proshansky, my friend Leah's husband, couldn't help asking me:

"Puah, have you gone completely crazy to marry a fellow who is ten years younger than you?" "Chaim," I answered, "you have known me ever since I came to my in-laws in Pinsk as an eighteen-year-old mother of a three-month-old boy. You were a friend of Yitzhak Machlin, my first husband's younger brother. Now you are my close friend because you are my best friend Leah's husband. I can talk about it with you candidly. Birnbaum is very interesting, not your average man, and I like him very much. Moreover, I chanced upon him in the so-called dangerous Balzac-age of a woman. For sixteen years I have been a free person, in the highest sense of the word, a truly respectable Jewish woman. Whether you believe me or not, I don't care. But very often even I had forgotten that I belong to the supposedly weak or beautiful sex until Birnbaum recalled the woman in me. Is this really the dangerous age or is it his great love and strong personality? I don't want to rummage around in that now. As for the only defect — the fact that he is younger — I feel intellectually and even physically no older than he, because I have not lived fully. For ten or fifteen years, I will still be a young woman, and then — as soon as I feel the difference in our years — I will leave. I am not seeking a nursing home in Birnbaum. I hope to be able to work even in my old age."

How did my children react? When we were still just friends, my daughter Sheyndl treated Birnbaum like a father, and he was a father to her throughout her short and sad family life, and was later a devoted father to her unfortunate orphans. As for my son, once during an intimate conversation, he said to me: "I like Birnbaum very much, but it often seems that he is taking some of your love away from me . . . " That frank statement did not surprise me. I knew that a feeling of jealousy had emerged in my son. But it soon passed, and he and Birnbaum became and remained close friends and later even shared the same political convictions.

In 1902, at the age of seventeen, my daughter took her teacher's

---

11. The standard statement when the groom takes his bride in the Jewish marriage ceremony. A traditional Jewish wedding does not require the presence of a rabbi.

examination and started working in the school. In the same year, for the first time, my financial situation improved to some extent. All four of us were working in my school for the entire six-hour day, as good and responsible faculty members.

When I met Birnbaum in 1901, he was a Zionist, not an active one but a strong sympathizer with our movement. At that time, my son also agreed with the principles of Zionism. My daughter was a deeply committed Zionist who resisted all attempts from the revolutionary currents that later played themselves out in my house. In Russia at that time, it was strictly forbidden to express the opposition's political opinions openly. The authorities persecuted people who took the slightest step in the direction of social activity. They were also suspicious of the Zionist movement, but turned a blind eye to it, depending on who was conducting the activity, how it was done, and how great a danger it posed for the regime and social order.

Despite the unfavorable atmosphere, the Zionists managed to get permission in the autumn of 1902 for Russian Zionists to hold a meeting in Minsk. Then the authorities changed their mind and ordered the meeting interrupted in the middle. Nonetheless, it was a significant and very interesting meeting. As one of the participants in that first and last meeting to be permitted by the Russian authorities, I was particularly interested in the reading of the "culture question" at that time. At the Minsk meeting, the same factionalists consisting of the "Youth" — Herzl called them the "Young Turks" — who had protested at the Fifth Congress in Basel against the opportunism of official Zionism, especially concerning religious "judgments," reached an understanding with the rabbis about *what* should really be considered "judgments."[12] The rabbis agreed to include "culture" within Zionist activity; and the "Youth" recognized the right of cultural autonomy for every trend within Zionism. That is, everyone would work in his own way. They agreed to let the rabbis educate their children in their way, in the old rabbinical manner. The agreement was "sealed" with a symbolic handshake by the representatives of the two generations and the two views of the cultural question — by Dr. Chaim Weizmann and Rabbi Yitzhak Reines.[13] At that conference the agreement was presented along with a lecture by Ahad Ha-Am about "culture." Ahad Ha-Am had previously

---

12. The issue at the Congress and the Minsk Conference was opposition to Herzl's recognition of rabbis as the definers of what constituted Jewish culture. The "Youth" argued for a definition of culture that included secular forms of cultural production.

13. Head of the Mizrachi (religious) trend within Zionism (1839–1915).

avoided both official Zionism and the "Youth." He simply did not recognize political Zionism.

In November 1902, Birnbaum's older brother divorced his wife and came to Warsaw with his four-year-old daughter. To make it easier for him to find a job, we took in the little girl. It didn't take him long to get settled, but his daughter stayed with us until he left with her for North America shortly before World War I. Obviously, he felt at home in our house, and my children were very fond of him. One fine day, he got up in the morning and told the children: "Listen, children, today is the last day of the Polish lottery. I bought a lottery book, so buy a 30 kopeck ticket from me, and maybe we'll win."

My children knew I was strongly against betting on the lottery. I always said that people should work and earn their money and not get involved in adventures by trying to win money in the lottery. They glanced at me, but this time I didn't say anything. They gave him 30 kopecks, and he wrote their names on the ticket. That evening, he ran in with the good news that a big sum had been won by that number and, for their 30 kopecks, they had won 2,000 rubles; and he, for his 60 rubles, was now a rich man with 4,000 rubles. For the first time in my life, I saw the joy of a person who had won the lottery. My children were also happily surprised, and almost at the same time both of them said: "Now, Mama, when school is over, we can go to Switzerland for a year to study pedagogy."

The very next day, the 2,000 rubles were deposited for them in a bank. At that moment, what delighted me was how the proletariat intelligentsia wanted to use their winnings. I thought that it was not in vain that our sages said: "Beware the sons of the poor for learning will come from them."[14]

Now as I write about that, I remember the tale my grandmother, the rabbi's wife, once told me while I was preparing for the examination in Mariompol. One of her grandfathers, a great rabbi in a Polish city, once went on a mission for a community matter. On the way — naturally, they traveled by oxcart — he met a Polish prince. They chatted a little and looking into the face of the prince, the rabbi suddenly said: "You will someday be king of Poland."

The prince wrote that down in his notebook along with the rabbi's name. My grandmother, may she rest in peace, remembered exactly what year that happened as well as the name of the prince, who later became king. Years later, it turned out that that Polish king issued a

14. Babylonian Talmud, Nedarim, 81.

harsh decree against the Jews. Once again, it fell to my great-great grandfather, the rabbi, to go to the king to get the decree rescinded. The rabbi didn't remember that the king was the same prince whom he had once predicted would be king. Only when he came into the throne room did they recognize each other. Of course, the king immediately cancelled the harsh decree and asked the rabbi what he demanded as a reward for his former prophecy. The rabbi answered that he wanted the king to appoint him rabbi of a whole district and not just his little town.

This is they way our grandfathers, the rabbis of that time, thought back then. And their great-great grandchildren apparently inherited the same ideas.

As I noted before, the years 1901–1903 were comparatively the calmest of my life. When, on the 21st day of the month of Adar that year,[15] I gave birth to a girl — my daughter Sarah, who now lives with her family in Haifa — my joy was boundless.

As I said, it was the emergence of the Jewish National Fund that drew the Jewish woman into building the Land of Israel. When a woman is interested in something, she works for it with all her heart and soul. To depict the development of the participation of Jewish women in the Zionist Congresses before the creation of a special Zionist woman's organization, it is useful to present the following facts.

At the first Congress, there were eleven women, most of them wives of Zionist leaders and a few students at Swiss universities who were interested in the movement. Even though they got equal voting and election rights, without any discussion on their part, the women kept quiet and merely watched and listened. It was not until the later Congresses that the women delegates began to exhibit some activity, which increased over the years.

Starting in 1921, after the establishment of WIZO [Women's International Zionist Organization] in London in 1920, the women's conferences were held at the same time as the general Congresses. Like the Zionist movement itself, the Zionist women's movement was at first exclusively bourgeois, and it engaged initially in purely philanthropic work, mostly for the Land of Israel. But the bourgeois origin of the movement is not particularly shocking since, at that time, the phenomenon was not exclusively Jewish. If the science of socialism is still beginning to criticize the roots of social injustice, middle-class women know more about that than any expert. The philanthropic impulse is supreme in them as compared to others. And those same women are

15. 1903.

ruled by the childish belief that charity and good will are sufficient to eradicate social misery. Despite the existence of the Miriam Organization from 1885 in Vienna; of the "Association of Jewish Women in Berlin for Cultural Work in Palestine"; and of the appearance of several high-society Jewish women at the first Zionist Congresses, I must confess that no Jewish women's movement, in the real sense of the word, existed at that time.

The initiative for the establishment of a separate Zionist women's organization in Russia-Poland at that time came from a group of Jewish women in Warsaw, not, God forbid, from the top ten thousand, but from real middle-class circles. The first Zionist women's organization, Bnos Tsiyon [Daughters of Zion], emerged in Warsaw at the beginning of the twentieth century, shortly after the establishment of the Jewish National Fund. Its program was in fact a copy of the men's organization, Bnei Zion [Sons of Zion], and its activity consisted mainly of work for the Jewish National Fund, the offering of Hebrew courses for women and female youth, and the promulgation of Zionist thought among the various classes of women to increase the ranks of organized women members.

But if the organization didn't take on any special women's missions and didn't present any special demands, wasn't its existence superfluous? Couldn't the work be carried on along with male comrades? One aspect, a very important one, underlined its justification. Those Zionist women's associations turned out to be necessary prerequisites and educational institutions to train the different classes of women to work socially and politically for our liberation movement.

Although it doesn't sound remarkable now, keep in mind that (at the beginning of the twentieth century) Jewish women, even young women and female members of mixed organizations, did not feel as free as they did in their own separate women's organizations. They were brought up with the old-fashioned notion of "All honor to the king's daughter within [her home]."[16] Seldom was a woman bold enough to appear in public or to take part in a discussion. Most of them were not yet liberated from the absurd notion that every man is smarter than every woman. Nor were they encouraged by the dismissive response of the men to the rare appearance of the women members. Even today, inside most of the so-called socialists, doesn't there stand an old reactionary philistine in relation to women? Quite often, after a woman gave a speech that was just as effective as that of a man, I chanced to

---

16. Psalm 45:14.

hear the degrading comment: "You can forgive her, she is a beautiful woman . . ."

Despite various obstacles, our first Bnos Tsiyon organization in Warsaw was very successful, and soon became a national association of seventy organizations in the cities and towns of Russia-Poland, numbering thousands of organized women members. Aside from its general activity in many areas, the association was primarily devoted to the goal of training and educating the masses of Jewish women. It created cadres of active, aware, educated women speakers, demonstrators, etc. As they engaged in their work, those women studied, developed, and frequently discovered hidden talents that were waiting to be developed. Those Zionist women's organizations among the Jews of Russia-Poland did not last long, and vanished at the outbreak of World War I in 1914. With the emergence of independent Poland after the war, broader horizons also appeared for the Jewish women's movement; new perspectives developed along with brand new tasks. It was the Jewish women's movement that created the "Union of Jewish Women in Poland" — Y.F.A.

The initiators and creators of that new movement, several aware and active leaders of the Zionist women's association, immediately concluded that the union had to deal with all the complex questions of the general women's movement and with the special demands of women. It had to engage in general cultural and educational work, and needed to recognize the importance of work on the ground so that positions in various localities would not be snatched up by others. Its main task was to organize the masses of Jewish women, and it did not subscribe to any party so that its ranks could include women of all trends. As a Jewish national union with a positive position on building the Land of Israel, the association had a special section for practical work in Palestine. But its main goal was to educate the lowest classes of Jewish women, to make young Jewish women productive, and to evoke in them an understanding of economic independence, a sense of society, and an interest in the collective.

No matter how hard the struggle of the women's movement was among other peoples, organizing Jewish women was many times harder. Unlike women in England, France, and America, we could not expect support from the men. Our movement was attacked from both right and left. The Jewish clerics, the Agude,[17] were terrified by the awakening of Jewish women. They saw the Jewish women's movement as an attack

---

17. The Agude, or Agudas Yisroel, was the organized party of Orthodox Jewry.

on their allegedly exclusive right to obscure and dull the minds of the women, so that women would never, God forbid, grasp how much undeserved grief and suffering they experienced, or what old-fashioned laws — like levirate marriage, the *agune* [the "chained" wife, whose husband will not grant her a divorce] question, the prohibition of the marriage of a Cohen and a divorcee, etc. — those men had created. The feat of depriving women of the right to vote in the community organization is a thoroughly anti-Jewish principle that originated in the Church's dictum — "the woman should be silent in the community."[18]

The left thought that women's organizations were harmful in general because the struggle should be conducted in common. Although the Bund did create Y.A.F. [Jewish Working Women], that organization was simply a means to get women's votes in the elections to the Sejm [parliament] and the city council. The regular democrats also stated that the women's organizations should first create a staff of women philosophers, social economists, and famous politicians, and then they would be worthy of claiming their right, which was recognized by the Polish constitution but incidentally monopolized by males.

Despite all obstacles, our movement progressed because we knew that you have to take power, that no one gives it to you voluntarily. And that you can take it only if you know how to educate, and organize the forces of, the masses. Therefore, our primary goal was to awaken a feel for "organization" among the women, to spread a network of Jewish women's associations over the whole country with a unified agenda. We hoped to educate the association's chairwomen not to substitute the *end* for the *means*.

Jewish women's associations also ran children's homes, held vocational courses, took care of children and orphans, engaged in social work, supported mothers and children, offered legal aid to deserted women, and established serious and honest cooperatives that were better administered by women than by men. In no case could those important works be dismissed as "just philanthropy," even by the purely Zionist women's associations. We never forgot that the so-called Galus [Exile] is the reservoir of human material for the Land of Israel, and it is thus extremely important that, in addition to being educated in a vocation, human material be physically and emotionally healthy as well.

Along with everything else, that work was an important means for keeping in close permanent contact with the various classes of women. Because the masses, especially the female masses, are drawn not only by

---

18. I Corinthians 14:34.

scientific ideas that move only a few; the masses are reached by con-crete, realistic acts derived from ideological struggles that improve the harsh conditions of their lives. Spokesmen for the most radical move-ments have recently reached this conclusion and are now trying to be involved in all possible areas of social assistance.

Our activities allowed us to organize and keep increasing and strengthening our ranks. Our goal was always to develop the conscious-ness of our own women's organization, to which nothing was foreign, whether Jewish or general. As an organization composed of common people, designed to protect their interests, it could demonstrate, through its agents, the ability of women and the great value of their work for society. It would be an organization with the broadest political goals, the voices of whose representatives would be able to influence the authori-ties to refrain from new horrible world slaughters that affected mainly women and mothers, who gave their husbands and children as cannon fodder.

The just demands of the extensive women's movement in indepen-dent Poland called for appropriate representation in the Jewish commu-nity organizations, the municipal councils, and the Polish Sejm. The women involved were not playing a game of political activism, of women's rights, or of rivalry with men; their demands were a revolu-tionary measure and a practical consequence of the urgent need and shameful oppression of the weak and helpless. As the difficulties in-creased, so did our strength. Practical necessity showed us the right path for the emancipation of the masses of women. We not only devoted our attention to the women workers, but were also concerned with all classes of working women, from the toiling to the so-called petite-bourgeoisie. We understood that, to this day, everywhere, the apoliti-cal, asocial, and emotionally blunted psyche of the masses of women, and their unconscious manner of life, held up the development of the radical women's movement. Therefore, among these very women, an intensive program of enlightenment had to be conducted.

We did get our Jewish women representatives into the Sejm and the city councils after the war; but, despite our constant, persistent struggle, we could not break through the Chinese Wall to get into the allegedly modernized Jewish community organization [kehile] in War-saw, although Jewish women had entered the community organizations in such places as Vilna and Bialystok.

Initially, even the progressive members of Mizrachi [the religious Zionist group] voted against women's suffrage in the community organi-zations. Soon they realized that this position was completely antidemocratic, so they rescinded their decision. And then the real orgy of the rabbis began, with the Agude representatives in the lead. They were apparently terrified of evil [sexual] passions, Heaven forfend, for "the greater a man than his fellow, so is his evil impulse greater."[19] Consequently, they categorically rejected the possibility of sitting with women in the kehile; they had no objections to sitting with Polish women in the Sejm and the Senate; but with Jewish women—"one should choose death rather than sin."[20]

During every community organization election we would hold public demonstrations and protest meetings, publish articles in the press, give speeches, and issue appeals, leaflets, and so on. In short, we carried out a grandiose electoral campaign since we wanted to participate actively in the election. But we had to make do with a moral success, convinced that our educational work would not remain "a voice crying in the wilderness."[21] The times were changing, and victory had to come at last.

(After a gap of 15 years, I came back to the Land of Israel for the second time, and in 1938 was active in the election campaign for the kehilla in Jerusalem. I was amazed at how indifferent the various women's groups were to the whole election. That abnormal phenomenon once again underlined the lack of awareness and the political immaturity of the masses of Jewish women, who still don't know how to use their right [to vote]. Is it not our own fault if only two women are in the Jewish community organization of Jerusalem, despite the intense campaigning of women leaders?)

At about the same time as the Jewish women's organization emerged in Poland—in 1918—so did a new radical women's "Pioneer" movement. The "Pioneer" girl, the simple Jewish girl from a good Jewish home, often even from Hasidic circles, whose one and only function was to sit and wait for her bridegroom—that girl suddenly created the first "revolution" on the "Jewish street." With all her until-then suppressed youthful fervor, she threw herself into a hard, stubborn struggle against her whole environment, wrenching herself out of her slavery, breaking through the Chinese Wall of moldy tradition, and preparing for a new life on healthy, normal foundations. It would be a new life whose religion was the religion of work and creation. It would be a life of economic independence and social equality, as a producer and not just as a con-

19. Babylonian Talmud, Sukkah, 52.
20. Babylonian Talmud, Pesahim, 25.
21. Isaiah 40:3.

sumer; as a creative, active element for a modern, working collective, where, in her new home, as a worker and comrade in the organization of working women, she would join the struggle for the just demands of women, the theoretical basis of the women's movement in every country and among all peoples. Although I respect that movement, I will remain objective and emphasize that it was not initiated by women. In Poland, it was not considered a separate women's organization, but merely an integral part of the growing Pioneer movement.

He-Halutz [The Pioneer][22] was born in Russia and moved to various European countries only after the Bolshevik takeover. It was mainly concentrated in Poland, where an intensive and massive training and education program was developed. From then on, a constant stream of Pioneers flowed to the Land of Israel. By that time, each branch of the Jewish Women's Association in Poland [Y.F.A.] had organized extensive training programs for women, particularly young women, in its separate Palestine section. The center in Warsaw got permission from the Polish authorities to offer courses for Jewish nurses and child-care workers; vocational courses for tailoring, laundering, embroidery, millinery, corset-making, weaving straw and raffia; and even for shoemaking. The courses were subsidized by the city council and other groups set up to provide aid. Naturally, we could not offer agricultural training. As soon as the He-Halutz movement emerged in Poland, we were in constant contact with its leaders and worked vigorously and intensively to educate young women in He-Halutz thought. And our youth sections provided the first Pioneer women for the coed work groups on the estates of Jewish landowners and for various land work in the fields and gardens of Polish peasants.

The propaganda campaigns of the He-Halutz leaders were effective, and the ranks of He-Halutz grew. Not only leftists, but middle-class youths, too, were imbued with revolutionary Halutz thought, the main goal of which was to shape the first labor army for the Land of Israel. Those young people were spurred by economic prospects for the future; those supposedly middle-class idlers, especially in the larger Polish provinces, became the vanguard of young workers who led the way to the Land of Israel to realize our efforts at putting Jewish life on new, healthy foundations.

But in the first phase of its existence, the He-Halutz movement in Poland encountered strong resistance from the parents of the Pioneers

---

22. An organization of Jewish youth, first established in 1904, that trained its members for settlement on the land in Palestine.

of both sexes. Suddenly the age-old struggle of fathers and sons was revived — and sons meant both sons and daughters. The fathers knew very well that they were constantly being pushed out of their economic positions by various combinations of the privileged within the larger population, and because of severe taxes levied by the government. Yet, the petit-bourgeois parents of the first Pioneers — shopkeepers, wholesalers, traders, merchants, and even artisans and craftsmen — absolutely refused to agree to the "lunacy" of their children, who were willing to throw away their more-or-less comfortable homes in the narrow streets of small towns, to go to *Hakhshara* [training camps] and prepare to be simple workers, mainly peasants, in the Land of Israel.

The sons waged a harsh battle with their parents, and the sons finally emerged triumphant: They left their homes and parents behind. But, between the parents and their daughters — the first women Pioneers — serious tragedies were played out. As a secretary in the central office in Warsaw, I often had arguments with, and had to listen to sermons from, fathers who constantly claimed that we were leading Jewish girls astray, encouraging them to leave their homes and go off with boys to *Hakhshara*, to "work in the land" as they paraphrased the Halutz-formula of "Land and Work." Our big union offices frequently became shelters where our young women members could hide out until our long negotiations succeeded in convincing the father or mother that *Hakhshara* work was good for the daughter. She would then go to the Land of Israel and relieve them of any worry about her future. And that was really the only way to influence dissatisfied parents in that conflict between "fathers and sons."

Four

Winds of Revolution

For a long time, I was secretary of the Jewish women's organization of the Pioneer movement in Poland, and later was an official in the Warsaw Palestine office. But I have gotten ahead of myself and shall now go back from 1918 to the interrupted thread of my memoirs, to the beginning of the period of "Sturm und Drang": the early years of the twentieth century.

Between the late 1890s and the first years of the twentieth century — almost until the outbreak of World War I — our Jewish youth were growing up in a corrosive and savage atmosphere of brutal anti-semitism. The principles of [Jewish] national ideology were shaken during those years. Although Jewish young people were devoted to the national ideal, they were also caught up in the revolutionary spirit of the time. They were drawn into the struggle for universal ideals, for a new order in the world in general. They were also deeply convinced that the Jewish problem was not a particular, but an international, question that could and would be solved only when fairness and justice prevailed, not through power and violence.

In both ordinary and Zionist Jewish families, the eternal question involving "fathers and sons" surfaced again. Once again, parents and children started talking in different languages, and stopped understanding each other; once again, they started acting out tragedies, and often there were victims on both sides. In the first years of the revolution, families were torn apart by such misunderstandings. Jewish fathers, both the pious and the enlightened, and especially the Zionist, pleaded:

"Even if the revolution triumphs and socialism is realized, we Jews won't gain a thing. Why are you worrying about others and not devoting our strength, not concentrating all our work to realize our own national ideal?"

That struggle also took place in my parents' house in Bialystok in the early years of the revolution. My hometown of Bialystok once boasted many enlightened and intellectual Jews, and later many prominent Zionist figures; but it was also a major industrial center with a large labor force. Its residents were intensely involved in all revolutionary movements — including anarchism. Bialystok produced a considerable number of Jewish revolutionaries, including the famous international politician, Meir Litvinov.[1] The father of the former Soviet foreign commissar, M. Litvinov, was Moshe Volokh. He was not only a great scholar, but also a maskil, clever in the full sense of the word. My father and he not only prayed together in Bukovstein's study house, but were also close friends. The children of both families were also friends, and I attended school with Litvinov's oldest sister. As I now remember it, even at the age of thirteen or fourteen — in those days, that was considered being a grown-up girl — I liked to listen to my father's conversations with Moshe Volokh, who was a frequent guest in our home.

My father had his own business, but Moshe Volokh was a "man" for one of Bialystok's rich men — Elihu Maylakh. Three generations ago, the director of a big commercial company was not called an employee, or an official, but simply — a "man," and that kind of "man" not only managed the rich man's biggest deals, but also evaluated the potential brides and grooms for the boss's children. If *he* didn't give his consent, the boss didn't conclude a match. Rich men were generous with their "men," because they knew very well that those "men" were a hundred times smarter than their employers in every respect. Asher Ginsberg (Ahad Ha-Am), the creator of spiritual Zionism, was such a "man" in the big commercial firm of Kalonymus Ze'ev Wissotsky, in Russia.[2]

Meir, the oldest of Moshe Volokh's three sons, studied in *kheyder* with Rabbi Kalman Saperstein, and he gave a fine bar-mitzvah sermon in the Holy Tongue. One of Litvinov's classmates in *kheyder* in Bialystok, who heard his sermon, was the husband of my cousin, the veteran Hebrew teacher in Jerusalem named Rabbi Zalman Ben-Tuvim. Ben-

---

1. Maxim Litvinov (1867–1951) was a prominent Bolshevik and a close associate of Lenin. After the establishment of the Soviet Union, he became a Soviet diplomat.
2. An important merchant, philanthropist, and Zionist. He is remembered as the founder of the Wissotsky tea company,

Tuvim said that Meir Volokh was an awful brat, but that he was very bright. Rabbi Kalman Saperstein often said that that "sheygets"[3] would someday become an important person.

Either because of their own personal rebellions or due to the influence of the Zeitgeist — or maybe because of both — my younger sisters and brothers were active in various revolutionary parties. The oldest of my brothers had been a *Mizrachi* since that organization emerged in Bialystok, and was a distinguished social activist. The older of my two dentist sisters, Dina Shapiro, was a Zionist; and within ten years, she and her family had moved to Haifa. The younger one was an active Bundist, still living in my house in Warsaw in 1897, when the Bund was created. Two younger sisters, both middle-school teachers in Bialystok, sympathized with the Russian Social Democratic Workers' Party; and my two youngest brothers went over to the most extreme revolutionary movement, anarchism.

While they were still very young students in the upper grades of the Jewish commercial school in Bialystok, they were active socialists. It is easy to imagine what Jewish parents went through in those years, when their children were participating in various illegal movements and could be imprisoned or exiled for the slightest infraction. But my father, may he rest in peace, was a very tolerant person. For example, he knew that my brothers would sit with their friends in their room smoking cigarettes on the Sabbath, but he would stay out of their room all day. And though my mother, of blessed memory, became less tolerant and sometimes criticized them, he would tell her that she was wrong, that they wouldn't obey her anyway and that she would make them violate the commandment to honor thy father and mother.

One fine day, the oldest of my brothers, Berl, was arrested and sent to the Predvorilke, the jail for political criminals in Petersburg. He was detained for about six months and released for lack of proof. All the time he was in prison, my father wouldn't let anyone else pack the bundles of food and objects he was allowed to send from time to time. And when someone once asked him why he didn't let anyone else do this, he answered: "So long as a person is alive, he has the choice of being different." Upon coming home from the Predvorilke, my brother naturally dropped out of school and devoted himself completely to revolutionary work. He resigned from the socialist party to be one of the organizers of the first anarchist group in Bialystok. Eleven young men,

---

3. Yiddish for non-Jewish male, but in this context, a non-believer.

his sadly famous colleagues, were shot unjustly in 1905 at the execution square of the Citadel in Warsaw by administrative order of the Warsaw General-Governor Skolan; almost all of them were from Bialystok — children of the finest Jewish families.

I will devote a few lines here in my memoirs to the memory of my young brother Berl and his short tragic life, although it is not easy even now for me to describe, after so many years, these personally difficult, bitter, and sad events. My brother Berl was a very high-strung person: a fiery, clever, handsome, tall fellow, born in God's grace with a gift for oratory. His speeches could grab and hypnotize the largest audiences. In Petersburg, he met a Russian revolutionary activist, the daughter of a municipal councilor. They worked together, for a time even among the factory workers in Bialystok itself. Later, they went abroad for a while and we didn't even know where they were. One fine day, in 1904, an elegant Russian lady came to see me in Warsaw, carrying a letter from my brother that told me how this woman would be bringing me a personal message from him and that she would spend only one day with me, on her way to Petersburg. Naturally, I gave her a warm welcome. But that evening, she was arrested in my house and taken to the investigation-prison in city hall, on Teatr Square. The next morning, I learned that no compromising materials had been found on her, except for a first-class express train ticket to Petersburg. They escorted her to the train, waited until she was gone, and didn't even search my house. A few days later my sister, the Bundist, visited a friend, who was another dentist and active Bundist (the wife of a popular Jewish doctor in Warsaw) in that same prison. There my sister learned that my guest, the Russian lady, had spent the night in this other woman's cell. She told my sister that the police had talked about calling on Madame Rakovsky and finding out who had sent such a high-class foreign guest. But nothing came of it. In late summer of 1904, my brother suddenly reappeared in Bialystok on a party mission, but he didn't accomplish much because he was arrested again in our parents' home in early October.

My father, may he rest in peace, who had been afflicted with heart trouble for eleven years, suffered a severe heart attack at the time of the arrest and spent six weeks in bed. But his sick heart gave out and on Sunday, the fourth day of Hanukkah in 1904, his pure soul departed, while he was at the young age of fifty-seven. Earlier that week, on Thursday night, Mama had taken the Hanukkah lamp to him in bed, but he had only prepared three oil wicks. Why not all? asked Mother.

He answered calmly that he didn't need any more. On Sunday morning, when they sent us a cable to come, we arrived in Bialystok from Warsaw in the afternoon and barely saw Father in his last hour.

That sad picture is still vivid in my mind's eye: My father sitting in an armchair — he could no longer lie down — and I, his oldest daughter, his firstborn daughter, his mainstay of strength and force, only seventeen years younger than he, his favorite, despite my alleged "great sin," stood helpless next to him. (The other children would say, not without jealousy, that Puah had Father's love more than all of them). I heard his last words: "Don't let them torment me anymore in vain . . . "

For many years, my father had been a very prominent wholesaler of herring, salt, and kerosene. Years later he represented the large oil company Mazut for the district of Bialystok. My father was not only an extraordinarily capable merchant, but was also a highly virtuous man. After his death, following the practice of Jewish businesses at that time, the management hired my oldest brother, the Mizrachi member, who had previously represented Mazut in one of their large Polish provincial cities, Ostrolenka.

At the age of fifty-five, my mother was a widow, with seven grown-up, unmarried but independent children — four daughters and three sons. But my mother's tragic experiences did not end with my father's premature death. In 1906 and 1907 she suffered two horrible misfortunes, which she survived only because of her deep belief and genuine piety.

It wasn't long after the relatively short pause of 1903 that revolutionary winds began invading my Zionist house, and they were devastating. My son Yud-Ber felt constrained by our national liberation movement, and was drawn to the ranks of the revolutionary fighters for the liberation of all mankind. Once this decision was made, he had to determine in a reasonable time which party to join.

How did I react to that metamorphosis of my son? First, I responded as a rational person tolerant of someone else's conviction, and as a mother who was a revolutionary to the depths of her soul. His change didn't come as a surprise to me. Could we Jews, especially our young people, remain indifferent to the horrors of the tsarist satraps and executioners against Russia in general, and against her Jews in particular, under the rule of the narrow-minded, dull last Nicholas, who believed God gave him "absolute rule" and told him to fight against the liberation movement?

By then, a revolutionary mood had found its way into my Zionist house, and we baked Homentashn[4] to celebrate every act of revenge anywhere in Russia against some Russian hooligan minister whom we considered equivalent to Haman's lawmakers. Even my two-year-old daughter Sarah — whom we called Sorele — would raise her childish fist and proclaim: "Woe unto you Tsar, I will kill you!" upon entering a classroom where the school authorities ordered the portrait of Nicholas II hung on the wall.

Unlike many of my contemporaries, I was not stuck in middle-class Zionism. I never preached the doctrine that said "make a fence around the law of Zionism."[5] As far as I was concerned, Zionism never contradicted socialism. Perhaps before many of our ideologues — the creators and bearers of Zionist socialist thought — I was convinced that our popular movement was revolutionary; that Zionism was not simply meant to build a national home in the Land of Israel for our persecuted and suffering people, but was also rebuilding all Jewish life on new, healthy national and social foundations.

And now my son helped me understand that the Jewish problem was part of a complex world issue that can and will be solved on an international scale; and, only then, will honesty and justice rule in the world, instead of brute force and might. Obviously, I did not work actively with my son, but I did accept one difficult task, the task of not taking my vigilant eye off of him so he would remain intact.

My Bundist sister became very active in her party at that time, and not wanting to compromise me, she moved to another apartment. I warned her not to, but to no avail. On May 1, 1905, during a labor demonstration, she attracted the attention of the police, and they came to arrest her that evening. As they were searching her room, the police officer asked her: "How come you moved out of your sister's house? We know your sister," he admitted. She answered that her sister had gotten married and that there was no room in her flat.

When she was taken to the famous tenth pavilion of the Citadel, another police officer at headquarters asked her the same question. That made her mad and she answered proudly that it was her private affair and none of their business. She was imprisoned for a few months and then released. But by then she could no longer remain in Warsaw. I went to my mother and my oldest brother in Bialystok and persuaded them to arrange a permit for her to leave the country. Following my

---

4. The triangular pastry baked on the holiday of Purim, it was named after Haman, the adversary of the Jews in the biblical book of Esther.
5. An extension of the rabbinic dictum that one should "make a fence around the law," i.e., be stricter in practice than the law demanded.

advice, they sent her to Berlin and then to Paris. Having one less person to protect made life easier for me.

My "rescue" operation did not end with my sister's departure. My nineteen-year-old daughter Sheyndl was working as a teacher in my school, and, as I said, was an avowed and outspoken Zionist to the last day of her short and tragic life. My house became uncomfortable for her too. As soon as the school year ended, I got a permit for her to travel abroad and made all the preparations for her trip. We decided that she would go to a teacher's seminary in Bern. In those years of Russian revolutionary activities, Bern, the capital of Switzerland, was a genuine city of refuge for Jewish students. Hundreds of young people from the Pale of Settlement — mostly women — went to Switzerland, to study medicine and to take advantage of the liberal attitude of the Swiss universities to modern young scholars yearning for higher education. The vernacular of that world was Yiddish, laced with Hebrew expressions, to emphasize erudition and literary knowledge. The clothing and external demeanors, especially for the girls, smacked of "nihilism." They lived a high spiritual life; ate once a day, and one dinner every other day. They never ate to their fill, but were full of ecstasy and were ardent revolutionaries. Day and night, they constantly listened to lectures and counter-lectures and discussions, and were faithful to the maxim: "The Law exists only for one who kills himself for it."[6]

When my daughter was about to leave, I had to overcome an unpredictable obstacle. At a Purim party in 1904, one of my closest friends, Mordechai Lederer of blessed memory, introduced my daughter to a student in his second year of law school, Alexander Elshvanger. He was very impressed with her and asked her to allow him to pursue their friendship. For a while, I had no idea of what was going on. They would meet at assemblies and at Lederer's house. Before long my daughter told me about her new friend and admitted that she liked him very much. However, she said that she didn't know him very well, and so she wanted him to start coming to our house so that they could become closer. Naturally, I had no objections. He visited us often and I saw at once that their relationship was more than a simple acquaintance, and that they liked each other. I was happy that he would be in school for a few more years so my daughter could study and not get married at the age of nineteen. At the same time, they would have more opportunities to get to know each other. But as soon as my daughter planned to go away, I couldn't control my feelings and couldn't imagine how hard it

---

6. Babylonian Talmud, Berachot 63.

would be to part for a while. It wasn't easy for me, but my daughter was convinced that she shouldn't stay in Warsaw, and so she left.

It was no surprise that, after long hesitation and some internal conflict, my son joined the most extreme revolutionary movement, anarchism. His choice was an obvious result of his radical, uncompromising approach to the problems of the Russian revolution and his whole attitude in general. Enraged and embittered to the depths of his soul by the cruel counter-revolution against the Russian people in general and the Jews in particular, he thought a new socialist regime could emerge only on the ruins of the decadent tyrannical rule. The constant propaganda activity of my two youngest brothers also influenced his decision. In late 1903, when the smell of gunpowder was already in the air — the Russians were preparing for war with Japan — my son went to Pinsk and got his father's help to be released from military service as an only son.

By an order of the school authorities in Warsaw, I almost lost my school at the beginning of the Russo-Japanese war, which broke out in January 1904. The school board ordered all principals of Jewish schools to dismiss every Jewish teacher of Russian and Russian history immediately, and to hire instead the wives of Russian officers who had gone to war. That order was a death knell for me, an issue of to be or not to be.

The faculty room at my school was intoxicated — more precisely, electrified — by a revolutionary Zeitgeist. At recess, current political issues were discussed, understandably in connection with Jewish troubles. How could we admit a Russian lady, the wife of a mobilized Russian officer, into such an atmosphere? Never mind the question of whether she could teach! How could I entrust — even temporarily — the education of my three hundred Jewish children to a total stranger? And I decided that, unless that bitter decree were repealed, I would close my school.

So I went to the authorities and was able to arrange an appointment with the inspector-general. I calmly informed him that, to my great regret, I could not follow his order. First, I could not dismiss my teachers in the middle of the school year. Second, I could not do that, simply on principle, because, if the Jewish schools didn't employ the Jewish teachers, these teachers went hungry, since they were not allowed to work in the Christian schools. The inspector-general listened to me with a serious expression and answered briefly: "I have my subjects and you have yours" — as kings talk to one another. I resisted his frown and wasn't surprised by his answer. I replied: "As you understand.

But I cannot follow your order." I wished him a good day and left. Although most Jewish school principals did follow the order, I absolutely refused to. Nonetheless, my school was not closed.

❖

On July 15, 1904, on his way to court in Petersburg with a report to the Tsar about political matters, the infamous minister Plehve[7] was murdered by a Russian terrorist bomb. The revolution simply came upon us and the Tsarist coterie grew afraid and lost its head. On August 11, it published a manifesto of "Pardon" for the nation and even granted some concessions for Jews. But the Jews accepted those gifts coldly because their eyes were more focused on the broader horizons then opening for Russia.

The enslaved people aspired to freedom. But the dark forces of reaction prepared horrible vengeance for those who took part in the liberation movement. With their incitement of the embittered benighted masses against the liberal intelligentsia and the "Zhids," the reactionaries wanted to achieve three goals: to frighten the liberals and socialists indirectly; to demonstrate the will of the "people" against changing autocracy for a constitution; and to compromise the whole liberation movement as an alleged trick of "foreigners," especially Jews. They campaigned openly for a pogrom with the slogan: "Beat up the revolutionaries and the Jews. The wonderful time is coming when there will be no more 'Zhids' in Russia!"

At Pesach, there was open preparation for pogroms. On April 9 and 10, in the industrial city of Bialystok, which was a center of the revolutionary labor movement, the Cossacks murdered Jews on the streets, burst into schools and private homes, and robbed and beat up men and women. After the Russian fleet lost the battle of Tsushima,[8] and caught up in the general fire of the Russian revolution that blazed in the summer of 1905, the Jews responded to the pogroms by a stronger commitment to the revolutionary struggle. Jews were active in all camps of the liberation army: among the Constitutional Democrats, the Social Democrats, and the Social Revolutionaries. It was a vicious circle: as the first victims of a horrible despotism, the Jews had to join the liberation movement; black, reactionary Russia therefore wrought

---

7. Vyacheslav Konstantinovich Plehve (1846–1904), reactionary Minister of the Interior, who suppressed liberal political activity and promoted russification and antisemitism.
8. May 1905.

its revenge on them by unleashing horrible pogroms; and that reaction intensified their devotion to the revolution.

In the summer of 1905, a new wave of pogroms broke, this time a military one. Irritated and embittered by the constant defeats of the Russian army in Manchuria, the soldiers and Cossacks tried to find satisfaction through easier victories over the alleged "internal foes." They beat and killed Jews in the streets of Minsk, Brisk, Siedlice, and Lódz. In Lódz, they shot at the participants in a joint Polish-Jewish labor demonstration. The enraged soldiers carried out a horrible blood-bath in Bialystok, simply shooting at innocent Jewish pedestrians; throughout the day of June 30, fifty people were murdered and several others were wounded.

Three days after the pogrom, when I arrived at my hometown on the first train from Warsaw to Bialystok after the bloody events, the sidewalks were still covered with the blood of the martyrs. In many houses, including my mother's, the front wall was shattered by bullets. I will never forget the horrible picture of the masses of wounded people jamming the halls and even the courtyard of the Jewish hospital. Scores of wounded men, women, and children, had been shot in the legs, the hands, or other parts of their bodies. To dilute the bad impression of that horrible bloodbath, the local authorities spread a rumor that a Jewish terrorist had shot the Bialystok police chief, and that the pogrom was Christian vengeance against Jewish terror.

In late July, about a month after another pogrom in Bialystok, the anarchist group in that city sent a few "activists" to Warsaw to initiate activity in the capital of Poland. One of the anarchists they sent was my youngest brother Moshe, who didn't stay long in Warsaw (my son took over his work). But the other Bialystok members remained in Warsaw and were frequent guests in my home.

I was well aware of the dangers facing my family, but I had to take the anarchists in because most of them — among them, girls — were the children of families we knew in Bialystok. My house became a refuge, and even the cellar under the house was turned into a hiding place for illegal literature and other necessary instruments . . . If, during the later frequent house searches, what was hidden in my "kosher" Zionist home had been found, everything would surely have fallen on my head . . . Fortunately, the Polish janitor was also an "organizer," and we were frequently saved from death by my Polish housekeeper, Mariana, who came to work for me at the age of seventeen and stayed for twenty-eight years. She was so close to my family that she was ready, as they say, to walk through fire and water for every one of us. We called her "a true blue Jew" from a rabbi's family, and I would often say: "Mariana, you must be Jewish." She really did have "a Jewish head . . ." During searches, she would divert the police and cunningly remove what they were looking for; it was only because of her that they never found any compromising object.

Naturally, my son was very active and so was Birnbaum, whose political position and worldview drew him to the anarchist idea. He helped write proclamations, leaflets, and so on. Things got so bad that neither of them could sleep at home; they would come out in the morning only to teach classes, grab some lunch, and escape. This was how we lived during the last two months of 1904. The "final failure" took place in January 1905. Eleven people were arrested and my son was supposed to be the twelfth. At four that afternoon, he came into the dining room wearing a winter coat and told me: "Mama, fast, take Sorele, and come with me to the Petersburg railroad station."

I grabbed my two-year-old daughter, dressing her warmly — there was a good frost and a sleigh path which we seldom saw in Warsaw. My son picked up the baby, and we got into the first available sled and went to the Petersburg railroad station. Holding the child in his arms, my son bought a ticket to Malkinia, four stations from Warsaw, where my aunt, my father's sister, lived. Still holding the child, he boarded the train, handed her out to me through the window, and went to Malkinia. From there, my aunt sent him to Ostrolenka to my oldest brother, and that very night my brother took him over the border to Berlin.

At eleven o'clock that night, they came to search my house. Police were in the room; soldiers were at the gate. The "mining engineer," as the officer of the Nalewki city quarter was called, came, and so did the commissioner himself, as well as some civilian secret police. They found nothing, and asked me: "Where is your son?" Putting on a naive face, I answered almost calmly that my son hadn't been in Warsaw for a long time. At that, one of the spies gave a loud angry shout: "That's a lie, we saw him today. He couldn't have gone away. Get him here!" "Take him, if you can!" I answered.

The spies left and so did the "mining engineer." Only the "commissioner" remained, and he came over to me, took both my hands, and said very emotionally: "What a lucky mother you are that you got him out; what a good thing you did to save him!" I stood dumbfounded before him and could not produce a sound from my throat. (How hard it is to believe now that that commissioner was a *German*). I had lived in his district for almost twenty years; my school was there. He knew me and my family well, and he now celebrated my success in saving my only son from death. When I recovered from my paralysis, I thanked him warmly for his sympathy and he left.

But the police were still at the gate waiting for my companion Birnbaum. The secret police had ordered them to arrest him as soon as he arrived at school in the morning. After the commissioner left, Mariana went down and started chatting with the police and soon found out who they were waiting for. She knew that Birnbaum was spending the night at his aunt's. She asked the police to let her go to the nearby pharmacy, to pick up a prescription for her mistress, who had suddenly fallen ill and had to be saved. Incredible as it sounds, the police let her go, and she managed to warn Birnbaum not to show up in Kopiecka Street any longer. For two straight days, he stayed at his aunt's. On the third day, he went to Grodno to his sister's, where they procured a passport for him in a different name. Then they transported him over the Grayeva-Prostken border to Berlin.

That wasn't the last search. At three o'clock in the morning, the same agents came back with an order to arrest everybody in my house. I had two couples living in two rooms in my house, one with a child. In a third room lived the journalist who wrote for *Haynt*,[9] Riklis. All three men were arrested in the middle of the night, but were released because they were law-abiding citizens.

A few days later, I was summoned to the office of the general-governor. At first, I declared that I would take my little girl with me, but I soon realized that if they were going to arrest me, they would have come to my house and not summon me to the office. The political policeman who ordered my interrogation simply asked: "Where is your husband?" I answered that my husband had left me a long time ago because he was younger than I, and unfortunately I didn't have the slightest idea where he was. Perhaps he understood from my ironical tone that he wasn't going to get anything out of me. In any case, he didn't waste much time chatting with me. He asked a few more formal questions, and I was permitted to go home.

Various rumors circulated in the city about the sudden "misfortune" of the group and their frightening and tragic end. According to one persistent version, there was a provocateur in the group. But the real reason has not been determined to this very day. As I said, all eleven who were killed so tragically were children of close friends; they had come to my house almost every day. The youngest of them, an eighteen-year-old, had finished gymnasium that May. His father, Mr. Shapiro,

---

9. Established in 1908, it was the leading Yiddish daily in Warsaw before World War II.

was the principal of a Polish official grammar school for Jewish children in Warsaw. He was a man of great Jewish erudition, a former yeshiva student, and an outspoken type of the Haskalah period, who not only devoted himself day and night to Torah and prayer, but also created a whole "study house" of young people, who left their homes every year to come to study in the big city, Warsaw. One of his "study house" pupils later became his son-in-law, Sholem Asch.

It is easy to imagine the difficult life of such a government teacher two or three generations ago. Yet his house was open to those young people from the provinces. Anyone who came in hungry went out full. It was his wife who took care of that "study house." Everyone living in the large courtyard and surroundings in one of the truly proletarian Jewish neighborhoods of Warsaw called her the "little teacher." A village girl, the daughter of an innkeeper, she had studied neither in high school nor university, but had an innate intelligence, a social sense, and a revolutionary spirit. She was a real "woman of valor" of a few generations back, a person with healthy common sense, a strong character, and most important, a good Jewish heart, which, our sages tell us, is the highest of all virtues. What that woman did for the provincial Jewish youth in Warsaw, despite her difficult life, put her in the second volume of Sholem Asch's trilogy, *Before the Deluge, Warsaw*.[10]

The Shapiro family had two sons and two daughters. The older son, an extraordinarily talented boy, was sent to Siberia for revolutionary activity, and his unfortunate parents lost all trace of him. They had had such high hopes for their gifted older son, but in the end, they never even knew what became of him. The two daughters became teachers. The younger daughter — Sholem Asch's wife — was my student. The younger son, David, completed the gymnasium in 1905 at the age of eighteen. After the "misfortune" of the group, the Shapiro house was searched from top to bottom in the middle of the night. They rummaged in the straw mattresses, tore up the floor, threw out the dishes and pots in the kitchen; and in the end, among the books in the boy's schoolbag, they found a bundle of proclamations. He confessed that it was his, and he and his father were arrested and were taken to Pawiak. There the two of them were locked in a single room, and the father turned white as a sheet overnight.

A defense was organized, but no one had access to the men — not a lawyer, and not even their family, who were only allowed to bring them food. We learned that the case was not to be tried in a regular court, but

---

10. The trilogy was published in 1931–33 and was translated into English (1933) as *Three Cities*.

in a war court, and that it was in the hands of the Warsaw General-Governor, the brutal Skolan himself. According to the authority of the Tsar and the exceptional laws that had prevailed in the country for a long time, he could sentence to death all those who were on administrative arrest. And the Tsarist murderer did use his authority, unjustly shooting eleven Jewish young men.

After the boy's death, they didn't keep the father very long, and didn't put him on trial. They arrested him only because they held him responsible for his underage son. Unable to communicate with his family, the father didn't even learn what had happened to the boy. Only when he came home did he find out his son's fate, which broke him completely for a period of time. But he pulled himself together and devoted himself to his school. He drugged himself with constant study; and the inexhaustible youthfulness that he had preserved from his early years in a Hasidic study house helped him overcome his distress.

The broken mother reacted quite differently to her great misfortune. She was so shocked that she couldn't even weep. Her tears were dried up. A kind of bitterness poured out of the corners of her mouth, and her spirit changed radically. She became quiet and frozen, and her eyes gazed off into the distance, as though they wanted to see things others couldn't. She also became completely indifferent to the revolutionary movement she had once espoused so ardently; she lost almost all interest in life around her. Only in one area did she concentrate all her energy, and that was on helping her neighbors in her own proletarian environment. The focus of her unfortunate and crushed life was now on alleviating the cares and suffering of tormented people.

About a month after the horrible execution of the "eleven," my son left Berlin for Switzerland. I was suddenly summoned to an interrogation by the investigating judge "for particularly important matters." Since I knew that my son was out of danger, I went calmly to that "fighter for right and justice." As soon as I entered his office and told him my last name, he took out a picture album, put it on the table next to me, and said: "All those people used to come to your home. I want you to identify them." I glanced casually at the album and answered him calmly:

"For fifteen years, I have been the principal of a gymnasium with three hundred students. I know a lot of people. Moreover, I have an active life and am in touch with hundreds of people. I have grown children whose friends come over. I myself am not an old woman and scores of people visit me every single day. How can I identify somebody from a photograph, and tell you if he came to my house once?" Hearing my evasive answer, he suddenly said to me: "Where is your son?" "In America," I answered calmly. "What did he do in Warsaw?" "My son is a teacher who worked in my school." "Do you know about his work to escape from Warsaw? Do you know about his participation in expropriations?" "This is the first I've heard of it. I know that, until the day before his departure, he worked in my school." "Now, as you state, he is in America. Can you give me his address?" I didn't answer, but simply cast an expressively ironic glance at him. "America doesn't extradite anarchists, so why can't you give me his address?" he repeated. "If America doesn't extradite, why do you need his address?" "Right. But, understand me, as an investigating judge, I need to know everything." "And as a mother, I have the right not to tell you." With that, my remarkable, rather foolish investigation ended. And nothing happened.

❖

When he reached Switzerland, my son started studying languages and auditing courses in economics and social science. His lottery winnings were enough for a year and later he supported himself by making cigarettes. His financial situation was difficult, but he didn't despair. He continued his education and waited patiently for the final victory of the Russian Revolution, which would certainly change his personal life as well.

My companion Birnbaum stayed in Berlin where he gave Hebrew lessons in Zionist homes and did pretty well financially. In the summer, his employers vacationed in Colberg—a spa on the sea, not far from Poland and suggested he come along so the children wouldn't have to interrupt their Hebrew studies. He gladly agreed. My daughter stayed in Bern for another year, attending the teachers' college.

The year 1905 affected me strongly, not only emotionally, but also financially. My three loved ones, the best teachers in my school, all left at the same time. My subtenants were frightened and gave up their rooms. I was left with my three-year-old daughter and comrade Riklis, the editor of *Haynt*. Although I knew that my loved ones were out of danger, every time the bell rang at the gate at night, I was scared they were coming back to search us. (In Warsaw, when the gates were locked at night, you had to ring for the janitor to open them up and let you in.) My sensitive little girl was also badly shaken by what had happened.

In general, it was a bitter time. The economic situation was almost catastrophic; and the revolution brought complete stagnation in commerce and small trade, among artisans and workers. Those were the parents of my students, and they were impoverished. The number of children in the school fell constantly. Though I made valiant efforts, I could barely hold onto my school. I had worked so hard for it. I lasted until the vacation, but then I went to Colberg with my daughter to meet Birnbaum and to make plans together.

In truth, I had begun to think that the time had come to finally leave for the Land of Israel. A while before, I had been offered a position at the Herzliya Gymnasium in Tel Aviv. But my friends dissuaded me; they pointed out that there were enough Hebrew teachers in the Land of Israel while right now I was running the only Hebrew girls' school in Warsaw and shouldn't throw away my work. And it wasn't easy for me to break up what I had built over fifteen years, under very difficult emotional and financial conditions, to go to seek new work. How would it look if I didn't find any? I would lose on both accounts.

I spent two months in Colberg and, after a long deliberation, we concluded that Birnbaum would come back to Poland with me, but not directly to Warsaw. We didn't cross the border at Kattowice-Sosnowice, but at Mlowa, toward Ostrolanka. At Rosh Hashonoh, we went to visit my oldest brother. Birnbaum stayed in Ostrolanka all winter, not for free, but as a tutor for my brother's children. Right after the holiday, desiring to be closer to Warsaw, he moved to Otwock, which at that time was a "refuge" for many "illegals" from various revolutionary movements, because there you could live unregistered. As a spa for patients with lung diseases, Otwock in the early years had no police force, since the Tsarist regime was not afraid of the physically ill.

In Otwock, Birnbaum offered Hebrew lessons. In those years, there were a lot of old-style *khadorim* in Otwock, but there was only one single private Jewish co-educational primary school, with Polish as the language of instruction. When Birnbaum got to know the principal of that school, Mrs. Kaminsky, as well as its spiritual and financial situation, he suggested that he join her as a partner, if she agreed to introduce Jewish and Hebrew studies into the school. Mrs. Kaminsky gratefully accepted. Birnbaum started teaching Hebrew in all classes, and he soon changed the nature of the school. The previous half-assimilated spirit became a national-Jewish one. The number of children increased significantly, and the financial situation improved.

The trip to Otwock from Warsaw took forty minutes on the regular train and only twenty on the express. At first I went there only on Saturdays, lest anyone was following me and could discover Birnbaum's whereabouts. Initially, I couldn't sleep soundly there at night either; every time a dog barked, I was sure they were coming to search. Though the winter and the following summer passed quietly, Birnbaum stayed in Otwock all year and never risked a trip to Warsaw.

In early 1906, my daughter Sheyndl returned from Switzerland. She went back to teaching in the school, and I was relieved to some extent. Her feelings for her young man Elshvanger hadn't changed, and he began visiting, almost every day. Meanwhile, he had finished both the university and his military service, where he was a "privileged soldier" in the cavalry.

One fine day, my daughter told me she loved him and had decided to marry him. I told her — nothing. But I had a feeling it would be better if the marriage didn't happen too soon. When relatives and friends learned of their plans, one of my good friends, a doctor, who had been a classmate of Elshvanger's brother in a gymnasium in the city of Suwalki, tearfully pleaded with me not to let that wedding take place. I replied that not only could I not prevent it, but I couldn't even protest it, because I wasn't even asked, but had simply been confronted with a fait accompli. For me, personally, the man was always a complete stranger, because I felt that we lived in two different worlds, even though he was a Zionist — that is, he shared my political perspective — and even though my lineage was no worse than his. But I had uprooted in myself the "delusion of greatness" and my children hadn't been raised in that senseless spirit either. I told my friend that my only hope lay in the fact that I had heard his mother was also against the match. Regrettably — to be precise, unfortunately — that hope was dashed.

It wasn't only the match with my daughter that the mother didn't want; she was also against the match of her older son. As I said, Alexander Elshvanger's older brother Jacob was also studying medicine in Warsaw. In his fourth year, he contracted typhus and was treated in the university clinic. His nurse was a student in the *feldshers'* [medics'] and midwives' courses at the university — a Jewish girl from Kharkov. She was very beautiful, and as often happens in such cases, they fell in love. When the two boys finished school and came to their mother for her consent — or as we say in simple Yiddish, for a blessing — for their marriages, she wouldn't hear of it and wouldn't even meet the girls. So, in the summer of 1906, the two boys married against their mother's will. The older, the doctor, went off with his wife to Kharkov; and the younger one stayed in Warsaw, practicing as an apprentice and later as an attorney.

My daughter and son-in-law moved into a flat with my friend Leah Proshansky—at Solna 6. My daughter continued working six hours every day in my school. She received the same salary as all the other teachers—like me, 60 rubles a month—and led a decent life. Her husband paid the rent and she took care of the household expenses. She was a successful teacher, remained an active Zionist, and fulfilled her duties as a wife and later as a mother.

Five

Family Tragedies

In late 1906, we experienced a horrible tragedy. One of my two younger sisters, Feygl—a pure person of unusual abilities, one of the best teachers at a Jewish gymnasium in Bialystok—committed suicide in Paris by shooting herself in the head. She had debated suicide for a long time, and a year earlier, while still in Bialystok, had tried to poison herself but had been forcibly rescued. Two days after that attempt, my mother, may she rest in peace, cabled me to come to Bialystok, where she begged me to try to persuade my sister not to do it again.

I carefully attempted to get my sister to tell me why she wanted to kill herself. She told me candidly that life was so empty and so dirty that one should get out of it. As I talked with her, I felt that she was speaking not just idle chatter, but words from her heart. It was a well-thought-out conviction and a strong decision. But I did try to dissuade her: "If you really want to get out of life, at least sacrifice it for the revolution. Do it for the liberation of the enslaved, suffering masses of humanity." She answered that humanity wasn't worth it. I stayed in Bialystok a few days talking with my unfortunate sister but concluded that there was no force in the world that could keep her from that fatal step. Her notion of life was distinct from that of normal humanity—in short, she wasn't suited for life.

I did accomplish one thing: I convinced her to ease our mother's anxieties by saying she "wouldn't do that" again. Feygl agreed, but on condition that she be allowed to go to Paris, where she supposedly wanted to study. Naturally my mother consented at once, and my sister left. My sister Tsirel, the Bundist, also came from Berlin, and they made their plans together. At first, she really did attend school as an auditor, and my older sister's letters convinced us that a miracle might happen. It isn't hard to imagine what my unfortunate mother was going through. Her only consolation, she used to say, was that at least Father didn't have to live through this.

Feygl's tragic death occurred under the following circumstances. During the few months in which they lived together in one room, my older sister protected her unobtrusively, trying as much as possible not to leave her alone. They didn't eat lunch together, but right after lunch both of them would come straight home. On the fatal day, while my older sister was dressed and ready to go out for lunch, the younger one said: "You don't have to come straight home from lunch today because I will be busy." My other sister didn't suspect anything because Feygl was as calm as she always seemed to be. Without worrying, Tsirel calmly went to lunch, strolled around a while afterward, took care of some errands, and came home at five o'clock.

When she opened the door, she saw our younger sister sitting in an armchair, as if she were alive, dressed up in her best clothes. Next to her was a small revolver, and from her temple a stripe of blood flowed over her face. Tsirel shouted and the neighbors came running. The doctor was sent for, but he only confirmed the death. The police also came and found a letter saying that no one was to be accused of her death. A second letter in Yiddish was to our mother, asking forgiveness for the grief she had caused her. She had waited for an illness, she wrote, like typhus or tuberculosis, in order to die a natural death. But unfortunately she couldn't wait any longer and had to take her own life. A third letter, to Tsirel, was accompanied by a batch of postcards addressed to our mother in Bialystok. In that letter, she asked her older sister to make sure that Mother found out only later; and so she left postcards addressed in her own hand. Tsirel took care of all the formalities and did the final work — the "true grace" — making the funeral arrangements for her younger sister who had died so tragically. Then she went back to Berlin and ultimately took a position as an assistant in a dentist's office in Lausanne, Switzerland. My sister's suicide was neither the first nor the only sad event heard about in Bialystok at that time.

The first edition of the landmark book by Otto Weininger, *Sex and Character*, appeared in Berlin in 1903. The young author — of Jewish origin — a "genius" psychopath who took his own life at the age of twenty-three, was very popular. Between 1903 and 1919, his book went through seventeen editions, and was translated into almost every European language. And young people of both sexes, especially women, admired it tremendously. They drank in all his words, not only reading them, but poring over them with fatal results. The twisted meanings, weird conclusions, and humiliating appraisals of the value and meaning of women in general ended up embittering mature people. And it is no wonder that the book shook the spirits of the young people at that time of *Sturm und Drang*, especially of young women who held high ideals and strove for education, self-development, and social equality, and who also struggled stubbornly for the freedom and equality of all mankind. And then there came someone who chopped off their wings.

In Bialystok itself, seven victims fell under that blow, including my unfortunate sister. They were girls with middle and higher education, almost all independent and from intellectual Jewish homes. The epidemic afflicted a great many cities. Aside from those suicides in Bialystok, I myself know of several that occurred for the same reason in Warsaw, in Uman, and in other places.

❖

In 1907, while my broken mother was still mourning the tragic death of her twenty-five-year-old daughter, she experienced another tragedy. Since 1904, my brother Berl, the anarchist, had been in hiding. He had probably been sent somewhere, but we had had no news of him; it seemed like he had simply disappeared. Then in the winter of 1907, one fine day, he suddenly came to Bialystok for a short, clandestine visit. He told us he had come to see Mother, and that he was proposing our older brother take a life insurance policy on him, if he could do it quickly, and give him some money as well, because he wasn't going to live long. My brother responded that he wasn't into that kind of business, but as the Bible says, "In his heart he guarded the matter."[1]

After his short visit, Berl left Bialystok for Paris, and again we didn't hear from him. But suddenly we read in the papers that the son of the late Menachem Mendel Rakovsky of Bialystok, the twenty-four-year-old Berl Rakovsky and his wife, were found shot to death in a suicide pact at a Paris hotel. Various versions of his death circulated in Bialystok. The revolutionaries thought he committed suicide because he was disappointed in his work. Others stated that when Berl found out about the death of his father, for whom he had an extraordinary love, he was

---

1. Genesis 37:11. The words "in his heart" were added by Rakovsky.

so horribly depressed that he was led to kill himself. Whatever the reason, it didn't change the sad fact.

My saintly mother found consolation by devoting all her time to her charitable institutions. And one more thing relieved her suffering: She believed with perfect faith that after her death, she would surely be in the World of Truth, with her beloved husband. Not only did she believe that, but she also prepared herself for it, and waited for it as a bride waits for her bridegroom . . .

How differently our people experience such tragedies . . .

In the summer of 1908, my son Yud-Ber, who was having a hard time living in Switzerland, suddenly suffered an attack of nerves that made him write incessantly. He composed poetry and prose on various subjects, day and night, and was unable to tear himself away from the paper. The doctors diagnosed this as a chronic illness, but could not determine its cause. Ultimately, they concluded that his writing reflected a strong yearning for his mother, strange as that may seem in a twenty-five-year-old man. For a while, the whole thing was concealed from me, but then the doctor (my son's friend) sent a letter to my daughter advising a meeting between my son and myself. When I heard the story, I wrote him immediately that I was going to Colberg, and asked him to meet me. By the time I got my exit visa and reached Colberg, he was already there.

When I got off the train and he saw me, he said only one word: "Mama!" Nothing more. And at this moment, thirty-three years later, I still hear his voice calling "Mama!" And to my dying breath, I will not forget it.

I stayed with him in Colberg for the entire vacation. He swam in the sea, recovering his appetite and his health. Naturally, returning to Poland was out of the question. Nor did he want to go back to Switzerland, for his doctor friend insisted that he cease all mental endeavors and shift either to physical labor or at least to something more technical, like office or commercial work.

In Berlin at that time lived the Rotshkovski family from Warsaw, who were friends of mine. Their daughter had attended my school, and some years later their son, an agronomist, married Nahum Sokolow's daughter (they have been living for some years now in Jerusalem). Before they married, Mr. Rotshkovski and his wife had both worked in a big tie factory in Warsaw, he as a bookkeeper and she as a tie-maker. Then while they worked together in the company, they fell in love and married. Both of them had a good business sense. They opened a factory and soon amassed considerable capital. Years later, they moved to Berlin, where they set up an extensive commission business. The Rotshkovski Company was very popular in Berlin, especially among nationalist and Zionist circles because both the husband and the wife knew how to run their house and their business. There was scarcely a Jewish student in Berlin who needed work who did not get a job at their company while attending school. They were genuinely warm people and over the years, their house in Berlin became a gathering place for scholars, as indicated by the fact that Nahum Sokolow married into that family. When my son told me he planned to look for office work, I immediately wrote to the Rotshkovski family, asking them to hire him, and I soon received an extraordinarily friendly answer. They were delighted to be able to serve me in any way possible, and invited my son to come to their house as soon as he returned from Colberg. He would surely feel at home.

In late July, I went from Colberg to Berlin with my son. The Rotshkovskis were overjoyed to see me, and my son went right to work in the office. At that time, Elshvanger's older brother, still a medical student at Berlin University, was also working there, along with some other Jewish boys from Poland. I returned to Warsaw happy that I had settled him so well and especially with our own people. Only one thing worried me: How would my son adjust to such simple work? He was a teacher by profession, immersed in his studies, and had no idea of trade or business.

How great was my surprise when, a month later, Mr. Rotshovski came to Warsaw on business. Bringing regards from my son, he told me: "You know, Mrs. Rakovsky, your son is an excellent worker. In one month, he has grasped the entire technique. And I must tell you that a young man from Kutne has been working for me, and he hasn't learned in three years what your son has learned in one month."

As for my son, he was at first not very enthusiastic about his new employment. But his view soon changed completely, especially since he managed to divide his time between gainful employment and his self-education. The Rotshkovski family's friendship was especially important to him. Whenever they visited Warsaw, they would always tell me my son's virtues and that they loved him as their own child. Yud-Ber worked in the Rotshkovski Company in Berlin for six years, from 1908 to the outbreak of the war in 1914.

As the previous chapters show, my life — even aside from the extraordinary family tragedies — was not easy. The revolutionary years, from 1905 to the outbreak of the war in 1914, were especially hard. But one thing did please me — that my son spent those difficult years abroad. I could at least correspond with him and know that he was safe. My life was hard, but interesting, full, and rich; and it had aspects of the highest satisfaction that can come only from an ideal you believe in with every breath. Because if you are devoted, first to the interests and life of your own people, and at the same time to the problems of mankind in general, you feel different even about your own personal suffering.

The brutal counterrevolution that was kindled at the same moment as the Manifesto of October 17th[2] drove the revolution to extremes of terror and anarchy. Everyone became horribly angry at the treacherous policy of Nicholas II. With one hand he signaled an agreement with liberal society, and with the other, he stuck a knife in the back, not only of the left, but also of the moderate democratic parties who didn't believe the tsarist promises would be kept.

❖

As I said, my older daughter Sheyndl married Alexander Elshvanger, the attorney, in 1906, and as I had unfortunately predicted (more correctly, felt), her choice of a mate was a failure. At first, my unhappy daughter tried to hide everything from me, and shared her suffering only with her stepfather, my companion Birnbaum. Soon that became impossible because she started suffering economically as well as emotionally. Her husband wanted twelve children, like the patriarch Jacob. In the first four years, my daughter, may she rest in peace, gave birth to two children — a boy, Arye-Shmuel, and a girl, Shoshana. Their expenses increased and their economic situation grew worse. My daughter taught in my school for 60 rubles a month. But not all at once, only two rubles a day for expenses. In those years, that was how principals of seven-grade schools with three hundred students lived. At first, when my school was a "primary" school, students studied over the whole year — all twelve months — without a vacation. Later, when I changed it to a middle school, the students had to take vacations — one month in winter and three months in summer. The teachers were paid for all twelve months, but we couldn't charge the children for the whole year. Well-to-do parents who understood that the faculty had to eat even during vacation would pay; but most parents didn't want to consider the situation of the teacher. As the saying goes, "A Jew gives himself

---

2. The declaration of the Bolshevik Revolution in 1917.

advice." In summer we lived on credit and in winter we had to work to pay off the summer months. It wasn't easy, but Jews are used to difficulties.

However, the situation became harder when two families—my own and my daughter's—needed to be supported by the school. People usually had to find work as private teachers in the summer to earn enough to cover their expenses. We came up with the idea of running a boarding school during the summer in one of the villages on the Warsaw–Otwock line. Among the three hundred parents of our students, there must have been fifty or sixty who sent their children away to get fresh air. That idea had come from my son when he taught in my school; he saw the summer plans as an opportunity for the children to study for three or four additional months under our direction. The parents were mainly interested in whether their children ate well.

We opened the first boarding school for children in 1906, in Szwider, one station before Otwock. Since we weren't sure the undertaking would succeed, we didn't rent a very big building, and we advertised in the newspapers over Passover week. Since no one in Poland had ever before come up with the idea of such an institution—in Germany such children's boarding schools had existed for years—our announcements evoked a lot of interest; and right after Pesach, many middle-class children enrolled, in addition to our own students.

In those years, middle-class Jewish women in Poland were very active. They often worked in their husband's shops and factories. In Warsaw, some women even ran big businesses and various crafts workshops on their own, employing hundreds of Jewish girls and teaching them a skill. Those middle-class working mothers couldn't leave their businesses to go to a summerhouse. Entrusting the children to the Polish maid was also impossible, so they were glad to be able to send the children for "fresh air," with the supervision of teachers and educators thrown into the bargain.

In short, we hit the target and took advantage of the right moment. At that time, there was no special building for a boarding school on the Warsaw–Otwock line. But from the number of children enrolled, we foresaw that the rented building would be too small so we immediately rented Jaretsky's villa in Szwider from the same landlord. At that time, it was a famous Jewish place. There were a few more small houses nearby and our child boarders made that villa very popular.

To allow us to devote ourselves exclusively to teaching, I formed a partnership with a good friend of mine from Bialystok and her husband, who owned a grocery store in Warsaw. He was a good merchant and a capable buyer — and with food, that's the most important thing — and his wife was an excellent hostess and an efficient worker.

The experiment yielded good results the very first summer. We enrolled eighty children, not only school-age kids, but also three- and four-year-olds who didn't want to eat at home as usual. We ran the boarding school — as far as conditions in that building allowed — according to the best rules of hygiene and education. A few dozen of the children had a Fröbel[3] teacher. The ten older girls had a woman teacher and the ten boys a male, all under our supervision. There was also a special doctor in the institution — a woman — and a female surgical assistant. With proper organization, the work wasn't hard, and it gave us a certain spiritual satisfaction. It may sound strange to idealize such simple work as feeding children. But — as many are convinced, not only every mother, but also every maid — the process takes on a completely different character when it is done by intelligent teachers and responsible educators.

I should point out the important social aspect of our achievement. Our initiative soon evoked a response. Famous Jewish doctors from Warsaw, especially pediatricians, were the first to open children's boarding houses on the "line." Some of them even set up year-round sanitaria for sick children. Soon, aside from the private boarding school for the rich and middle class, Jewish cultural and political organizations also opened children's boarding schools and sanitaria for poor, working-class children.

In Szwider, we ran the boarding school at Jaretski's for four years, from 1906 to 1910. Attendance increased from year to year, and that institution soon became as popular as my school. It was called P. Rakovsky's Children's Boarding School. Our situation improved economically. The boarding school was open almost all summer, from the month of Iyar until the holiday of Sukes.[4] Our partners lived in Otwock during the winter, and right after Passover they would go to Szwider to make the necessary preparations and repairs, and even to prepare food that wouldn't spoil. My daughter Sheyndl's economic situation grew much better, but emotionally she suffered more.

In 1911, Warsaw celebrated the twenty-fifth anniversary of the newspaper Ha-Zefira. It commemorated the event with the performance in the philharmonic auditorium of a Hebrew play, The Age of Gold, starring my daughter, who was a talented actress, and Uri-Nissan

---

3. Friedrich Fröbel was a German pioneer in kindergarten education.
4. Approximately from May to October.

Gnessin.[5] Soon after, my daughter told me in secret that she had decided to take her children to the Land of Israel. But first she wanted to be fluent in Hebrew, so she hired her friend Uri-Nissan Gnessin to teach her. Needless to say, I was thrilled by her decision. She began a serious study of Hebrew literature. After she made that radical decision, she came back to life and her whole mood suddenly changed for the better.

Our children's boarding house continued to develop and prosper. In 1910, a rich Warsaw Jew built a magnificent modern two-story villa with thirty-three rooms and big glassed-in verandas in Mikhalin — on the "line," right near Warsaw — in the middle of a wonderful forest. We rented it, bought special children's furniture, and ran the boarding house on a genuine European standard for four years from 1910 to 1914, until the day before the war broke out. Because they attended the summer boarding house, a number of school age children also boarded in the city during the winter. Some were girls from the provinces who came to study in Warsaw. Our new flat at Nowoliepke 40 had big, comfortable rooms, and we converted it into a boarding school for young people. Our partner's daughter and son-in-law — a childless couple who worked as employees in the boarding school in the summer — managed the place. Applicants beat a path to our doors and had to wait weeks for a place to open up.

My daughter was planning to go to the Land of Israel as soon as possible, and was secretly making preparations to leave at the end of summer 1912. Unfortunately, she became pregnant with her third child and all her hopes were shattered. Despite her difficult physical condition and unusually oppressed emotional situation, she wouldn't stop working even for an hour and taught until her last day.

The greatest misfortunate of my life happened one Thursday afternoon, the eighteenth of Adar, 1913. It was then that my daughter Sheyndl died of pneumonia in childbirth, at the age of twenty-eight. The child, a girl, was born alive, and two hours later, my unfortunate daughter gave up her own pure soul. All Warsaw lamented my great misfortune with me. I did not want to see an obituary notice for my daughter in the newspaper; for me there was no consolation. I didn't see her corpse; I wanted her to remain always alive in my memory, beautiful and with a good, clever smile on her bright face. I did not want to see them put her in the ground. My old mother came to the funeral of her dear young granddaughter.

---

5. A Hebrew writer (1881–1913).

What happened to me? I really died with my child, but she was put into a grave and I remained walking around as a living corpse. For eight straight months I didn't have the strength to cross the threshold of my school. I was unable to live with the thought that I wouldn't find her coat in the corridor on the hanger, because she had always arrived at school earlier than I did. She was twenty years younger and wanted to ease her mother's burden as much as possible. For me, the question at that time was "to be or not to be." At first, I thought that I might have lived long enough. I told myself that living without her was harder than leaving the world altogether, and I decided to drink the bitter goblet of the poison of my hard fate to the last drop. Yet now I had new obligations: I had to bring up three little orphans. That thought may have eased the harsh suffering of her last minutes. I had to carry out her wish to take the children, hard as it was for me to live without the light of my daughter.

My ten-year-old Sorele took the tragic death of her sister very hard. The two sisters had loved each other very much. The little one would wake up in the middle of the night so no one would see, and write poems — in Russian — about the tragic death of her sister who died young. She would follow me around, not letting me lament, and kept repeating: "Mama, we have little children."

My companion Birnbaum did the actual, hardest care and work for the unfortunate little orphans. At night, the cradle of little Sheyndl — she had her mama's name — stood next to his bed. He dedicated all his free time to the children, like the most devoted father in the world.

Right after Passover, the boarding school reopened. I went with the children, and Birnbaum came there every day after school. Sheyndl was a copy of her mother. After a while, it seemed to me that I was twenty years old again and raising my own Sheyndl, not her orphan. I didn't leave her alone for a moment. Once — I remember it as if it were yesterday — in Mikhalin, I was alone on the veranda, holding the child in my arms and looking at her bright face. I suddenly felt confused, and a moment later, seemed to black out. But then I jolted awake as after a nightmare, hugged the child to my breast to keep her from falling, and said to myself: Puah, get a hold of yourself! What will become of the poor orphans?

That year we stayed at the boarding school through the holidays. The children improved, and the baby became more and more like her mother. Where was the father? Right after the catastrophe, he left the house; he didn't leave Zalna Street, but just rented a room across the street, at number 18, with our old friend, the journalist Riklis. Riklis told us that during the day, Elshvanger would stand at the window for hours looking at number 19. At night, he would run around the rooms, shouting: Charlotte! (the name he called Sheyndl). Riklis felt sorry for him and didn't want to leave him alone. Now and then he would come to see the children for a few hours and then go back to the city.

One day, soon after Sukes, he came in holding a four-year-old boy by the hand and said to me: "I found this little orphan on the street and brought him to you. Let him be raised with my orphans." And then he left. Naturally, I kept the little boy for a while, until we got him into an orphanage.

As if those experiences weren't enough, a few months later I received another blow: I lost little Sheyndl within three days. She lived only nine and a half months and died on the ninth day of Teves,[6] her mother's birthday. One evening, I put her to sleep, cool and healthy, and in the middle of the night she jolted awake with a horrible shout: "Babtshe!" (She babbled in Polish because she had a Polish wet nurse). To this day, her horrible shout still rings in my ears: *Babbe!* We called the doctor at once and he diagnosed a concussion. On the third day, the baby passed away. To this day, I don't know what caused it. The people in the house whispered that the little orphan stranger had pushed her through the room in her buggy and that she had suffered a blow. But I couldn't be sure of this. One fact, however, I do remember. Strange as it may sound to modern people, even according to Freud's theory of dreams — a few days before that misfortune, I saw my daughter, peace be with her, in a dream, wearing a black dress with a long bow — which was the fashion — and a light blue blouse. Her face beamed. She bent over the child's cradle next to Birnbaum's bed, picked up the sleeping child, and disappeared. I woke with a start and wanted to call her back, but she wasn't there anymore. I told that dream for the first time only three days later when the child had passed away. Maybe my devoted daughter thought she had left me too heavy a burden and wanted to ease it, and took the little one to her.

That second death in such a short time terrified me. I asked my friends for advice about what to do now, and how to protect the other two children. I was almost crazy. Then the days became bearable again. I went back to teaching in my school; I drugged myself with work and social activity, and was always with people, but I suffered from permanent insomnia. For a while, I couldn't get control of myself. Living with my companion Birnbaum became hard. I could live again for my duties,

---

6. Hebrew month that falls in December or January.

but enjoying life was beyond me. I wanted to separate from him, and I stayed only because of gratitude for his fatherly relations with my beloved daughter's poor orphans. Their own father hardly cared about them, and he didn't give me any money to bring them up. They loved Birnbaum and were closer to him than to their own father. This went on until the outbreak of the war. It wasn't easy. I was forty-eight years old; Birnbaum no more than thirty-eight. A strong and loving man, he had married me ten or twelve years before. But I could hardly be with a young man when my twenty-eight-year-old daughter was in the ground. He often said to me: "You have no right to leave me because we have a child. She loves both of us and you may not destroy her life." (Sorele loved her father very much.) His reasoning was right but it only increased my suffering. I realized that I was unfair to both of them, yet I couldn't take anything more from life. We stayed together because of the orphans; because of our only child; because of our mutual economic interests. But it was no longer an ideal life together.

Six

Winds of War

When the war broke out in August 1914, we spent our last summer in Mikhalin. A hundred children and eighty young people attended the boarding school. For a week the situation was tense. Rumors circulated that the Germans would destroy the Vistula Bridge and that it would be impossible for us to get into the city from the Line. On Friday and Saturday — the first and second day of the war — all the mothers came down, grabbed their children, and left, leaving everything behind and, of course, not paying their bills. Naturally, at such a moment we couldn't protest, but we had to stay through Saturday and couldn't just leave everything behind. On Sunday morning we rented a cart, packed up whatever we could take, and went to Warsaw. We still got there a long time before the Germans captured the city. Even though the parents paid to get their things back, we still suffered a significant loss.

The school remained open. There weren't many children, but we taught as always. One day, Alexander Elshvanger came and told us he was going off to war. He said goodbye to the children and left. We didn't even know where he was sent. In Warsaw and many other Polish cities, people who had relatives in Russia fled to them, but we didn't get out.

All of a sudden, a good friend of ours brought a letter from Elshvanger, saying that his mother and her family had fled from Grayeva to Vilna. He wanted us to send the children to her in Vilna at once. I was thunderstruck at the idea of parting from my daughter's children! How could I send the unfortunate orphans to Vilna? To whom would they go? To his mother, who wouldn't even meet my unfortunate child? No power in the world could make me do that. I told the messenger, Rapoport, categorically that I absolutely refused to give up the children, because my daughter had left them with me, and nobody else.

But Rapoport didn't give up either. He sent other people to talk to me, and they told me that I had no right to keep the children in such a dangerous place as Warsaw, that I shouldn't risk their lives. You can imagine what I went through. Naturally, I didn't want to risk the children's lives; yet I couldn't live without them; so I went to Vilna with them. But what was I to do with my own daughter Sarah? How could I leave her in Warsaw? Her father absolutely refused to let her go. So, we asked her what she wished to do. After considering briefly, she announced that she was not going, that she was staying with Abba (as she called her father).[1] I decided to go alone with the two other children. The situation was growing worse by the hour. Rapoport didn't leave me alone. I went to the office at the Citadel to get a pass and took one for my Sorele too.

Bullets were already flying over Warsaw. I ran home to pack so that I could leave on the next train. When my Sarah saw me packing and heard the bullets, she said that she was going too. This time, her father didn't say a thing. I grabbed the children, ran to the railroad station, and took the last train out of Warsaw. The cars were crammed full of civilians and soldiers, and there wasn't a single seat available. The train moved. I was standing with the three children when I heard a soldier say: "Where are you running, you vile Jewess, with your three pups? I'm going to throw all of you out the window and put an end to you!" I was dumbfounded. And what would they do to him if he did indeed carry out his threat?

To this day, I still don't know how we traveled all night long and got to Vilna alive the next morning.

I traveled with fifty rubles in my pocket. I went to my sister-in-law's aged mother — the mother of the Cohen they hadn't let me marry twenty-five years before. There was no room in her house for the three children and me so I had to let Madame Elshvanger know that I had brought the grandchildren. An aunt soon came, an old Fräulein, who wanted to take them. The children cried, and so did I. I told them they would see me every day, and they went with the aunt.

My sister-in-law's aged mother lived alone with a maid, who was not young either. Both old women seemed to be good people, which was the most important thing for me. I recovered. Things were easily arranged. I rested from the trip for a day and then started looking for

---

1. Hebrew for "Daddy."

work; but with the few rubles I had, you couldn't get far. My hostess's son, the engineer Frenkel, was the director of a large craft shop, called "Help Through Work." He knew me well and hired me right away as a teacher of Yiddish and arithmetic in the school.

In Vilna at that time, there was a "Yehudia" school, just as in Warsaw. The director of the school was Rachel Goldberg, an active Zionist, whom I had met at Congresses and with whom I had become friendly. The principal of "Yehudia" was the teacher Mordechai Mazo, who later established and administered the "Vilna Troupe."[2] I went to see Rachel Goldberg, who introduced me to Mazo, and I joined Yehudia as a teacher of Hebrew. That took care of my financial concerns. I rented a room for me and my Sarah from a young family named Berlin, who came from Kovno. At that time, Vilna was full of refugees. I moved in and started working in both schools.

My grandchildren came to me every day. I enrolled my Sarah in a Jewish gymnasium, and I calmed down a bit. Soon after I came to Vilna, Birnbaum wrote to tell me that a few days after I left Warsaw, a bomb had hit the house at Nowoliepke 40. The only damage to our apartment were some knocked-out windowpanes, but no one was hurt. He was happy that I was in Vilna with the children and that we were spared such a horrible experience.

I taught for two months, and my work was satisfactory. I was registered with the board as a teacher in both schools so that I could get a permit. But bad luck always followed me: The schools received a notice from the board that the teacher P. Rakovsky was not permitted to teach in those schools. I went to the inspector and explained to him that I ran a seven-grade school in Warsaw, that I was a refugee and that I wanted to know why I was not permitted to teach. He answered me coldly: "You have the right to teach only in German, nothing else. Your specialty is the German language, so try to get hired as a German teacher."

I understood that there was no point complaining. When I had taken my teacher's examination twenty-five years earlier, I had known German very well and chose it for my specialty. People usually chose mathematics for the examination because they had to know the whole course anyway, but I had never liked arithmetic and had a facility for learning languages. At the time of my examination, I planned to open a school in Bialystok where German was widely taught, because a lot of Germans lived there, but there wasn't one licensed teacher specializing

---

2. A Yiddish theatrical company, established in Vilna in 1916 and relocated to Warsaw in 1917. It was considered a symbol of high-class Yiddish theater.

in the German language. I explained to the inspector—although I understood it wouldn't help—that in our school in Warsaw, I taught all subjects, with the permission of the head of the school board. But he grew angry and repeated coldly: "You have the right to teach only the German language."

I went directly from the inspector to the head of all educational institutions. That official was a more intelligent and politically mature person. He listened to me attentively and answered me very politely: "You may be right, but I can't do anything against the law." I commented: "Excuse me, Professor, but twenty-five years ago, I couldn't know that a war would break out between Germany and Russia." He answered calmly, with an eloquent smile: "But that fact can't change the law."

You can imagine my situation. It was clear to me that I would not be a teacher in Vilna. But what was I to do now? I came home dejected and told Mrs. Berlin about the result of my visit to the head of education. "Don't despair, Mrs. Rakovsky," she said. "You won't be helpless in Vilna if you can't teach in the school. Since you won't leave the city and can't leave your grandchildren, we have to find a solution, and I think that I have some advice for you. You ran boarding schools for children, so you know how they work. We have decided to leave Vilna; I'm giving you my apartment with everything in it, as it is, and I shall go. Take in a few boarders, arrange a homey lunch. Vilna is full of refugees; food, as you know, is dirt-cheap. I guarantee you that you will get through the war just as well as if you were teaching. Food for the body may be as important as spiritual food. Why, "if there is no flour, there is no Torah," she concluded with a pleasant smile.[3]

My friends, Rachel Goldberg and L. Frenkel, the engineer, naturally sympathized with me, but I did have to leave the school. If there had been no emergency, a solution might have been found. But due to my financial situation, I couldn't wait; before long the Berlin family left Vilna and went deep into Russia, and I opened a boardinghouse and lunchroom in their four-room apartment. My enterprise succeeded beyond all expectations. I rented two rooms to lodgers, and the number of lunch boarders increased not by the day, but by the hour. At that time, my lodgers, my lunch boarders, and generally frequent house guests were refugees in Vilna. They included teachers and writers, along with the local intelligentsia and the initiators and founders of the famous "Vilna Troupe." My home became a copy of my home in Warsaw.

---

3. *Ethics of the Fathers*, 3:17.

In a few months, along the same courtyard in the city center on Great Pohulyanke, a building became vacant when the railroad administration left Vilna. It contained eight large rooms on the street and even a few sizeable halls. I soon rented it. The rooms were let. Within a few days, there were two hundred people at lunch each day. I brought my manager and my cook from Warsaw, along with the four local house servants, and I myself served as bookkeeper and cashier. And food in Vilna really was extraordinarily cheap; it flooded the market. My little children lacked nothing. My Sarah studied diligently and saved her allowance for a piano so that she could learn to play — she had considerable musical talent — and my grandchildren were at my house almost all day long, and went to their other grandmother's only to sleep. For the first time in my life, I saved 200 rubles from my work — to become a capitalist in wartime . . .

My companion Birnbaum came to see us and asked me to go back to Warsaw. He spent a few weeks with us, and then went back home. The prosperity lasted just one year, until the Germans came. The front was inching closer and closer to Vilna, and the situation was growing tense. Anyone who could flee went deeper into Russia. The big Jewish middle school moved to Yekaterinoslav. Some of my young boarders were destitute, so I brought them into my house as waiters. I thereby created a small house commune. As the situation became more serious, I came up with the idea of going into Russia, because I learned that some of our family members were already there. The first ones to go to Astrakhan were the wife and children of my oldest brother, who lived in an especially dangerous place, right next to the German border in Ostrolenka. People thought it was no place for women. My brother didn't waste any time and as soon as the war started, he sent his wife and four young daughters to his brother-in-law in Astrakhan, who was the engineer Frenkel, "the Cohen." He himself stayed in Ostrolenka. Both my sisters, the dentists, also fled to Russia, first to Yekaterinoslav, then to Astrakhan. In short, I had family there.

The main point was that I no longer had my school in Warsaw. During the first year of the war, from 1914 on, Birnbaum had been principal of the school, as I had turned it over to him. Who thought the war would last for years? Everyone was sure it was a matter of months, at most a year, and people hoped that the end would come soon. In 1915, my companion Birnbaum liquidated the school and gave all the equipment of the school library, etc., to Jewish schools in Warsaw. He didn't even keep the license; he just didn't take it off the wall. He got work in Jewish schools as a teacher of Yiddish and Hebrew, and at the same time started writing textbooks in Yiddish and Hebrew for primary and middle schools. His books quickly became very popular; his Hebrew textbook, *Yaldut*, in three parts, was used in schools and *khadorim* throughout Poland. Only the *Tarbut* schools[4] boycotted it because it didn't have a Zionist character. But because it was written in such a pedagogically modern way, children easily learned the language.

I struggled with the idea of going to Russia. My son-in-law's family certainly wouldn't give me the children, so how could I leave them, maybe never to see them again? It would have been hard to steal them away from their other grandmother, and I wasn't sure I could carry out this plan. I had no one to talk with and felt awful. Somebody let the children know about my plan to leave. One day, both of them came running to me, very sad and frightened. They fell on my neck and said only "Bobbe, how can you leave us alone?" That was enough. Even now, twenty-six years later, as I write this, I still hear the grief in their voices. I didn't go and we all stayed in Vilna, waiting for the Germans.

The Germans entered Vilna on Yom Kippur night, during Kol Nidre [the evening prayer service]. We were sitting in a dark room, watching the street from behind the open curtains. It was a bright, moonlit night, but the city seemed dead, with not a living soul on the street. No one went to bed. Instead, we sat hiding in the corners of the big rooms, waiting for dawn. I have to tell about my difficult experience the day before the Germans came. I went to see the Elshvanger family in a suburb of Vilna that was separated from the city by a bridge. I begged them to give me the children for a few days until power changed hands. The bridge could be torn up, I pleaded tearfully, and we would be separated from one another. At such moments, I said, the center of the city is just as safe as the suburbs. I had a flat with young people, with lots of food, and I didn't want to worry about the children and not know if they were all right. But the Elshvanger family turned down my request.

I still remember that Yom Kippur in Vilna. That whole night we heard the trudge of the retreating tsarist foot soldiers and the horseshoes of the cavalry resounding on the stone bridge.

I trembled at the sight of the fleeing tsarist army: They were torn up, locked up, barefoot, and scared to death. I can still see the Cossack on his horse, who was probably lost and separated from his unit. I can still see the mortal fear on his face. As soon as he disappeared, the German Death Hussars, in their special uniforms, were the first to enter

---

4. A network of Zionist-oriented elementary and high schools in interwar Poland in which Hebrew was the language of instruction.

the captured city, followed by an endless procession of German infantry and cavalry. Rumors circulated that Kaiser Wilhelm himself had come to Vilna with his army . . .

Order prevailed in the city. Necessary foodstuffs simply vanished overnight. The seven good years[5] were over. The exorbitant prices for any food you could get rose by the hour. Instead of beef and veal, people started eating horsemeat.

In my house, we didn't yet feel the change. But there was a sense of dejection. I stayed in Vilna all winter, and Birnbaum came to join us, thinking I might go back home. But without the children, I couldn't go.

In the spring of 1916, my Sarah suddenly fell ill. The doctor—a good friend of ours—said she was longing for her father, and advised me to go back to Warsaw. Once again, I had a hard time: I could hardly leave the children, so I had to beg their father to let me take them. Elshvanger didn't spend much time at the front. He wanted to join the cavalry, but they didn't take Jews. What had moved him to go to war? His relatives thought he went out of despair, that he was fed up with life. In late 1915, he fell ill at the front, ran a high fever, and was sent to a military hospital in Russia. I didn't know exactly where he was, only that it was deep inside Russia. I got his address and wrote him that I was going back to Warsaw because of Sarah. I asked him to consider her this time and not me, and to write to his mother to let me take the grandchildren to Warsaw.

I waited a long time for his answer, but, fortunately, it was positive. I didn't liquidate my business—only left it to my old, very good friend Zilla Levin, and returned to Warsaw with all three children.

When I came back to Warsaw, I did not find my big apartment at Nowolipkie 40. Birnbaum lived with our partners in a smaller apartment at Karmelicka 11. The boarding school still existed, but on a smaller scale; the apartment was not comfortable, and I soon moved into a bigger and nicer flat on the first floor of Dzieka 6, along with our partners. I enrolled the children in school and started looking for work in private schools, as a Hebrew teacher. I didn't have to search very long. In the same building as my new apartment, a certain Mendel Kagan, who had once been a teacher in my school, ran a primary school, and hired me to teach. I soon got an additional job teaching Hebrew in a Left Poalei Zion school. Birnbaum also had enough work, and to some extent, our economic issues were solved.

During my two years in Vilna, I hadn't been very active in Zionist

---

5. Reference to the story of Joseph in Egypt, Genesis 41.

and social work. But now that I had recovered a bit, I began to take an interest in what was happening in the Zionist world, in Warsaw in general, and in the women's organization in particular. Understandably, I was planning to throw myself energetically into work, since I am one of those people who can't sit still. One day, Mr. Alexander Elshvanger came to me and took the children away again and put them in a boarding school. Despondent, I decided to leave Warsaw.

One day, I placed an announcement in the newspaper saying that I was looking for a job as a principal or Hebrew teacher in a school in the provinces. I got offers from seven provincial cities, including Plock, where I ended up taking the job. Plock was the city where my grand-father had been a rabbi for seventeen years (and always had trouble with the Hasidim), and where I had my most pleasant childhood fan-tasies, where my children had lived and attended the gymnasium, where I still had close relatives who would accept me with open arms, and where I would feel at home.

We moved out of the apartment. Birnbaum and Sarah — who was now fifteen years old and as close to her father as she was to me — took a room with his childless aunt; and by the new school year of 1918, I was working as a Hebrew teacher in the Jewish co-educational gymnasium in Plock. Transportation between Warsaw and Plock was good, and I could spend every holiday with my family. So I calmed down somewhat.

I soon got involved in social work, first creating a Zionist women's branch of the "Bnos Tsiyon" — that was still before the Jewish Women's Association [Y.F.A.] was formed. I'll mention a comical episode: Once, after a meeting of the Jewish National Fund, a rumor circulated in the town that Comrade Rakovsky taught the women that they could even steal money from the men, if it were for the Jewish National Fund . . .

But I stayed in Plock only for one school year, and then went back to Warsaw. I came back at the right time. The men's gymnasium, Askala, had just opened a girls' school. I took a position as a Hebrew teacher in the beginners' class of the men's gymnasium. I was offered this level because I was known to be a specialist in early education and always found the greatest intellectual satisfaction in watching how the youngest and most delicate innocent children mastered the difficulties of learning. They developed slowly, but in time started to understand how important it was for them to study. As for the work itself, I am a born teacher, and I knew how to make my lessons easy, interesting, and lively for the children, who loved both the lessons and me. When I started teaching at Askala, I enrolled my granddaughter as well, so she was with me for the first half of the day. Her father didn't object because she was exempt from tuition. I taught at Askala for two years, until I immigrated to the Land of Israel in 1920.

When I returned from Plock, I did not rent an apartment, but sublet two rooms from a young couple who had a four-room apartment at Karmelicka 5, near the school where Birnbaum and I taught and near the gymnasium that Sarah and my grandson attended. I privately entertained the idea that it was high time for me to go to the Land of Israel. For almost thirty years, I had lived and worked for a land I had seen only in my dreams. I kept my decision to myself. But I waited for a good time to realize my idea.

In 1916, soon after I returned to Warsaw, my son Yud-Ber wrote me from an internment camp that he was to be freed and allowed to return to Warsaw. He was able to return only if he had a job in his profession as an employee in some business. If that did not work out, he hoped to be deported to Russia. But first he wanted to see us. I sent him a certificate stating that he was being hired by a manufacturing firm in Warsaw. But in late 1916, he didn't get the permission to leave, so he remained in the internment camp. Not until early 1918 was he exchanged for a German prisoner and sent to Moscow.

In August 1918, he and one of Chaim Weizmann's sisters, Dr. Mina Weizmann, were sent to Vienna in an exchange between Austrian and Russian prisoners of war. The delegation traveled in a special train that stopped in Warsaw, but he was there only for a few hours. My son obtained the proper permission to go into the city and he came to visit us in the flat where we no longer lived, though he asked for our new address. It was vacation time and I was in a summerhouse, one station away from Warsaw. By the time I got to Warsaw, he had to go back to the train. I spent only one hour in the railroad station with him, after eight long years, for he had left for Berlin in 1910. It was another eight years before we were to meet again, in 1926, in Danzig, where my daughter Sarah and I spent three whole days with him.

The cease-fire after the armistice of November 1918 threw the countries into chaos. We lacked essential items like food, clothing, and heating materials. Dangerous epidemics, uncertainty, inflation, and other negative things made the people despair. Not only the defeated, but also the victors, lost their heads. If that was how the people acted even though they remained on their own soil and needed only to rebuild their destroyed homes, one can easily imagine the catastrophic situation of our own homeless, persecuted, and tormented Jewish people.

In the middle of that chaos, a new and horrible misfortune befell the Jews. As always and everywhere in history, when the aggressive lusts of the people reach their apogee (and never did it happen so intensively and in such a broad scope as during a world war), the military collapse in the eastern countries after the armistice was accompanied by bloody pogroms — and a few persecutions of Jews even took place in central Europe. But the most horrible atrocities took place in Poland and the Ukraine, where for months the so-called "white" camps[6] carried out dreadful slaughters of Jews.

The first postwar years were especially difficult for the Jewish masses of Poland. The smaller towns and cities were destroyed. The capital city of Warsaw was flooded with scores of ruined refugees. In the Jewish quarter, groups of orphaned and abandoned children lay about, wandering the streets chanting heartbreaking songs of lamentation that they composed themselves. Despite the superhuman efforts of the rescue-and-help committees that were created, need and wretchedness increased. The necessary money was lacking to create at least a temporary roof over the heads of the miserable refugees. No one could build a few children's homes for the wretched orphans.

Returning to Warsaw from Plock in May 1918, I threw myself fervently into the work of our women's organization, Bnos Tsiyon, and called on the members of the committee first of all to start a campaign for abandoned children. But we hadn't yet considered the different ways to deal with that issue, when one day my friend's brother, Levi Levin-Epstein, may he rest in peace, came to me and, without any introduction, said purely and simply: "Come, Puah, let's go together to take the abandoned children off the Jewish street. To a certain extent, you have a claim to that work. At last we have gotten a free building suitable for a children's home from one of the rich landlords on Twarda Street. And we have to make all efforts to open that rescue institution as soon as possible."

It wasn't long before those wretched children not only had proper food and a roof over their heads, but also a warm home. But that work was not easy, especially at first. The suffering, the misery, and especially the horrible street life had had a catastrophic effect on the children. With various combinations and tricks, they would get away, would sneak out and get lost for a few hours and start their previous profession of begging. Thanks to the efforts of the teachers and educators, we finally succeeded in uprooting that harmful tendency. In time, that institution, called "Eshel," served as a model for the considerable number of such children's institutions that came into being in those difficult

---

6. Opponents of the Bolshevik Revolution.

years through the initiative of various social and party organizations in Warsaw and in other large cities of Poland. The catastrophic refugee period during the war of 1914 and in the early postwar years, with its brutal acts, was merely a prelude to the economic ruin that the power brokers of liberated Poland later prepared for Polish Jewry.

As for my personal situation in those difficult postwar years, I can also be considered, in a certain sense, to have been among the refugees. Even though the question of bread was solved, I was no longer able to rebuild my school or my destroyed home. As in the good old days, I threw myself again fervently into the party and social welfare activity. At that time, there was enough work in all areas.

Seven

To the Land of Israel

During the world war, the Jewish socialist parties were very active. As was true for the general socialist groups, the world war served as an important transition period for the Jewish working class movement. The feverish pace of the movement itself, as in socialist ideology, evoked an internal change. In that atmosphere of socialist activity, the news of the Russian Revolution came like a bolt out of the blue and was important to the Jewish socialist movement, as it produced complete freedom of activism in word and deed. All the incendiary materials, the illegal propaganda that had been collected for decades, exploded all at once and allowed the most intensive, although the shortest, period in the history of the Jewish labor movement in the Diaspora which changed overnight into a popular movement that won over multitudes of workers.

The political significance of the Jewish socialist party increased for another reason as well: From the very first, the Russian upheaval had a strong socialist tone. The power and the meaning of the "Workers' and Soldiers' Councils" were very strong. In those councils, which were a kind of "kingdom within a kingdom," the socialist parties dominated. Jewish workers participated in the Councils as active members with equal rights from the beginning. The Jewish parties also sent several members to the newly elected city councils, where they reinforced their influence there too. The Revolution brought equal rights to Russian Jewry, both on a local and a national scale, and that factor influenced the democratization of Jewish life in the country.

As for the internal development of the movement until the Communist upheaval, two factors stand out. On the one hand, the S.S. [Zionist Socialist Workers Party] and the Sejmists were unified into one party (the United Jewish Socialist Labor Party);[1] and on the other hand, the crystallization of the new socialist Zeirei Zion movements introduced nuances into the Jewish socialist world-view and later developed into a world movement modeled on "Poalei Zion."

That crystallization of the socialist Zeirei Zion movement was an important phenomenon. I emphasize the word *socialist* because the Zeirei Zion movement had existed for years, but took on a socialist tinge only at the time of the Russian Revolution. The movement itself, like so many others, had emerged in the first decade of the twentieth century as a radical Zionist youth movement dreaming of immigration to the Land of Israel. It was ideologically linked to the labor movement in the country — that is, to an important part of the Jewish Yishuv. Its ideological proximity to the "Poel Ha-tsair" movement[2] had increased in particular; and almost all the immigrants to the Land of Israel from the Zeirei Zion had joined the latter party in the years before the world war. At that time, there were various unsuccessful attempts to organize Zeirei Zion as a special group within the general Zionist movement. At almost every Zionist Congress, there were meetings among the Zeirei Zion delegates devoted to the discussion of ideological and organizational issues.

In Russia, the Zeirei Zion were concentrated in special associations that were also called Zeirei Zion or "Ha-Tikvah" (the first associations in Pinsk and Kishinev), and they organized joint conferences from time to time. At the Eleventh Zionist Congress in Vienna (1913), during the first joint consultation between the delegates of Zeirei Zion and Poel Ha-tsa'ir, they elected a joint central council of all groups based in Warsaw, and published the first journal of the movement, called *Shaharit* [Dawn]. But the movement, as such, had no connection with any socialist efforts. It was satisfied simply with the democratization of the Zionist movement and with supporting the workers in the Land of Israel. Now and then, individual groups did show a certain tendency to socialism, but their sympathies remained only platonic.

The illegal Zeirei Zion conference in Pinsk in 1906 did declare its socialist world view, but did not reach any practical conclusions, aside from creating a resolution that the Land of Israel should be built on

---

1. The United Jewish Socialist Labor Party was a working-class party that advocated national minority rights for individuals.
2. Ha-Poel Ha-tsair [the young worker] was a labor party founded in Palestine in 1905.

socialist foundations. But that uncertain position could not be implemented. The differentiation process within the movement itself soon began and constantly brought a large number of people to socialism. That internal development received a strong impetus from the course of events in Russia. And at their second national conference in Petrograd,[3] in August 1917, Zeirei Zion declared itself a socialist faction, stayed in the general Zionist organization without making an attempt to create an independent political line. By late 1917, Zeirei Zion appeared as a new socialist movement with its own ideology and with a large enough number of supporters (twenty thousand at the time of their second conference). In fact, it took a while for the faction to liberate itself completely from the influence of the general Zionist movement and to proceed to independent political activity.

Political events at the end of the world war and the development of an independent Poland shifted the center of that movement to Poland, where the greatest masses of European Jews were concentrated. The Polish Zeirei Zion organized as a separate faction during the third national conference of Zionists in Poland (November 1918) and I myself joined the Zeirei Zion faction at that time. At that Zionist conference, I was even reproached for that step by Comrade Abraham Podlishevski, himself a strong supporter of the socialist youth movement: "Comrade Rakovsky," he said, "we didn't expect you to lead the youth away from us." "I am very proud," I replied calmly, "that I am strong enough to influence the youth."

The center of the movement had been in the Ukraine in 1917–1918; afterwards, when it moved to Poland, that section was considered to be the strongest Zeirei Zion group. At the second conference of Zeirei Zion of Poland (Warsaw, February 1919), which proclaimed the socialist agenda and thus caused the resignation of a certain number of members, there was an attempt to unite all parts of the movement into an international association.

From the very first, the organized Jewish workers' parties participated actively in Polish politics. When the workers' councils emerged in November 1919, representatives of the Jewish socialist parties joined them. Jewish socialist representatives presented general socialist and special Jewish demands to the municipal councils including the equality of the Yiddish language, and the democratization and secularization of Jewish community organizations.

---

3. The former St. Petersburg, the city was called Petrograd from 1914 to 1924, when it became Leningrad.

The change in the political situation of independent Poland, the democratization of the government and municipal institutions, and, especially, the declaration of political equality for Polish women, evoked a response in the ranks of Jewish women in Poland, too. The significance of that important event was properly appreciated by the organized groups of Jewish women. Our leftists — that is, the middle-class Bnos Tsiyon association — were the first to react. But it was not easy to implement an intensive propaganda campaign among the masses of members of our seventy chapters of Bnos Tsiyon in the Polish cities and towns. We had to persuade the women to take advantage of our rights as soon as possible, and as a first step to that goal, we had to expand the framework of our own organization. To enable us to participate actively in the political and social life of the country and in the life of our Jewish people, we had to attract more women from the various classes, and therefore the Bnos Tsiyon association had to become a broad and extensive Jewish women's organization (Y.F.A.)[4] with a positive position on Zionism and a special section for practical work in Palestine. After a strong propaganda campaign, the proposal to transform the national assembly of the Bnos Tsiyon Association for that purpose was adopted almost unanimously.

A short time later, the Bund also established a special "working women's organization" (Y.A.F.)[5] in Warsaw. But that new group was initiated by men and not women. It was our socialist comrades of Zeirei Zion who were against these initiatives; they were in general the sworn opponents of special women's organizations at that time, because they thought the idea contradicted the principles of socialism . . .

Despite my total involvement in social and political activity at that time, my thoughts moved in one direction: that I mustn't stay here any longer, and that now was the time for me to leave for the Land of Israel, to see with my own eyes the land of the most beautiful dreams of my youth. I wanted to work to restore the land. Another consideration influenced me as well: I felt constrained in independent Poland. I was envious of the Poles, and was unable to rejoice at their victory or participate in their happiness. I hope my friends, the warm sympathizers and outspoken supporters of Poland, forgive me for telling the truth: for forty-four years, I lived in the capital of the Polish state, in Warsaw. But I never believed the promises of the Polish rulers or the integrity of the Polish people with regard to us. Intuitively, I always felt that we Jews

---

4. Y.F.A. stands for Yiddishe Froyen Organizatsie, Jewish Women's Organization.
5. Y.A.F. stands for Yiddishe Arbeter Froyen, Jewish Working Women.

would suffer if they regained power, and my premonition, unfortunately, came true.

Even though my trip to the Land of Israel was a matter of life and death for me at that time, only at the end of the summer of 1920, with the greatest of exertions, could I realize my decision. It was not so easy to leave my seventeen-year-old daughter — she was then in her first year of law school in Warsaw University — and my orphaned grandchildren. But my journey was a holy obligation to carry out the final wish of their dead mother, that her children be educated in the Land of Israel.

How did I go? In June 1920, I was elected in Warsaw to be a delegate at the impending Zionist conference in London. I didn't tell my family of my decision to leave from there for the Land of Israel. I had money for expenses to travel to London and to spend time at the conference. But how was I to go on? I hadn't thought of that; the main thing was to obtain a visa for the Land of Israel in London. The rest, I would probably figure out on the spot. In late June, I went to the conference with the group of delegates. The situation in Poland had become very tense. It was the time of the Polish–Bolshevik war, and the Red Army was at the gates of Warsaw. Our delegates from Poland were very nervous. But, as we know now, their fear was groundless; the Bolsheviks retreated and "calm and joy"[6] reigned once again in Poland.

The London conference was serious and sometimes stormy. The first Zionist assembly since the Eleventh Congress (in Vienna, 1913) was held twenty months after the end of the Great War. The London convention was not a Congress, but only a so-called annual conference (a small Congress). At first, they thought of holding that conference in Carlsbad, closer to the big Jewish centers. But since the executive members had to negotiate the text of the Mandate[7] about the borders of the Land of Israel, they weren't ready to leave London, and the conference met there from June 7 to June 22, 1920. It was considered to be a constituent assembly.

After the Balfour Declaration[8] and the Mandate, and after the appointment of a Jew with Zionist sympathies (Lord Samuel)[9] to the post of High Commissioner in the Land of Israel, the world organization now had to elect an authoritative and capable administration, prove

---

6. In Hebrew in original (*menuha v'simha*).
7. The political control over Palestine, which was given to the British after World War I.
8. The Balfour Declaration was issued by the British Government on Nov. 2, 1917. It endorsed Zionist activity to establish a national home for the Jews in Palestine.
9. Herbert Samuel (1870–1963) was a British Jew who was appointed the first High Commissioner of Palestine.

the validity of its own constitution for the new conditions or determine if it had to be changed, sketch out the building plan, and find a way to implement it.

The most important decision of the conference — the establishment of the Keren Ha-Yesod, the institution for financing reconstruction [in Palestine] — passed unanimously. In fact, that fund was of the greatest consequence for the building of the Land of Israel, and that positive phenomenon outweighed the negative aspects of the conference. I want to emphasize that it was the Russian Zionist leaders, Naiditsch and Zlatapolsky, who initiated the idea for the Keren Hayesod.[10]

A second important decision was the establishment of a world organization of Jewish women, "The Federation of Zionist Women, WIZO," led by Mrs. Vera Weizmann, Mrs. Rebecca Sieff, Mrs. Ramona Goodman, and Mrs. Dr. Edith Eder. The conference also took cognizance of the political successes [of Zionism] and thanked world leaders on behalf of the Jewish people.

As I was an avowed supporter of separate women's organizations, the creation of WIZO was a pleasant surprise for me, and of course I took pains to participate actively in the WIZO conference. When both conferences came to an end, I began to contemplate my immigration to the Land of Israel. The main thing was to get an English visa. First, I appealed to a relative of mine, a member of the Zeirei Zion in the Land of Israel. Then it occurred to me to appeal to the leaders of WIZO who had been living in London for years as English citizens, and surely had "connections." So I appealed to Mrs. Dr. Eder, a bright woman and a leftist, to help me get a visa. She listened to me carefully and said: "A remarkable coincidence. You want to go to the Land of Israel, and what we need most is a person to organize a WIZO chapter there. I suggest you take the job of secretary of the future federation, and that will easily allow you to get an entrance visa to the Land of Israel. Our office will work out all the necessary papers to get the visa. Just give us your foreign passport." I needed no better results from our conversation. At last I was going to the Land of Israel.

A joyous surprise awaited me on the ship in Brindisi, where I met Rachel Weizmann, Chaim Weizmann's smart and vigorous mother. We had been friends for years. Rachel Weizmann did not have a modern, secular education, according to contemporary concepts, but she did have a native intelligence, a modern worldview, and a sharp mind; she

---

10. Isaac Naiditsch (1868–1949) and Hillel Zlatopolsky (1868–1932). Both were industrialists as well as Zionist leaders.

was a clever woman in the fullest sense of the word. Experience has taught me that to appreciate the son, you first have to meet the mother, because it is she who forms the soul and shapes the spirit of her children. I had met Rachel Weizmann through our children. Back in Warsaw, two of her daughters had been close friends of Sheyndl, my daughter who died young. When the war broke out, Rachel Weizmann and her younger children went to Moscow where she had met my son.

During my time in the Land of Israel, one of my greatest joys was visiting with Rachel Weizmann whenever I happened to be in Haifa. She often surprised me with her opinions about various painful questions in general and about the Yishuv in particular. Her understanding of youth and her tolerance of their weaknesses are also amazing. It is scarcely believable that hers are the thoughts of an old lady, born three generations ago. On her own, through intuition, she has reached the highest level of the understanding of life. In September 1920, when we met on the ship to the Land of Israel, Rachel Weizmann was traveling with her oldest son, Feivel. We spent all our time together on that ship. She sailed directly to Haifa and I disembarked in Alexandria and went to the Land of Israel by train a few days later. Our delight at that unexpected encounter was unbounded.

One of my cousins, a prosperous grain dealer named Jacob Goldin, was living in Alexandria at that time. Although I didn't know him personally and didn't even have his address, I managed to find him. An official from the Zionist organization in Alexandria came to greet the Jewish passengers on the ship, and gave me the address of a restaurant where I could meet my cousin at lunchtime. Even though I had never seen him in my life, I recognized him among the crowd because he looked just like his father. I had gotten off in Alexandria for two reasons: First, I hoped to find my cousin's mother and three children who were supposed to be visiting him from Lublin (Poland); second, I wanted to satisfy my childhood fantasy and have a look at Egypt. I didn't meet my cousin's mother in Alexandria (she came only several weeks later), but I stayed at his house a few days, and saw all the sights. From Alexandria I sailed to Tel Aviv, a good twenty-four hours away.

Words cannot describe how I felt. You have to experience it firsthand. When I saw the Land of Israel, I didn't believe it. It took some time until I realized it wasn't a dream. I arrived there a week before Rosh Hashonoh, in September 1920.

Right after Rosh Hashonoh, I went to Jerusalem to teach in a school. At that time, the head of the Education Committee was Dr. Joseph Luria, a friend of mine from Warsaw. Years before, he and his wife — a relative of mine — had come to Warsaw where he had opened an "Improved *Kheyder*,"[11] and ran it until his trip to the Land of Israel. With Dr. Luria I didn't need any recommendations. He simply asked me if I wanted a job in an agricultural settlement or in one of the cities. I told him I wanted to live in Jerusalem itself, to be in the center of political and social life. Even though I had seen very little of the country, I was most impressed by Jerusalem — it feels more like the Land of Israel than even the purely Jewish city of Tel Aviv.

"If you really want to settle in Jerusalem, Comrade Rakovsky," Dr. Luria told me, "I have a suitable job for you. Mrs. Yellin[12] and Mrs. Miyukhas have recently created a vocational school for girls and they need a teacher of Hebrew and other subjects. I advise you to take that job. The work will surely be interesting for you, both socially and educationally, because these won't be small children, but young people you can surely influence even outside of school." "I like your proposal very much, Comrade Luria. Confirm me as a teacher in that position; I leave the conditions up to you. School won't start until after the holidays, and meanwhile I will look for a room and move in, and when you call me, I will report for work." I spent a week in Jerusalem, and I found a room in Zikhron Moshe, the most aristocratic quarter, with a family called Levin from Warsaw. I looked up relatives and friends and learned about the Jewish women's organizations in the country and the addresses of the branch representatives in Jerusalem so that I could start to establish a WIZO chapter.

I came to the Land of Israel for the first time in 1920 but with a thirty-year internship of Zionist activity, from Hovevei Zion on. So I had some idea of the political and economic situation in the country. But there's nothing like hearing and seeing for yourself, so I decided to use my free time until the school year started to get to know the Yishuv as much as I could.

Even though there were no middle-class, politically organized groups in the Land of Israel in 1920, there were Jewish women's associations. The first national political organization was the "Union of Jewish Women for Equal Rights," founded in 1918, and incorporated in 1920 into the International Federation of Equal Rights for Women, with its central office in London. Another association emerged in 1920, the "Histadrut Nashim Ivriot" [Organization of Hebrew Women], established by Dr. Rachel Kagan, who was later chairman of WIZO in the

---

11. A modernized version of the traditional *kheyder*.
12. The wife of David Yellin, a distinguished educator and writer.

Land of Israel. The third association, a purely philanthropic one, was "Ezrat Yoldot," [Aid for Women in Childbirth], directed by Mrs. Hochstein, who was one of the most popular social and philanthropic activists in Jerusalem, even before "modern" social work. And last but not least, there was Hadassah, led by its worthy initiator and founder, Henrietta Szold.[13]

There was no organization of working women in the Land of Israel in 1920 because it was still the so-called era of "before the giving of the Torah"; and the Histadrut Ha-Ovdim [Organization of Workers] was not established until the summer of 1921. I participated in its founding assembly in Balfouria. We sat on the ground under boxwood trees the first day, until they brought a bench and a table from somewhere. Next to me were A. D. Gordon[14] and Yosef Chaim Brenner,[15] who, even back in Warsaw, had been one of my daily visitors. The conversations and passionate discussion at that conference were so fascinating that we weren't even aware of our uncomfortable conditions. Comrade Brenner even forgot that a living person has to eat.

I was especially interested in the heated discussion of the proposal to create a separate section for working women with a special "women's council" in the Histadrut. The opposition of some comrades to that proposal didn't surprise me because I had "known" of that position in Poland for years. But what did surprise me was that even one of the most active leaders of women's groups, Manya Shochat,[16] also opposed it. As a former member of the Russian Social Democratic Party, she argued that a separate section for working women contradicted the principles of socialism. More than twenty years later, I met Manya Shochat at the splendid Fifth Working Women's Conference in Tel Aviv (February 1942) and heard her fervent speech about the extraordinary achievements of the working women's organization in the Land of Israel in various fields. I reminded her of that argument in Balfouria at the founding conference of the Histadrut in 1921. And I noted with some satisfaction that the results confirmed which of us had been right back then.

I spent the month of Tishrei [September/October] in Tel Aviv and

13. Henrietta Szold (1860–1945), founder of Hadassah, the most important women's Zionist organization.
14. A. D. Gordon (1856–1922), Zionist philosopher and Zionist pioneer, a Tolstoy-like figure.
15. Yosef Chaim Brenner (1881–1921), an important Hebrew writer and Zionist pioneer.
16. Manya Wilbushevitch Shochat (1880–1961), Zionist pioneer and founder of the first collective settlement in Palestine.

the surrounding colonies with friends and relatives from Poland; and on the first of the month of Heshvan [October/November] 1920, I started teaching at the girls' vocational school in Jerusalem on Meah Shearim Street. As I sat in class, I often could not believe that I really was in the Land of Israel. Particularly at first, I walked around like a dreamer, because my life hadn't changed completely; in Warsaw, I taught at Kopiecke 5, and in Jerusalem I teach on Meah Shearim. There was a slight difference: there my students were only Jewish children, but here there were some Arab girls who were not simply learning a vocation, but were accepted on condition that they also learn Hebrew. The twelve- and thirteen-year-old Arab girls looked just like their Jewish classmates and spoke Hebrew, and at first it was hard for me to distinguish which of the children were not Jewish, and even when I did know, I wouldn't treat my Arab girls any different than the Jewish ones.

My work in the school soon became routine so I started my social welfare activities, first by organizing the WIZO chapter. I invited the chairmen of the existing women's associations in Jerusalem, presented the goals and tasks of the international WIZO organization, proposed the formation of a joint committee to work more intensively with a unified force and to create a broad WIZO chapter in the country. I tried to persuade them that that activity would be neither competition nor contradiction to their previous work, but could in time contribute to the development and reinforcement of their already existing institutions. After some discussion, my proposal was accepted by Henrietta Szold, Mrs. Hochstein, and Mrs. Kagan, and we created a joint committee and worked intensely. Only the "Union of Women for Equal Rights" remained an independent organization.

I myself worked hard to enlist in our organization a few active individual working women, who were very popular in the Yishuv. Thus, I met the distinguished Rachel Yanait[17] and tried to influence her to join WIZO; I felt that this would enable her to develop her professional activity and create a network of agricultural institutions for girls. But our attempts failed. Rachel Yanait thought — and this was her main motive — that if WIZO supported the working women's institution materially, it would try to influence it spiritually. I was not convinced of that. I attempted to create that committee, not because the end justifies the means, but because I had learned from experience that only

---

17. Rahel Yanait (1886–1979), Zionist pioneer, labor leader, and educator. She was the wife of Israel's second president, Yitzhak Ben-Zvi.

teachers and educators, and not financial committees, create the soul of the educational institution.

The initiators and founders of the many working women's settlements and pioneer women's farms in the Land of Israel soon found the right way to work with the "bourgeois" WIZO. Neither side yielded, but necessity and the advantage of working together led to mutual understanding and successful achievements. The work of our joint committee was soon extended and developed, and we decided to rent an office. At that time, I got a letter from my cousin Goldin that she and the three children were now with her son, the agent in Alexandria, but under no circumstances would she remain in Egypt. She asked me to give her the possibility to come to the Land of Israel. She had a good profession — making children's clothes — and she hoped to get work. I answered at once that I was living alone in a big room and would welcome her as a guest, and thought that I could also find work for her in her profession. Even before she came, the committee suggested I rent a two-room flat along with the office, thus lowering the cost both for me and for the organization, and creating more comfortable conditions. I liked the proposal. Apartments were plentiful in the Land of Israel at that time and I soon found a two-room apartment with a small kitchen (of course, without today's modern conveniences) on Meah Shearim Street, not far from the vocational school.

My cousin from Alexandria did not allow herself to wait long, and she came when I had just moved into the new apartment. We used boxes and crates as furniture for the two rooms. Some bigger crates in the middle of the room, covered with tablecloths, were the "table." Around the walls were long narrow boxes with mattresses on top, covered with linen blankets, to sit on during the day and to sleep on at night.

The office was in the first room. Committee meetings took place once a week, and office hours were from four o'clock to seven every day, because I worked at school until noon. I didn't need to learn Hebrew, so I started learning Arabic. Friends recommended an Arab teacher who had a Jewish wife, and I easily learned to read and understand the language. Writing was harder.

A week after my cousin came, I found work for her as a seamstress in the vocational course of Mrs. Leah Berlin. Within a month, she brought her eighteen-year-old daughter and younger son from Alexandria. Her older boy stayed behind to study in the commercial school in Alexandria. The daughter, who had completed gymnasium in Berlin and knew several languages, soon got a job in the Jerusalem post office. The family circle increased and a homey atmosphere was created. When the daughter started earning money, the son demanded that his mother stop working. But she didn't want to sit idle, and since she already had to run the house, she decided to open a lunchroom. I was on full pension and soon brought her more customers, including my friend's two sons, Shmuel and Joshua Proshansky, who were then studying surveying in Jerusalem. People started coming to my house, mostly my friends and acquaintances from Poland.

Working in the school gave me more time and opportunity to get to know the real situation of the Yishuv at that difficult period. I was able to examine the complex questions of rebuilding the Land of Israel and of our prospects and hopes for the future. It was hard for me to understand our leaders' positions on some vital problems. For example: the explicit attitude of contempt of our leadership at the time to the Arab question. My relative Chaim Kalvarisky, whom I had known since I was a student, introduced me to that urgent problem. It was also hard to agree with the explicit negative stance to the so-called Exile [the Golah, or Diaspora]. One of the currently popular and distinguished leaders of the Yishuv surprised me back then with his statement that the Jewish people would be constituted only by those Jews who would live in the Land of Israel. This notion of Zionism was completely alien to me. Even under ideal conditions, the Land of Israel cannot accept all the Jews from the Diaspora, and most of them will have to live in other countries. Is the final goal of our efforts to turn into a sect, even a purely Hebraic one?

One direct consequence of such a notion is contempt for our folk language, Yiddish. At the time, the extreme chauvinism about that issue was expressed in bizarre ways. An incident from that time in Jerusalem has remained in my memory to this day: One Saturday, a delegate from Poalei Zion from Poland was to deliver a lecture in the Zion Cinema in Jerusalem in Yiddish. The organization of "Defenders of the Language" found out about it and a few young gymnasium students spread the rumor that the speaker was a Communist. At the appointed time, a police troop surrounded the cinema building. Naturally, the scheduled talk didn't take place because the speaker had been warned in time. But what marked the incident for me was that a few hours later, in my presence, one of the gymnasium students bragged to his mother that he was an initiator and leader of that "heroic act." I won't mention any names — the memory of my friends, his parents, is too dear to me—but that gymnasium student later became the right hand of one of the most popular Revisionist leaders, Ze'ev Jabotinsky.[18]

My own personal experiences in the catastrophic month of May 1921,[19] are some of the bitterest moments of a life filled with suffering. Using my free time to travel over the land during the Passover vacation, I first went to see my friend Leah Proshansky in Tel Aviv, and from there to Rishon le-Zion, to visit Ze'ev Gluskin, my oldest friend from Warsaw. Ze'ev Gluskin, one of the veteran members of Bnei Moshe in Poland, devoted his whole life to the Zionist movement. He was one of the founders and most active members of the Carmel Society in Poland. In the Land of Israel, he had been the director of the wine cellar in Rishon le-Zion for a time. He donated his house on Montefiore Street to the famous municipal library in Tel Aviv.

During the week of Pesach, shortly before the outbreak of the pogrom, I walked to Rehovot. On the way, I encountered Arab men and women, and it never occurred to me that the whole population, even the women, were preparing for an attack. We later learned that the Arab women hid bandages and various other instruments in their roomy clothing to save their wounded men. And we also discovered later that none of the labor leaders or the Haganah [the defense organization] had any notion of the preparations for the pogrom, which had been crafted so secretly.

I remember it as if it were now. On Saturday night, on the eve of May Day, a large group of us took the train from Rehovot to Tel Aviv. We were in a holiday mood, noisy and singing, and no one expected the *fatal* surprise in store for us the next morning. Holiday spirits still prevailed in the home of my friend Shapiro. And Leah Proshansky told me, as a curiosity, what the Arab maid had said to her that day in Yiddish: "It won't be good." They had laughed as at a joke, and calmly went to bed.

At six in the morning, I woke with a start, hearing strange noises. Everyone in the house was already up. But since I didn't feel very well, they wanted to hide the reason for the uproar from me, and tried to persuade me that two fellows were fighting about something in the street. But the noises didn't stop. I got out of bed and went into the dining room. When I saw the faces of the people in the house, I insisted they tell me the truth. Incidentally, I noticed that my friend Shapiro's

18. Vladimir (Ze'ev) Jabotinsky (1880–1940), Zionist activist, founder of the Jewish Legion during World War I and leader of a right-wing faction of Zionists that became known as Revisionism. It called for a struggle against British rule in Palestine and for the creation of a Jewish state.
19. Time of the Arab riots in Jaffa.

two oldest sons intended to go away somewhere. They told me the noise was nothing; the Jewish workers in Jaffa were holding a May Day demonstration in the street.

"Too bad," I remarked, not without resentment. "In Warsaw, I always participated in the May Day demonstrations, and here in the Land of Israel, I can't go out in the street today. But the day is long," I admitted. "The demonstrations will probably reach Tel Aviv, and I can still join them." I calmly went back to the bedroom, but I soon heard noises, and of a different sort. Then I started shouting at them to tell me the truth or let me go myself to see what was happening. Only then did they tell me that a pogrom had erupted in Jaffa against the Jews and that the Arabs wanted to invade Tel Aviv. The main street of Tel Aviv at that time was Herzl Street. At one end it was separated from the road to Jaffa by an iron gate, and at the other, the Herzliya Gymnasium stood rather awkwardly, blocking the broad street. At night, the iron gate was closed to keep strangers out.

At that time, you traveled from Tel Aviv to Jaffa in carriages, because there were still undeveloped areas between the two cities. Since the rioters couldn't get in through the closed Herzl Street, they threatened to enter through Neve Sha'anan, but they didn't succeed there either. The Jewish Haganah and the English military put up a strong resistance, but the pogrom was really stopped by the Hindustan units that came to help.

At dusk, the dead and wounded were brought from Jaffa. These were the most horrible moments of that catastrophic day. Even decades later, it is hard for me to relive the event. At that time, there were no hospitals in Tel Aviv, so the Herzliya Gymnasium was turned into a temporary hospital. This was during Passover, when schools were closed. The wounded were placed in the classrooms and until the dead were buried, they were laid in the cellar of the gymnasium. Among them was the writer Yosef Chaim Brenner, brutally murdered.

A large number of women and youths immediately organized to tend to the wounded. They worked devotedly, day and night. I stayed in Tel Aviv and worked with that group of volunteers until the vacation was over. Right after the sad event, Nahum Sokolow, who was then in the country, came from Jerusalem and delivered a heartbreaking eulogy for the fallen, encouraging the thousands of people gathered in the square beside the gymnasium building.

In despair, morally and spiritually beaten, I returned to work in Jerusalem after the Pesach vacation. I simply could not accept the idea that I had experienced a pogrom in the Land of Israel and now had to go on working. I had seen enough pogroms in my life; in my hometown of Bialystok, more than one, as well as in Warsaw and Siedlice. But a pogrom in the Land of Israel? How could that be? That was the most terrifying, that pogrom of our hopes and dreams; of our work of many years; of the Zionist movement in general. It was very hard for me to get back to my everyday routine right after the events. Everything seemed so small, so trivial, so superfluous.

Once again I recovered from great shock by working at school, among my students. My internal struggle of "to be or not to be" — that is, to stay in the Land of Israel or to go back to Poland — was aggravated by the bloody events that may have been the decisive factor. I had not come to the Land of Israel to solve my personal issues; I never sought a sanitorium there. I believed with complete faith that the Land of Israel must and would solve the painful Jewish problem. Even in its destroyed condition, the land made a grand impression on me. The gorgeous blue sky, seen nowhere else; the white nights, especially in Jerusalem; the remarkable sunsets with their seemingly endless twilights; the pure mornings; the splendid sunrises — in short, all nature shows why only that land could produce such great spirits, God-seekers, and prophets.

Yet my suffering increased by the day, by the hour. I constantly felt the pain that, "because of our sins,"[20] by our own fault, others had grabbed the Land; we had come here too late. The pious Jew who could not hasten the end of Exile, recited laments and waited for the Messiah; our youth, our most aware element, found satisfaction by struggling for a universal ideal for mankind; and some Jews saw the Promised Land wherever they could make a living. But no matter what, the Jewish people in general lacked the passion for a homeland; they lacked love for their own fatherland. Perhaps there were objective reasons — because we haven't lived long enough as an independent people on our own soil; or because the long years of wandering atrophied that sense. Whatever it was, the fact was that we had no feeling even for our few remaining sacred places. The Western Wall was abandoned to foreigners who knew that you can do anything for money in the Orient while in Russia and Poland rich Jews donated money for Greek Orthodox churches and convents. Strolling around in Jerusalem at dawn every Sabbath and looking at the German, Italian, and Russian colonies with their convents and various other buildings, I couldn't help but weep with despair at the destruction of my life's ideal. I was especially vexed by the loud church bells. Nowhere else did they shock me so

---

20. From the Festival Musaf liturgy — "because of our sins we were exiled from our land."

much as in Jerusalem. Naturally, in such a mood—even though my economic situation was fairly good—I could not accept the responsibility of bringing my seventeen-year-old only daughter Sarah, who was then a student of law at Warsaw University, or my unfortunate orphaned grandchildren (the twelve-year-old boy and the ten-year-old girl) to the Land of Israel. Not to mention that I couldn't achieve the latter without a struggle. At that time, my grandchildren were temporarily with their father. In addition, my only daughter suffered emotionally from the political opposition between her mother and father. She was, as they say, between two fires, and didn't know which of us was right, since she loved both her parents.

As soon as I decided to go back, I felt very isolated; some people started to consider me a "traitor." The Weizmann sisters were especially angry. One of them even told me: "You're running away, Puah, because you haven't achieved a place here like Chaim Weizmann." Even my old beloved friend Leah Proshansky and I often spoke in different languages. Naturally, my decision to go back hurt her very much. An avowed idealist, even at the age of eighteen when she visited the Land of Israel for the first time, she often showed me the beauty of the Land and its splendid sky. I listened to her quietly and kept silent. But once— I remember as if it were now—I couldn't restrain myself but said to her: " 'The sky is God's sky, and He gave the earth to human beings.'[21] It's not the sky we need here, but the earth, the ground; meanwhile we're sitting on a volcano, and are guilty of not seeing the others, only ourselves. Remember when I used to always tell you that there may come a time when we will be able to create a national home in the Land of Israel? I believe we will obtain large territories there along with money. But I don't believe in our people, in their will to take advantage of those possibilities. And I have the courage to say that I saw it correctly."

The only one I could talk to at that time, in especially difficult moments, who understood my difficult internal struggle, was my friend from Warsaw, the wife of my friend Michael Halperin.[22] She was one of the most idealistic types in our movement. I had met Michael Halperin in 1893, a year after I came to Warsaw. On his first visit to my home, he had impressed everyone there with his bearing, his Jesus-like face and wide blond beard. He spoke Russian. Before long he felt at home in our house. I know details of his life that he personally told me. He came

---

21. From Psalm 115, recited in the Hallel prayer on festivals and days of the new moon.
22. Michael Halperin [or Helpern] (1860–1919), Zionist activist and pioneer.

from a distinguished Jewish family and was the only son of his widowed millionaire mother. When young, he had married the daughter of a rich man in Grodno, a famous beauty. But she left him because of his idée fixe to give his whole fortune to rebuild the Land of Israel. At her request, he gave her a divorce, and in the rabbi's house, after the divorce decree was issued, he paid her ten thousand rubles for a kiss.

By the time he came to Warsaw in 1893, he had a second wife and three small children. For a while, he lived alone in the city and later he brought his wife and children from Smolensk. At that time, he was hardly a rich man. His wealthy mother was dead. He had already managed to squander her fortune, and his family was in big trouble. He came to Poland at that time not from Russia, but from the Land of Israel. He came back not with personal goals but with a great project for a Zionist enterprise. He planned to organize a large joint stock company in Poland to produce wine in the Land of Israel, and hoped to export it to Europe and overseas to the Americas, on a large scale. His initiative soon won supporters from a group of Zionists in Warsaw, from the wealthier merchant members of "Bnei Moshe." They formed a group to advertise the project and attract stockholders. The project achieved its hoped-for success, and soon the first joint stock company in Warsaw, named "Carmel," was established to export wine to Poland from the wine cellars of the Land of Israel in Rishon Le-Zion, all according to the plan of the "extravagant" Michael Halperin. But note that comrade Michael Halperin, the initiator of the whole project, was *not* one of the first stockholders in Poland, because that sort of idealist was considered a bad merchant who could only hinder . . .

The Halperin family had a hard time economically in Warsaw; his wife suffered especially. She was from Russia and couldn't adjust to life in Poland. With a degree in archaeology, she was a very educated woman, and couldn't find a place for herself, as they say. With his temperament and his wild, unbridled energy, Michael couldn't find a place for himself anywhere. He would get lost for days in a chess game.

When their financial situation became really critical, they started preparing to go to the Land of Israel. As I recall — but I don't remember it precisely — her father was in the Land of Israel at that time. Shortly before Halperin made *aliyah* [literally, ascended] to the Land, he came to me once, very excited, to tell me a secret he wouldn't reveal to another living soul. He had come up with the happy idea of raising enormous sums of money to build the land. When he got there, he would expropriate treasures from a place where they weren't doing anybody any good, and those treasures would constantly increase in value. I corresponded with the Halperins during their first year; later they regularly sent regards through my friend Leah Proshansky.

In 1920, as I said, I looked up Halperin's wife in Jerusalem and we soon became very close once again. At that time, they were living in a remote neighborhood, in an Arab courtyard, in two small rooms with no facilities. She cooked in the courtyard on an Arab stove. I did not find Halperin and hadn't seen him since his departure from Warsaw. She told me he was wandering around in the Galilee, dressed in a sack, belted with a rope, and she hadn't heard from him in a long time. Her young son Jeremiah, who was in the eighth grade at the gymnasium, lived with her. Her older son had fallen in the past war as a soldier in the Jewish Legion.[23] At that time, her only daughter was studying art in Paris. Halperin's wife, herself, worked as a nurse, because she couldn't get any work as an archaeologist. However, she did not find a position in a hospital, because there weren't any hospitals there at that time — Hadassah had only just started organizing its sanitaria.

What kind of work did a nurse do in the area of public health? Every one of them supervised a certain district, visiting the flats and courtyards, examining the diseased eyes and heads of the Jewish children. The work was very hard. Aside from the primitive working conditions, those nurses had to struggle, first of all with their half-wild little patients, whom they sought to heal, and then with horribly backward mothers, who thought that if the child's "ulcer" were cured, all the Torah he had learned would fly out of his head.

Halperin's wife was one of those nurses in Jerusalem. Her salary had to support her and her two children. That was how I left her in 1921, when I went back to Poland. Later I heard that she was living in Paris with her daughter. Not until 1935, shortly before I came to the Land of Israel the second time, did a tall, handsome young man come to my home in Warsaw and introduce himself as Jeremiah Halperin. He came from Paris, bringing warm regards from his mother to whom he had promised he would look me up. He told me that his mother was doing well, that she lived with the daughter — who was studying at the Sorbonne — along with the daughter's family, and that she was generally content. As a Revisionist, he thought it best not to mention that his sister had married a Christian Frenchman.

Some time ago, someone came to me in Jerusalem to ask for mate-

---

23. Organization of Jewish soldiers who fought in the British Army during World War I.

rial for a biography of my friend Michael Halperin, which was subsequently printed serially in *Ha-Mashkif*. At that time, I refused because I planned to mention him in my own memoirs, and now I have.

During my first time in the Land of Israel, in 1920–1921, I did experience two interesting positive incidents. I participated in the founding assembly of the Histadrut Ha-Ovdim [Workers' Organization] and in the election for the highest institution of the Yishuv, the first Assembly of Representatives.

Of course my greatest interest was the issue of women's voting rights and eligibility for office in that high institution. Knowing the composition of the Yishuv at that time, with the representatives of the Agudah [Hebrew version of Agude, the anti-Zionist Orthodox Union] at the head, I knew that Jewish women would have to wage a grim struggle for this elementary human right. The initiators and organizers of that struggle were the representatives of the first (and at that time the only) political women's association, the "Union of Women for Equal Rights." The contest was long and difficult. The women demanded the right to vote not only for the Assembly of Representatives, but also for the community organizations and committees of the colonies. They were opposed most bitterly by the Orthodox. But the Mizrachi [Orthodox Zionist] party also opposed giving women the right to vote, and tried to make "party capital" with that step.

After a long hard struggle, the "committee pro tem" finally agreed to grant the women the right to vote for the Assembly of Representatives, but only "provisionally"; the final resolution of that issue was turned over to the future Assembly. Between 1920 and 1942, there were only three elections to the Assembly.

In 1920, of 314 delegates, there were fourteen women (4.5 percent): seven were members of the "Union for Equal Rights for Women" and the other seven were workers. During the five-year term of the Assembly, the women elected to it sat on hot coals, as it were. From one session to the next, the Orthodox opposition to the participation of women in that national institution increased. They demanded categorically the "liquidation" of the women. Finally, the Mizrachi came up with a proposal to hold a plebiscite on the question of voting rights for women, but only among the men. The results could have been predicted. The Hitahdut — that is, the "Union of Equal Rights for Women" — fought that proposal with all its might. In early 1925, it appealed for support to Jewish women's organizations all over the world. The large and important ones responded with letters and telegrams to the National Council, demanding equality for women in the Land of

Israel. The demand by Hadassah in North America carried serious weight.

In 1925, the elections for the second Assembly took place. Of 201 delegates, twenty-six of those elected were women, representing 13 percent, including thirteen members of the "Union for Equal Rights." At the first session of the second Congress, the women elected from the Union rebutted the arguments of Mizrachi against voting rights for women, arguments that were purportedly based on the Torah. With evidence in their hands, the women demonstrated that in the first elections the Mizrachi leaders appealed to Orthodox women to participate in the election on behalf of the Torah, and then the same Mizrachi spokesmen supported a strict ban against the participation of women in our national institution, once again on the basis of our holy Torah . . . At the same session, the dangerous referendum was defeated and a resolution was adopted, in the month of Kislev 5686 [December 1925] that ended the struggle for voting rights for women to the Assembly.

In 1931, elections for the third Congress were held. There were 94 delegates, seven of them women, including three from the slate of the Union for Equal Rights for Women and the Jewish women's organization. Meanwhile, because of the Union, the women won the right to vote in several settlement committees and in the community organizations (in Jerusalem and in the council of Petah Tikvah a few years later). Since I was present at the first difficult struggle of Jewish women for equality in the Land in 1920, when I came back to the Land of Israel for the second time in 1935, I was pleasantly surprised at the equality of women achieved by the "Union for Equal Rights for Women" in fifteen years through extensive social, economic, and political work.

The school year in the girls' vocational school ended in early August 1921, and I started preparing to return to Poland. I didn't have anything to liquidate because my cousin Goldin and her children were staying in the apartment with its "furniture boxes." Before I left, her daughter married. The younger son was at school in Mikveh Israel [an agricultural school in Palestine] and the older one was still in Alexandria. They took in boarders for lunch and were doing relatively well. After I left, my cousin brought her three older girls from Poland, and all of them are still in Israel to this day. That cousin Goldin remained a widow with seven children for thirty-seven years; and thirty years ago, she understood that girls also had to be economically prepared for life as independent people, especially in the Land of Israel.

With me in my return to Poland in 1921, also after only a year in the Land of Israel, were my friend Ts. Z. Weinberg, a teacher, and a member of the editorial staff of *Moment*,[24] Yosef Heftman. In 1920, Ts. Z. Weinberg was the principal of the school in Zikhron Ya'akov. He had come to the Land of Israel with his oldest daughter, leaving his wife and other children in Warsaw. As a veteran Hebrew teacher and pedagogue, he was deeply disappointed by the level of education at that time in the Land in general and in the schools in particular. The work in his school was not satisfying. His return was not a tragedy for him, and he went back to Poland with an easy conscience.

In August 1921, the elections for the Twelfth Congress in Carlsbad took place. At that time, there were about ten thousand shekel payers [members of the Zionist Organization] altogether in the Land of Israel. I could not hope to be elected as a delegate to the Congress, but I was appointed as an expert, which allowed me to participate in the Congress with the same rights as a delegate. And a few days after Tisha b'Av,[25] I left the Land of Israel with a group of delegates.

As I parted from my closest friends, who understood me to some extent, I simply said: "I came to the Land of Israel on Simhas Toyre, and I am going back on Tisha b'Av . . . " I was first reproached for leaving the Land of Israel, but in a relatively light form, during the Congress by two old friends, the most popular leaders of the General Zionists. "Comrade Rakovsky," they told me, "you may not leave the Land of Israel. By doing so, you bring the greatest shame to our movement." "You may be right," I answered. "But I want you to understand that I have considered this step thoroughly and have suffered greatly. At least I have been in the Land of Israel. But why haven't you gone? What are you waiting for? In your situation, you can do it easier than I." One of them replied that he couldn't go to the Land of Israel without a minimum capital of ten thousand pounds. The other said that he couldn't go and come back, so he had to wait a while longer.

The first did go there a few years later, bought a big house in Tel Aviv and planned to move in, but tragic family matters forced him to return. He later died in Warsaw. The second came, after a long delay, lived in Tel Aviv for a few years under unusually difficult economic conditions, and experienced much emotional grief. But he managed to die in the Land of Israel. Both friends were important for the growth and development of the Zionist movement in Poland in a variety of areas. They sacrificed a great deal of time and money; but as members of the

---

24. *Moment*, Yiddish daily newspaper founded in Warsaw in 1910.
25. The Ninth of Av, a day of fasting that commemorates the destruction of the First and Second Temples in Jerusalem.

old generation of the first "dreamers and fighters," they waited too long to come to the Land of Israel and were not properly appreciated there.

Entirely unfriendly was the attitude of my fellow party members in the Zeirei Zion faction at the Twelfth Congress. They regarded my return as an alleged "betrayal" of the Land of Israel. They simply "put me in *herem*"[26] and didn't let me participate in the sessions of the faction I formally belonged to, as one of its founders. I didn't react to that treatment at the Congress, but decided to wait until I returned to Warsaw.

---

26. The *herem*, or excommunication, was a form of punishment levied by the traditional Jewish community through its rabbinical court. Here it means "ostracized."

Eight

Organizing Polish Jewish Women

The Twelfth Congress, the first after World War I, was held in Carlsbad from September 1–14, 1921. Despite several negative points, I found the Congress exhilarating either because of the new milieu or the deep conviction permeating the enthusiastic speeches of our intellectual leaders. In any case, my depression abated, and I calmly traveled from Carlsbad to Warsaw. When I reached Warsaw, I found my family and friends healthy, cheerful, and pleased to see me back.

To maintain my cheerful mood, I used my old tried and true method: I immediately started looking for work. I first appealed to my friend, Dr. Shmuel Weinberg, director of the Askala Gymnasium. But he regretfully informed me that, right after I had left for the Land of Israel, the girls' school was forced to close because he couldn't find suitable teachers. And there were no vacant positions in the men's gymnasium. Unable and unwilling to wait a long time until I found work as a teacher, I accepted the suggestion of my fellow committee members of the Jewish Women's Association, Y.F.A., and took the job as secretary of the Association. In addition, a month later, my friend Leah Proshansky arranged for me to teach Hebrew to her cousin, Mrs. Tsirinsky, a wealthy woman who had just returned from Russia. I soon started finding work in my second profession, as a translator of foreign languages into Yiddish. And so, the economic issue was solved. My daughter was studying law, my orphaned grandchildren attended gymnasium. In 1921, they were still with their father, who spent an hour a day with them at lunch. They lacked for nothing since they spent more time with us than they did in

their boarding house, but, as is said, they had no "home." Even then —
the boy was eleven and the girl was nine — they belonged to Ha-Shomer
Ha-Tsair[1] in Warsaw, and so to some extent, they could forget that they
were orphans.

The Y.F.A. association in Poland grew into an extensive Jewish
women's organization that had a positive position on the Land of Israel.
It also had a separate section for practical political work. The Association was not apolitical; it worked actively in all areas of Jewish society
and political life in the country. One of its most important functions
was to train young Jewish women for productive work, not only girls
from the working class, but also from the middle classes and even
Hasidic circles. Several women pioneers were later recruited for the
Land of Israel from the girls in our vocational courses.

I came back to Warsaw at the time of the sharpest struggle of the
Jews in Poland for their national and civil rights. The country was
experiencing the "wars of the Jews of Poland," as the leader of that long
struggle, Comrade Yitzhak Grünbaum,[2] called his collection of articles
and Sejm [parliament] speeches — his oral and written activity on behalf of Jewish equality in Poland. As an elected representative of the
Y.F.A. organization in the Jewish national council, I became very active
in mobilizing the women of our association to struggle for our rights.
Like Polish women, we were granted voting rights and eligibility for
office in the Sejm and the municipal councils, but we had to fight
against our own domestic wielders of power for the right to vote for the
new, supposedly "secular" Jewish community organizations. In Vilna
and Bialystok, women had the same rights as men in the community
organizations. But in our cities, especially in Warsaw, the Orthodox —
Agude, the rabbis and even Mizrachi — absolutely refused to sit with
women in the kehile [community organization]. For almost twenty years,
Jewish women in Poland stubbornly waged a constant battle, from 1920
until the outbreak of World War II in 1939, but without success.

At a protest meeting of the Y.F.A. organization during the last kehile
elections in Warsaw, Dr. Schiper,[3] of blessed memory, correctly under-
scored with his exit the importance and necessity of women's activity in
the kehile. Even the Mizrachi representative, H. Farbstein, had the
courage to state that in the education department, the work of Comrade Rakovsky was very desirable, but . . . It was not yet the time.

---

1. Zionist-socialist pioneering youth movement, founded in 1916.
2. Polish Zionist leader, one of the main spokesmen for Polish Jewry between the two wars.
3. Ignacy (Yitzhak) Schiper, a historian and public activist.

Now, in June 1942, as I write these memoirs, I must note that not only in Poland but also in the Land of Israel did Jewish women fight for the right to vote in the municipal councils, the *kehile*, and even the Assembly of Representatives. For the last seven years since I arrived in the Land for the second time — since 1935 — I have participated actively in the community organization elections in Jerusalem. And now, I happen to be a passive participant in the Haifa community organization.

As I said, I went back to Poland right in the middle of the "Sturm und Drang" epoch. For years, the center of my life had involved my work for the national liberation of my people in its old home, as well as my struggle for equality in the world. So the catastrophic Jewish situation in Poland made me despair. I often felt trapped when Jews came to ask me about the Land of Israel, wondering whether or not to go. Since the situation was, in my eyes, bad there and even worse here, to be fair, I would give an evasive response: "Dear friend," I used to say, "a Jew who is willing and able to make aliyah to the Land of Israel packs up and goes. But Jews who come to ask for advice always stay where they are."

As always, my economic situation seemed secondary. In particular, in comparison with the general situation, it really wasn't very bad. Along with working in the Y.F.A. association and the well-paid private lessons, my companion Birnbaum had a permanent position in a Jewish school, and I also was able to work as a translator. The first book I succeeded in translating when I came back to Warsaw was Erich Maria Remarque's *All Quiet on the Western Front*. I emphasize the word *succeeded* because, looking back at my translation after a year, I decided that Yiddish literature had to be enriched first of all with more of the anti-war books that had appeared in the immediate postwar years in European languages. I considered it a duty to introduce Jewish readers, particularly mothers and young people, to the terrors and horrors of the first world slaughter in order to evoke disgust and resistance to the futile bloodbath, and to rouse and develop an anti-war spirit in them! Remarque's book was the first and, according to general opinion, the best work of that kind because it was written by a young man who had experienced all the bloody events that the human imagination can hardly fathom.

During the winter of 1921–1922, the two children of the Tsirinsky family became very attached to me. They had never attended school and were preparing for the examination to a French gymnasium in Warsaw. They loved my lessons so much that they told me that they studied no other language as eagerly as Hebrew. But can you teach children Hebrew without a connection to the Land of Israel? The children had not grown up in a Zionist environment. Their mother was from a very distinguished Jewish family, but she was not a Zionist. As for their father, he had absolutely no interest in Zionism, even though he contributed generously to the various national funds. In general, Mr. Tsirinsky was a vibrant and enterprising person. An exceptionally talented merchant in his forties, he had already managed to acquire an enormous fortune. The wood merchants said that when he came from Russia to Poland, he bought a large part of the Polish forests from the government. He also owned the largest textile factory in Poland. In his enterprises he employed many Jewish workers and administrators, and the whole staff respected him for his unusual honesty with all his workers.

There was only one "commercial" enterprise I couldn't interest him in, despite my constant agitation: I could not get him to invest some of his capital in the Land of Israel. I failed, even though he bought houses in Berlin and Danzig and villas in Copot and even in Italy, and had much capital invested in various foreign banks. The children often asked me to persuade their father to buy land in the Land of Israel. Before Pesach, when I studied the Haggadah with them, I advised them to steal the Afikomen[4] at the Seder and to relinquish it only on condition that he promise to buy land in the Land of Israel. The children carried out that "expropriation" and got a promise from their father. Soon after Pesach, at the demand of the children, I mentioned his promise to him. "Where should I buy land, Mrs. Rakovsky?" he asked me in a special tone. "In *your* Land of Israel?" "Oh, Mr. Tsirinsky," I answered tranquilly, "that *you* should speak with the tongue of the wicked son in the Haggadah,[5] I never expected this of you." And I left the room at once. When I went back to the children, they didn't ask me anything, for they already read the answer on my face . . . I present that fact only as an illustration of how atrophied the sense of a national fatherland had become, along with the idea of rebuilding the Land of Israel, even among respectable, nationalist-minded Jews.

In May 1922, before the school year ended, Mrs. Tsirinsky suggested that, instead of going to a summer house, I and my family stay in Copot, since she wanted her children to continue their Hebrew studies all summer. Since they knew a lot of people in Copot, she would recommend me for as many Hebrew pupils as I would accept. Food cost the

---

4. The piece of matza saved for dessert at the Passover Seder. It is customarily hidden and the children who discovers it ransom it for a reward.
5. There are "four sons" discussed in the Passover Haggadah. The wicked son distances himself from his family and his people.

same as in Warsaw, and the stay would be very interesting for my children. I agreed to the proposition and settled in Oliwe near Copot. I soon was hired to give lessons in Oliwe, and later got a job teaching Comrade Yitzhak Grünbaum's little boy. The Grünbaum family lived in Copot every summer. It took twenty minutes to travel by train from Oliwe to Copot. From eight in the morning until noon, I was busy in Copot, and in the afternoon I gave a well-paid lesson in Oliwe itself.

A few weeks later, my friend Leah Proshansky also came to Oliwe, and rented a flat in my neighborhood. At that time, her two sons were studying in London and she and her husband were living in Warsaw. The sons wanted to see their parents, but were Russian citizens who couldn't get Polish visas, so they decided to meet in Oliwe, near Danzig, because citizens from all over the world could come to the free city of Danzig.

The Proshansky family was very friendly with a family named Cohen from Lódz; the men had been classmates. The Cohens also had two sons. The older one studied in Brno (Czechoslovakia), and was also a Russian citizen who could not get a Polish visa; he hadn't seen his parents in three years. The friends agreed that the Cohen family would also come to Oliwe, and, as the French say, the friends of our friends were also our friends. I often would meet with the Cohen family too. These encounters were especially interesting for the young people. My friend Leah's children had grown up with my Sorele. They had spent summers with us at the boarding school and were as attached to her as if she were a younger sister; that was no wonder, since their mothers had been devoted friends for thirty years. The children were the second generation of friends. In 1914, right after the outbreak of the war, we were separated and didn't see each other for eight years. At that time, my daughter was eleven years old, Shmuel Proshansky was sixteen, and Joshua was fifteen. Now, in 1922, Sarah was a student at Warsaw University, and they were in London. It was a pleasant surprise, and they had much to talk about day and night. But, as usual, I was busy all week long, except for the Sabbath, and I was glad that Sarah was spending her vacation pleasantly with my friend and her children, Shmuel and Joshua, and their friend Zvi Cohen. I realized that Zvi Cohen was interested in my Sarah when I happened to notice that his mother was jealous of her. At the time, I wasn't seeking a bridegroom for my nineteen-year-old daughter, so I didn't react to the matter.

At the end of June — a month after we came to Oliwe — I suddenly got a telegram from Warsaw, saying that my grandchildren were coming and that I should meet them at the depot in Danzig. My surprise and uneasiness until I saw them is easy to imagine. The children simply said that their father had called them from Grayeva and allowed them to go to be with their grandmother in Oliwe. Naturally, they were glad to go, and my joy at having them was clear.

Throughout the few years that my daughter Sarah studied at Warsaw University, she wanted to travel abroad. She was very unsatisfied with the Polish professors and suffered from the open antisemitism that Polish academic youth directed toward their Jewish classmates. But it was hard for me to part with her, and I tried to persuade her to finish studying law. When she was twenty years old, she could travel abroad to study somewhere else in another faculty. Meeting students from other universities reinforced her desire to go abroad. In early August, the young people all left—first Zvi Cohen, and a few days later, the Proshansky brothers. Then, as my friend Leah and the remaining members of the Cohen family left Oliwe, I and my family moved to Copot; after the season, rooms were cheap and, because I gave lessons, it was much more convenient for me there. Another important issue that moved me to stay in Copot somewhat longer, at least over the holidays, was that I didn't have a house in Warsaw for my grandchildren, whose father finally had sent them to me. He himself first went to Berlin and later to the Land of Israel. I couldn't bring them to the two small rooms where my companion Birnbaum, myself, and our daughter lived; even if we crowded together, the sleeping arrangements still wouldn't work.

Meanwhile, Sarah began to be bored. One fine day, she told me that if I planned to stay in Copot through the month of Tishrei, she was going back to Warsaw by herself. I asked her calmly why she was hurrying back to Warsaw. The university, I said, didn't open until October. And what would she do there all alone? She paused before answering my question, and then revealed a secret: "Cohen made me a serious proposal, but I told him that I haven't known him long enough to make such a serious decision. I promised I'd write to him. But it's not convenient for me here, so I want to go to Warsaw." I wasn't surprised. My maternal instinct had recently told me that my daughter was going through something very serious. I didn't want to get in her way. Two days later, she went to Warsaw.

My companion Birnbaum and I stayed in Copot with our grandchildren for almost a month. They celebrated and were happy to be back with us. After we returned to Warsaw, the children and I slept for three weeks in the office of the Women's Association [Y.F.A.] until we finally were able to take a room in the same building where we had lived. The children attended school and everything went back to normal.

The correspondence between Zvi Cohen and my daughter grew frequent and lively. It certainly increased the income of the post office in Poland and Czechoslovakia. But it didn't keep her from studying, and she went back to law school. One day in early December, I got a personal letter from Zvi about his serious, honest love for my Sarah. He was happy that the feeling was mutual, and asked me not to stand in the way of their happiness. He wrote that he would like to come to Warsaw during the winter vacation, but since he was a Russian citizen, he couldn't get a Polish visa. But he knew that Sarah wanted to go abroad, and he thought it best if I agreed to let her attend a Czech university. If she came to Brno, he wrote, they would decide where and what she should study. He concluded the letter by telling me that he had written the same letter to his parents in Lódz.

About a week after they received their letter, his parents came to see us in Warsaw as in-laws. They asked me not to keep Sarah from going to their son in Brno. They also invited my daughter to come as a guest to their home in Lódz first. Hard as it was to part from my Sarah, I started preparing for her trip abroad. The various formalities — passport and necessary visas — took a few weeks. Shortly before her journey, she stayed with his parents in Lódz for a week at most. When she came home, she told me that if she had stayed there another few days, she would have run away, since it was so hard for her to play the role of their son's "bride," as they introduced her to their friends.

In early December 1922, she left for Brno, but stayed only a short time. From there, she went to Vienna, where she studied history and philosophy at the university. Since all that was going on didn't stop her from continuing her studies, I calmed down.

Among the various institutions and learning centers of our Y.F.A. federation, there was also — as I said — a vocational school for girls, most of whom came from the lower classes. Many of them studied for free. Naturally, the school also ran a big deficit. All our efforts to get a subsidy from JCA and later from ORT were unsuccessful.[6] In January 1923, the new inspector of ORT schools for Poland, the engineer L. Frenkel, came to Warsaw. He was a friend of mine from Vilna (and was a brother of my oldest sister-in-law). I invited him to visit our vocational school for girls, which was under my direction. He was very impressed by the school. I then told him quite openly that I had invited him to tell him the truth, that the school lacked means and its con-

---

6. JCA, a philanthropic association to assist Jews in economic distress, founded in 1891; ORT, philanthropic society established in 1880 to provide vocational training for Russian Jews.

tinued existence was threatened; I pleaded with him to try to get the ORT administration to give the school a monthly subsidy. He replied that with the best will in the world, he couldn't do that because ORT subsidized only its own schools, not those of other societies. But, he assured me, "I have a suitable proposal for you, Mrs. Rakovsky, for saving your school, if the party ambitions of your board members are not as important as the school itself. The ORT school for girls in Warsaw is looking for an academic director; the best solution, I think, is for you and all your students to transfer to the ORT school. ORT doesn't need the building, the machines, and the other school supplies. You can use the building for another enterprise, of which, I have heard, your Y.F.A. possesses a great number. You don't really risk anything. Simply allow your students to continue their studies and you'll have the right to accept new students in the future. We have only one demand for you, Mrs. Rakovsky — that you take the job of a principal in the ORT school."

I listened to him attentively, promising to put the matter to the board so that I could soon give him an answer. I immediately called a special meeting of the committee and invited some active members, to whom I lectured objectively and in detail about the matter. I said: "We now confront the alternative of whether to close down the school or transfer it to ORT. And I think that, of two evils, we have to choose the lesser. In the partnership with ORT, we don't invest anything. On the contrary, we only give our students a chance to study under better conditions. In fact, they remain under our supervision because the spirit in the school is introduced by the person in charge, and not by the administration of its financial institutions. My personal situation is not at issue because I will accept whatever decision this meeting makes; if our school continues to exist, I will resign from ORT. Aside from everything else, I think we can regard the whole issue as a kind of "first aid," a temporary solution, because I am firmly convinced that our chairman, Mrs. Rachel Stein, as a member of the Warsaw city council, will surely manage to get the necessary subsidy for all our institutions, and then we can re-open our vocational school."

There was a fervent and serious discussion, in which almost all our members participated; and although there were some votes against, the majority was in favor of the proposal. I sent Engineer Frenkel the text of the positive answer of our committee. Since all appropriate formalities were settled by ORT, I received the official notification from Dr. M. Silverfarb, the director of the ORT schools in Poland at that time, that, as of February 1, 1923, I was employed as a principal of the ORT school for girls in Warsaw with a salary of 300 zlotys a month for six hours of work a day. After I worked for ten months in the ORT school, our councilwoman, Mrs. Rachel Stein, did succeed in getting a subsidy from the Warsaw city council, along with other specially established philanthropic organizations for culture-work in Poland. And we again opened our vocational school for girls. We didn't lack students. After I left, the ORT school administration did not hire an academic but a qualified artisan, a Christian from Germany.

In May 1924, Cohen finished school, went from Brno to Prague to look for work, and soon got a job as a building engineer in a large private company. Because of certain problems concerning their citizenship — Cohen had a Nansen Passport[7] as a refugee from tsarist Russia and my daughter didn't want to give up her Polish citizenship — the rabbinate in Prague couldn't or wouldn't give them a religious marriage. After going through the proper formalities, they arranged for a civil marriage in Prague city hall. Only a year later did Cohen's parents, after a long procedure, manage to get him Polish citizenship, because he had been born in the town of Lune.

In August 1924, I left my job at ORT. The lessons with the Tsirinskys also ended because the children were attending the French gymnasium. Tsirinsky's big businesses got a harsh blow from the government; his match factory was monopolized by the state. The state also imposed extraordinarily high taxes on his various forest and wood businesses. His depression led to a serious and incurable illness — leukemia — which was treated for several years, but he died at the age of forty and a few years.

After he died, his wife liquidated the business. With whatever was left of the capital, she and her children went to Paris. In 1936, they came to the Land of Israel for a short visit. In 1938, the son came back to the Land of Israel by himself. He stayed at my house in Jerusalem a few times and told me he was going back to bring his mother and sisters. Fortunately, they managed to come here just before the war broke out. This time, the daughter came as a licensed airplane pilot. At the airport in Lod, she met a young Jewish pilot from a very rich family — a well-known commercial family in Tel Aviv — and those two pilots soon got married. And as the ladies say, may we say the same of all Jewish children — even in a socialist Land of Israel. . . .

In August 1924, I again got a job in the secretariat of the Y.F.A.

---

7. The identity card issued by the League of Nations for persons made stateless by the Russian Revolution of 1917.

association. I also worked at my regular translations. My grandchildren studied diligently. The girl, Shoshana, was in the fourth grade and the boy, Arye Shmuel, in the sixth grade of the gymnasium. He was also active in Ha-Shomer Ha-Tsair. His friends always told me that no one could do what Alec did — that's what they called him.

At that time, the poverty of the Jews in Poland strengthened the Zionist movement. In 1924–1926, the rate of aliyah [immigration to Palestine] rose extraordinarily, although this was only a temporary situation. The Palestine Office in Warsaw was not only an important national institution, but was also a large-scale, prosperous emigration company. I was in difficult economic straits, so I decided to talk to one of the party leaders in the Palestine Committee, Dr. Joshua Gottlieb, about a job in the Palestine Office. Like many party members, after studying in Switzerland, he had belonged to "Time to Build."[8] So in some sense, he was my ideological opponent. But he was a smart man, and after a short chat, he promised to talk to Comrade Barlas, the director of the Palestine Office.

The next day, I went to Barlas and was offered the job. The first few weeks were really hard for me, but I soon adjusted and it wasn't long before I made the work interesting for myself. Aside from the files, I began to get interested in the people for whom I filled out the various forms and whose passports I prepared. That work was not only interesting, but also necessary. At that time, seventy-four clerks worked in the Palestine Office, and I was the seventy-fifth. The staff were mostly young people, mostly single, but some with families, and I was the only older clerk. The office, at Marianska 7, took up three floors: the work, especially when the transports left, was unusually difficult. The clerks treated the immigrants bureaucratically, without empathy or understanding about the experience of wandering — even the voluntary wandering of a person who leaves his home to go the Land of Israel, his national home. But who can guarantee that this would be his last move? I considered it my duty to make the difficulties of moving as easy as possible for these people. To some extent, I succeeded, even though some bureau chiefs were not satisfied with my "intercession." Sometimes I reduced the fixed fees, or arranged deductions for ship tickets, cheaper train tickets, etc. But the chiefs always filled my requests.

There was a special plague that doesn't appear in the Torah.[9] During the time of increased immigration to the Land of Israel, strong gangs

---

8. A Zionist faction formed in 1923 and loyal to Chaim Weizmann's policies.
9. Reference to the ten plagues of the Exodus story.

and thieves' organizations would cheat the immigrants of their last few pennies, especially during the large transports, often even at the gate, and even on the steps of the Palestine Office itself. Repeated warnings in the press and all other means didn't help; the provincial immigrants regularly fell into the net of those swindlers. I still remember an interesting case that happened in 1934. One day, I managed to stop one of those people; externally, he looked like a middle-aged Jewish merchant, and it was hard to believe that he was capable of such acts. Interrogated by Comrade Shafar, then committee chairman, he behaved very calmly, listened attentively to everything Comrade Shafar said to him, and finally answered: "Give me a job like you have, Mr. Shafar, and I won't look for any income on the side . . ." He wasn't arrested.

Writing now, decades later, about my work and experiences in the Palestine Office at that time, I recall a pleasant, personal surprise related to my comrade David Remez, of blessed memory.[10] In the summer of 1925, an international workers' congress, including a delegation from the Land of Israel, was held in Moscow. The delegation [from Palestine] demanded to address the congress in Hebrew. The organizers hesitated a bit, but gave in. After the greeting, the chairman told the speaker that, unfortunately, none of the audience understood his speech. My son, who had worked for years at the translation office for all conferences and congresses, was then asked to translate the speech into Russian. Knowing that he translated from ten languages on the spot, the leaders were not surprised that, as a Jew, he also understood Hebrew. But the comrades from the Land of Israel were amazed. During the break, Comrade Remez wanted to know where they got a Jew who could translate from Hebrew into Russian on the spot; he went to the translator and asked who he was, and was told that he was my son. Returning to the Land of Israel through Poland, David Remez visited me and gave me personal regards from my son. Apparently childhood lessons come in handy even in the Soviet Union . . .

Work in the Palestine Office was not only satisfying, but fascinating. I was the first one to get to work and the last to leave. My comrades often commented that my sense of professionalism was undeveloped. To this I replied that I saw our office not as a personal welfare institution, but as a national institution to bring Jews to the Land of Israel. Another very important incident interested me when I started working in the Palestine Office. The Palestine Commission was comprised of party representatives and Halutz organizations that had a large number

---

10. David Remez (1886–1951), labor leader and political figure in the Yishuv.

of women members. However, not one single woman sat on the Commission. The Y.F.A. association, as an organization that was not purely Zionist, could not claim a seat on the commission. But why did the women members of the mixed organizations, especially He-Halutz, not react? Is it any wonder that [unorganized] women also give up their recognized rights?

A committee that determined eligibility for immigration was later formed within the Palestine Commission, and that body, which decided the fate of every immigrant to the Land of Israel, did not include one single female member. The section for practical Palestine work in the Y.F.A. association, as I said, mainly prepared young women through vocational education for the Land of Israel. At my suggestion, we demanded that the eligibility committee reserve a place for a representative of our women's association. The proposal was accepted. The Y.F.A. elected me to be its representative on that committee.

At the very first meeting, I grew even more convinced of the importance for women to participate on that committee. Women had to defend the interests of female pioneers and female emigrants in general, and even had to take notice of the attitudes of their own male comrades. In addition to everything else, the new decree about the system of scheduling and certificates also limited certificates for women, but every unmarried male pioneer, or any immigrant, was allowed to sponsor a girl on his certificate. This made young women completely dependent on the kindness of their male comrades. That humiliating decree had serious consequences and often even created tragic situations. It produced several fictitious marriages, and men who didn't know a girl would take one along. Some men took advantage of this situation in various ways. A few simply took money from the women they sponsored. Others — if they liked the girl — wouldn't grant her a pre-planned divorce when they reached the Land of Israel. Later, we came up with an invention: When the marriage ceremony was held, the divorce decree was prepared on the spot. Pious Jews were angered, for they considered this action to weaken the sanctity of marriage — and to some extent, they weren't altogether wrong . . .

In December 1924, over the winter vacation, my grandson Arye-Shmuel gave me a "pleasant" surprise. He came to tell me that he had completed the sixth class of the gymnasium and was dropping out of school because he had decided to go to the Land of Israel. At first, I declared that he couldn't mean this seriously, that he only wanted to know how I would react. But what he said next showed me that he had made a firm decision. For a week he had been working for a blacksmith, a very good craft in the Land of Israel, and was sure that I would help him carry out his plan. He was going with a group of members of Ha-Shomer Ha-Tsair, and he hoped that he would soon be able to bring me and his sister Shoshana to the Land of Israel.

Naturally, I didn't stand in his way, because I knew it wouldn't help, since he came from a family of dangerously stubborn people . . . But the leaders of Ha-Shomer Ha-Tsair did protest that he had not completed his internship in the party. And secondly, they argued that he had to finish his studies and immigrate to the Land of Israel not at the age of sixteen, but at eighteen. However, no one could dissuade him.

He studied diligently to be a blacksmith. At six in the morning, he had breakfast, didn't even take along a snack, and came home at five o'clock. He couldn't warm up his lunch, but ate it cold; otherwise he didn't eat at all. He didn't want to tell us who his boss was, but I found out through his comrades in Ha-Shomer Ha-Tsair because several pioneers studied with the same blacksmith. I then went to see this blacksmith, and told him that my grandson was starving all day, from six in the morning to five in the afternoon. I asked him to give him a snack and promised to pay whatever he demanded. The blacksmith listened to me and said: "He's your grandson? I didn't know that, although I knew he didn't come from ignorant people. Several pioneers study with me, but I must tell you that he has learned more in a month than all the others do in three. He can already shoe a horse. And what you ask me about food, I've been amazed all the time; all the fellows eat a snack at the nearby tavern, but he doesn't go, even though I pay for the food. It's a good thing you came! I understand that you don't want him to know about this. Don't worry. I'll find a way so that he won't go hungry all day."

In May, my grandson completed the blacksmith course and started preparing to leave. The committee of Ha-Shomer Ha-Tsair carried out all the necessary formalities and even paid his travel expenses. A few days before he left, he brought me the certificate from the sixth class, put it on the table, and said:

"Take it, Grandmother, I don't need it anymore." What he really meant to say is that he *wouldn't* need it any more. The next day, he packed his things to go. That is, he put a few pieces of clothing, some books, and a loaf of bread into a rucksack. He was barely persuaded to take a piece of sausage. But he absolutely refused to take a coat or a pillow or a blanket. "At home in Asia, you don't need all those things," he answered me. He put the rucksack on his shoulder and gave me his hand: "See you in the Land," he said, and was out the door. "Wait a minute! I want to go with you at least to the train," I said. "No, don't. If you go with me, I'll take another train." He held his hand out to me again — he didn't like to kiss — and left for the Land of Israel. I never saw him again. . . .

In early August 1925, I got a month's vacation from the Palestine Office to go to the Fourteenth Congress, which was held August 18–31 in Vienna. First, I decided to visit my daughter in Prague and bring her to my house in Warsaw on the way back — she was seven months pregnant. The university was closed for vacation. My daughter told me that her condition had not kept her from studying; she had completed the school year and had been promoted. I spent a week with the children in Prague and came to Vienna for the Congress on August 19th. The WIZO conference was held in Vienna at the same time. The Y.F.A. association had joined WIZO and sent our chairman Rachel Stein as a delegate. And, as a delegate to the Congress, I automatically had the right to participate in the WIZO conference.

In early September, a large transport of immigrants to the Land of Israel was supposed to leave Warsaw, including my younger sister from Bialystok, a dentist, her husband Shapiro, their three children, and our seventy-seven-year-old mother. They traveled as capitalists [not as pioneers] and therefore could take a mother along. In addition, the English Consul demanded that her other children sign a pledge to send their mother five pounds a month. We had already decided to do this, even before the Consul demanded it.

On September 1st, I was back in Prague. My daughter had arranged everything before I arrived because she knew I wanted to be with my mother when she left for the Land of Israel. All we had to do was buy train tickets to Warsaw. "But you know what I'm going to do?" said Zvi, as he went to buy the tickets. "I will buy tickets to Lódz, not to Warsaw. My parents have a three-room flat; and aren't so busy. My aunt Olya lives next door, and Birnbaum is also working in a school in Lódz now. And in Lódz there are maternity hospitals that are just as good as in Warsaw. You yourself," he said to me, "are very busy. It is better for Sarah to go to Lódz." I didn't protest because, aside from all those reasons, there was something else: Shortly before I had left for Prague, I had received a letter from my mother asking me to move. Sarah was to go to Lódz to have the child and not to Warsaw. The children, Sarah and Zvi, didn't know that. But since they shared that opinion, I told myself that the commandment to honor your father and mother has the side-benefit of lengthening your days,[11] and that I was obliged to carry

---

11. The fifth of the ten commandments.

out the demand of my old mother, who was not, in my opinion, an average person of her generation — and I went to Lódz with Sarah.

I was only one day late. The office thought that the Shapiro family and my old mother should leave with the transport, and there was no way they could postpone leaving. So they left one day before I arrived in Warsaw from Lódz. It is still hard for me to describe what I experienced that day. My friends told me that my mother had departed amid cheers. The young people included her in a dance on the train platform as the "youngest" pioneer ascending to the Land of Israel. The Jewish press devoted a few articles to my mother and her house in Bialystok, where children grew up to participate in both the Jewish national revolutionary movement and the general revolutionary movement. For a while, I couldn't forgive myself for not saying goodbye to my dear Mama. I never saw her again . . .

Five weeks later, on November 12, 1925, I got a telegram from Lódz, announcing that Sarah had given birth to a girl, who was named Hemdah after my daughter Sheyndl, who had died young (*Hemdah* was the Hebrew version of the Yiddish name *Sheyna*, of which Sheyndl was the diminutive). At that time, I had a premonition that that baby would grow up in the Land of Israel. (Right now, in July 1942, in Haifa, not far from the front, after a midnight alarm, as I write these lines about her birth, Hemdah is working in the lower Galilee in Moshav Sha'ara, along with a group of comrades in the eighth class of the Real School [a high school] in Haifa).

Between 1924 and 1927, I worked more intensively, eight hours a day: from morning to noon in the Palestine Office and in the afternoon in the Y.F.A. secretariat. In addition, I continued my translations. My work in various areas gave me such intellectual satisfaction that no personal interests existed for me. Materially, I lacked nothing. My granddaughter Shoshana was in gymnasium. Her brother was in the Land of Israel. As I had foreseen, kibbutz life didn't suit that hundred-percent individualist, and after a few weeks, he left. He couldn't settle down to any regular work. He surveyed the whole Land of Israel, drained swamps, suffered from malaria, became friendly with the Arabs and even lived among them, and became active in the Haganah and Ha-Poel.[12] He didn't write to me. I heard about him from my mother, may-she-rest-in-peace, my sister, and his comrades. In short, his idealism approached lunacy . . . He was very poor, and when I sent a few

---

12. The Haganah was the underground military organization of the Yishuv, established in 1920; Ha-Poel, workers' sports organization, established in 1926.

pounds to him through my sister, she could barely prevail on him to take the money. For a while, he worked in Haifa and slept beside a well. My sister heard about this and pleaded with him to come sleep in their house, where they had an empty room. But he refused. One day, my sister told me, he borrowed a pound from her and named the day when he would pay it back. A few days later, at one in the morning, the bell rang. At first, they were terrified, but they opened the door and found Arye-Shmuel repaying the loan. Since he had said "today" — even if it was in the middle of the night — it had to be "today." That was how he lived for ten years. His last work was at the Dead Sea in 1935. He worked where the temperature was 40 degrees Celsius, and fainted at work. He was taken to Hadassah Hospital in Jerusalem with pneumonia, and died three days later at the age of twenty-seven.

My Sarah took a year off from school. In the winter of 1925–1926, she was with her in-laws in Lódz with the baby. At Pesach, they went to Otwock for the vacation. In the early summer of 1926, Zvi completed his work in Prague and came to look for a job as a building engineer in Poland. In that year of the "war against the Jews of Poland," there were absolutely no prospects. He soon applied at the Russian consulate in Warsaw for an entrance visa to Moscow as a "specialist," and I asked my son to do what he could so that the process wouldn't take long.

At that time of the Fourth Aliyah,[13] when the Jewish middle-class was immigrating to the Land of Israel, threatened Jewish capitalists sought other countries for more profitable investments. Several rich manufacturers and large industrialists, mainly from Lódz, ran to "compassionate" Romania (where the "Iron Guard," led by Codreanu was raging, and the tone in Parliament was set by Professors Yurga and Kuza, who were famous at the time as avowed Jew-haters). These capitalists were not given citizenship and were not allowed to reside there permanently, only temporarily, to rebuild the destroyed city and develop commerce, manufacture, and industry. On the other hand, the Romanian authorities didn't want them to stay there.

That capitalist emigration opened a special source of income for the Romanian lower and even higher administration. I have never seen such open corruption in any other country as in Romania. For the slightest thing, the officials would simply demand it; and shamelessly report that nothing was done without "bakshish." With our pensions, they openly stated, we would starve to death without "bakshish." You

13. The Fourth Aliyah extended from 1924 to 1928.

could even get to ministers with "bakshish," through their gypsy con-
cubines. Because of that corruption, Jews did "business" and lived better in that country, which was only three days away from the Land of
Israel . . .

One of those wealthy Jews was Cohen's uncle, Isaac Gross, a Russian Jew, who moved from Łódz to Bucharest in early 1926. He was a
master craftsman and enterprising merchant, who took his brother-in-
law, Zvi's father, along to work for him. The mother stayed in Łódz for
the time being to sell the apartment and other property. When she
learned that Zvi was waiting for an entrance visa to Russia, she raised a
loud hue and cry: "How can it be?" she argued, "Akiva is a Communist
[the older son already in Soviet Russia] and if Zvi goes to Soviet Russia,
I won't have either of my two sons." Naturally, she wrote to her husband and her brother-in-law, and they started pelting Zvi with letters to
come to Bucharest and not wait for an answer from Moscow. In Romania, they wrote, there was a lot of construction and Zvi had the best
prospects there to make a career and become wealthy.

I didn't want to tell Zvi not to go to Bucharest, and to wait at least
for an answer from my son, even though my Sarah was more attracted to
Moscow than to Bucharest. But I said: "If I were an able-bodied, working engineer of 29, who didn't belong to any political movement and
wanted to specialize, I would, naturally, go to Soviet Russia and not to
the dark, antisemitic Romania. If you don't have to change your citizenship, you can go and come back if you don't like it. Just to look at
the country where such unprecedented great upheavals have taken
place is interesting for a young person, especially since you have a
brother-in-law there who will do everything he can for his only sister.
I'm just telling you what I think," I concluded, "and you do as you like."

Zvi went to his mother for a few days and then to the Romanian
consulate for a visa to Bucharest. But only Jewish capitalists easily got
entry visas from the Consul; an engineer, whose only capital was the
profession he carried with him, a foreign intellectual proletarian, who
might compete with one's own, isn't let into a country, even if he was
needed for a while. After much running around, they finally got the visa
because the uncle helped from Bucharest; and a month after Zvi left,
the papers from Moscow arrived. Obviously, my son was very depressed
about the whole thing, but I tried to calm him and wrote him that it
might be for the best because a person cannot easily change his attitude.

As soon as he got to Bucharest, Zvi got work on government buildings; that is, he didn't get the work himself, but a big Romanian con-

struction firm got the work and hired him as head engineer with a good salary, because they themselves were from the old school and appreciated his knowledge of modern construction.

In August 1926, Sarah returned to Prague to continue studying. I kept the baby in Otwock through the holidays and then sent her to her grandmother in Łódz for the winter. In April 1927, Sally and a group of students and professors went on an artistic and historical excursion for six weeks to Paris, Le Havre, Bordeaux, Lisbon, and Tangier. On the way back, through Strasbourg to London, and from there, at the end of May, at the end of vacation, she came to Warsaw. From the end of Pesach, the baby and I were back in Otwock. Soon after Sarah's arrival, I got a letter from my son that, as a high secretary of the "international cooperative movement," he was going as a delegate of Soviet Russia to the international cooperative conference in Oslo. On the way back, he would go through Danzig and asked me to come there with Sarah to spend a few days with him. In 1918, I saw him for a whole hour in the Warsaw railroad station; a second time, in 1922 — another hour in the railroad station during his trip from Moscow to Berlin. To get off the train for a day in Warsaw was dangerous in those years, both for him and for me. From 1922 to 1927, I hadn't seen him at all. In Danzig (more precisely, in Copot, which was safer), we spent three whole days with him. In 1905, when I saved him from certain death, Sarah was three years old. When he saw her twenty-two years later, he couldn't take his eyes off her. Day and night for three days, he talked with her constantly. She made a strong impression on him. We went back to Warsaw from Danzig together, but, of course, in separate cars. At the railroad station in Warsaw, my son immediately entered the international Paris-Warsaw-Moscow express. We said a quick goodbye and withdrew immediately. Naturally, there were secret police on that express train.

Sarah spent the vacation with us in Otwock, and in August she went back to Prague to finish school. Right after Sukes, her mother-in-law left for Bucharest with the baby.

In early 1927 my job at the Palestine Office was threatened. Danger confronted almost the entire staff of seventy-five persons. My colleagues assured me that even if only three officials remained, I would be one of them. I don't know about the others, but for me, this was not a personal matter. Aliyah rose from no more than 700 a month in 1920 to 1,800 in July 1924, and later was up to 4,000 a month. In 1925, there were 34,000 immigrants, 50 percent from Poland itself. By the end of 1926, the number of Jews in the Land of Israel had increased to

147,000. The sharp inflation of the Polish zloty in 1925–1926 and the economic depression in the Land of Israel at the same time suddenly reduced aliyah from Poland to a minimum. In the Land of Israel, they knew that the depression was not just a passing phenomenon, as they said. Back in Poland, the Palestine Office began to reduce its operations — not all at once, but in phases. First, various departments were combined, and the top two floors were liquidated, leaving only the ground floor. Every day, the amount of work decreased. We sat at our desks like "mourners for Zion"; my heart broke when I looked at the orphaned certificates in my desk drawer. I had been in charge of them for five years, and was proud of that trust. Now when I came to work in the morning in the almost empty rooms, I always thought of the biblical verse: "The roads to Zion mourn."[14] With my hundred-percent pessimism, that crisis was very hard for me. It did indeed last several years; then another increase of Aliyah was expected. I again worked in the Palestine Office for almost three years, until I finally immigrated to the Land of Israel in April 1935.

At that earlier time, I had worked from January to April 1927. When the crisis reached its climax — in April we did not receive any notice about the high unemployment levels in the Land of Israel — only a few of us were left in the office. I couldn't bear this, so I went back to my work in the Y.F.A. secretariat, where I was in demand. Aside from my translations, I also was able to work for the evening newspaper *Moment*, translating stories, writing the "latest news of the day," and performing other editorial work.

I moved in with my sister, the dentist. My granddaughter Shoshana was in the seventh grade. At the end of the school year, she wanted to follow in her brother's footsteps: that is, to get a sixth grade certificate and go to the Land of Israel. I absolutely refused. That wasn't easy, but my sister had a special influence with her and she also thought Shoshana should finish school first. Finally, my granddaughter gave in and completed gymnasium.

During the vacation, we built up a summer camp for the youth department of the Y.F.A. association, together with the vocational school in Kaszimiesz. It was a wonderful place on the banks of the Vistula. We rented a big house from a farmer, paid for by the general treasury; housekeeping was done collectively and food was cheap because the girls prepared everything by themselves. They slept on the

---

14. Lamentations 1:4.

floor on straw mattresses, and took just one bed from the landlady — for me. That was a unanimous decision by the entire collective and I had to give in to it.

Quite by chance, the Poale Zion youth of Warsaw also had a summer camp there. The groups met and held joint lectures, discussions, evening talks, singing, and dancing. In short, they became Jews. All through the next winter, our girls talked constantly of the lovely days of Kaszimiesz.

Nine

Russian Journey

In late winter 1927, I suddenly had the idea of going to see my son and finally getting a look at that wonderful country that covered one-sixth of the globe — the country building itself on such new and supposedly different bases, to which most other nations would not or could not agree. You couldn't travel there by sea, and the international express train trip from Warsaw to Moscow took twenty-six hours, without a change of trains.

One day in early April 1928, I went to the Soviet embassy and submitted a written request for an entry visa to see my son and Moscow as well. In 1928, the ambassador was named Voykov; he was later murdered by a criminal hand. When he approved my request, Voykov told me that he happened to be a personal friend of my son's and if I wanted, he could arrange the travel plans for me by telegraph within two weeks. I thanked him and told him that I was a teacher in a school and couldn't leave for a month. In early May, I got the entry visa. Three people were traveling from Warsaw. One was a Fräulein Press from Bialystok, a Bundist who taught in a Tsisho[1] school in Warsaw. She was going to see her younger sister who worked at the People's Committee for education. The second traveler was a member of Y.F.A., Mrs. Srebrik, whose husband was a partner in the Central book publishers in Warsaw (today he owns the Yizrael publishers in Tel Aviv). Like myself,

---

1. Yiddish acronym for Central Jewish School Organization, a network of secular, non-Zionist Yiddish schools, founded in Poland in 1921.

Mrs. Srebrik was going to see her son, an engineer, in Moscow. We left Warsaw at ten o'clock in the morning. The next day, at noon, we were in Moscow.

My fellow passengers were met at the railroad station by their relatives, but I hadn't sent a cable since I didn't want to disturb my son at work. Instead, I went to the address I had been given. When he came home after work, my son found me in the room where he lived with his wife and her older sister. But he also had another room in a house of the Comintern,[2] which he shared with the family of a Jewish doctor.

In addition to my son, my youngest brother Moshe was in Moscow, where he worked at a scientific institute. At that time, he and a friend were working on a major book, *The History of the Labor Movement in Russia*, and were gathering material from various libraries and scientific institutes. They did the work itself at home. My brother regularly sat long hours over his research,[3] like our grandfathers and great-grandfathers the rabbis (but with a distinction).[4] He was so steeped in his work that when he needed something to wear, his wife would bring his clothes right into his room. She was not Jewish but was the daughter of a middle-class farmer, and they had met at work in an office. She was such a good and dignified person that the whole house of Jewish tenants called her "the modest one." When I got to know her better, I told her that she was the first Christian I had gotten close to . . .

I was usually at my brother's until noon, first because my son and his wife were both busy in the office, and because my brother was, as they say, a wise Communist. With him, I could talk openly not only about the positive factors, but also about the negative phenomena that struck me at the time. And I did observe carefully because no one showed me around. I saw and heard everything on my own. My brother's wife had time (they didn't have any children); she was very familiar with Moscow, and went with me wherever I wanted to go. I also had a nephew living in Moscow—a son of my older brother, the "Mizrachi" member from Bialystok. That young man had a job and didn't want any problems; he would really have been more at home in his native Bialystok at his father's store . . . I also found many other relatives, friends, acquaintances, and even students in Moscow. For all of them, my coming to Moscow was an extraordinary event. Aside from my relatives in Mos-

---

2. An abbreviated term for the Communist International, or the Third International, an association of national Communist parties founded in 1919.
3. In the text in Hebrew, Torah v'avodah, literally doctrine or teaching and worship or work—a traditional formulation.
4. In the text in Hebrew, l'havdil, to distinguish, between the sacred and the profane.

cow, my youngest sister was living in the western Caucasus in Novorossiysk, a place that had been used for exile in tsarist times, but which was now a big suburb on the Black Sea.

In May 1928, I noticed a large building in Moscow that had a sign saying "Borochov Club." I started going there often to hear lectures and reports about Birobidzan.[5] The hall was always packed. But whom did that auditorium belong to? Did the audience have anything to do with Borochovian Zionism?[6] I couldn't find out: I didn't see anyone I knew there, and it wasn't proper to ask a complete stranger such a question.

My son's visitors were all people of another world. If I asked if someone were a Jew, I was answered with a friendly smile: "He is a person. We don't recognize any issues of race." As I said, my son was very busy, coming home from work at four or five o'clock in the afternoon. Everyone ate lunch in the cooperative kitchen of the institute or factory where he worked. Often my son was also busy in the evening, but he would find the time to chat with me. On Sunday, though, he gave me all his free time. During our intimate friendly conversations, he often said to me: Oh, in youth, if you and I had wanted to be social democrats, my life would have turned out differently.

My son never had a personal life, as it were. From 1905 to 1908, the best years of his youth, he lived far from home, first in Berlin and later in Switzerland, where he supported himself by making cigarettes and going hungry. From Switzerland he went back to Berlin in 1910, where he was better off economically but unhappy working as a clerk. He spent the war in a German internment camp. From 1918 on, he had been in Soviet Russia, clearing snow off the streets of Moscow and living on potato skins. Even in 1928, ten years later, he had a place in society but still had no personal life. His wife, a girl from a petit bourgeois home in Grodno, was married the first time as a gymnasium student to the only son of my younger sister. In 1914, when the war broke out, they had all fled to Petersburg. My sister, who suffered from heart disease, went to the Crimea to recover from pneumonia, but died on the way, in Feodosia. When her husband returned to Petersburg, he found their only son sick with typhus; and the boy died a few days later. At the funeral, the unfortunate man had a heart attack and died at the grave of his only son. Such a horrible tragedy could only have happened to one of my mama's "lucky" daughters . . .

---

5. Region in the Soviet Far East set aside by Stalin for Jewish colonization and to provide a counter to Zionism. The project was established in 1930 but was approved by 1928.
6. Ber Borochov (1881–1917), a Russian Zionist and Marxist theoretician of socialist Zionism.

The twenty-two-year-old widow then went from Petersburg to Moscow to be with her older sister, the wife of a doctor. She herself was a pharmacist. When my son came to Moscow and learned of that tragedy, he visited the two sisters and found work for the widow, who was then unemployed. In 1928, I found both sisters living together in one room; the older sister had separated from her bourgeois husband, but left her eight-year-old daughter with her rich father because of his better material conditions.

The six-story house on one of the main streets of Moscow, where the Lipshitz sisters lived, had once belonged to the big Wissotsky and Gotz Tea Company, but now a few hundred workers' families lived there. My apartment had seven rooms, but it was inhabited by seven families, most of them with children of various ages. In the common kitchen were fourteen Primus stoves. The tenants took turns cleaning the kitchen, bathroom, and other facilities. It was especially lively on Sunday, when the people were home and the kitchen smelled like a holiday with all fourteen stoves going at the same time. But relations among the tenants were comradely — in the fullest sense of the word.

Communists were the only friends who associated with my son. But I wanted to know how other circles of society were reacting to that unusual reshuffling and transformation of classes. I had enough time to visit friends and acquaintances. At the time, I was simply surprised at the upheaval that had occurred in the minds of most people in just ten years. I will present only a few facts to illustrate their attitude.

Among my several acquaintances in Moscow, I discovered a Gedenstein family. Mrs. Gedenstein had been a friend of my Bundist sister. In Warsaw, Mr. Gedenstein had owned one of the biggest fur stores on Bielenska Street. He transferred his big merchandise warehouse to Moscow just as the 1914 war broke out, and some time later, he went on doing business. When Russia started showing signs of revolution, all big fur stores moved to Leipzig, but Gedenstein stayed in Moscow. Shortly before the upheaval, he was offered a million dollars for his merchandise warehouse, but he didn't want to sell because he wouldn't make any profit. A few days later, all his merchandise was confiscated.

In 1928, I found them in a five-room apartment in Moscow. A Communist official lived in one room. The Gedensteins still had the Jewish servant they had brought from Warsaw in 1914. Aside from the fact that they were no longer capitalists, they had also lost their only son, who had volunteered for the Red Army and hadn't come back. How did such a Jew live in Moscow now?

His married daughter — a Communist — worked at making ties. She got cloth from one cooperative and supplied the finished goods to another one. The whole family, including the servant, worked on the ties. You worked, ran a house, and lived. I asked Mr. Gedenstein how he had adjusted, after his rich life in Warsaw, and he answered: "People want money mainly out of jealousy, because everybody has it. But when you know that nobody has it, in time that sense of jealousy atrophies completely." "But tell me the truth. We've known each other a long time," I said. "If you could now go back to Warsaw to your previous life, wouldn't you leave all this?" "No! Absolutely not. I have absolutely no yearning for that way of living. Look, we all work; we're healthy, cheerful, and contented."

I could present a whole series of facts to illustrate that my friends and relatives who had lived for years in Moscow back in tsarist times had adjusted easily to the new regime. They worked as businessmen in various areas and often told me they were happy that the government took care of things while they worked calmly at their professions and made a good living. But I want to be objective: There were also some dissatisfied people who kept arguing, "We remember the fish"[7] and demanded the tsarist "flesh pots." But their dissatisfaction was always about the new economic situation, never about intellectual or moral conditions.

The most positive aspect for me was that there was no antisemitism in Soviet Russia. The entire so-called "anti-religious" movement was mainly carried out among the Christians. If not for the *Yevsektsia*,[8] which consisted mainly of former Bundists, the schools for Jewish children in Soviet Russia possibly would have been operating in Hebrew. But most Jewish parents, who had their children's future careers in mind, did not send their children to Jewish schools, but to Russian ones. Privately, at home, they could study as much Hebrew as they wanted with the child. My friend Getterman, who had once run a *kheyder* in the Warsaw suburb of Praga, went to Moscow with his family at the outbreak of World War I in 1914; in 1928, he lived exclusively from giving private Hebrew lessons and even showed me how Jewish young men studied Talmud. I even heard a bar mitzvah talk in Hebrew from their thirteen-year-old boy, at a celebration with my Warsaw friends in Moscow. I also saw a lot of Jews, including students in their uniforms, coming out of the big Moscow Kor Shul at Simchas Toyre,

---

7. Complaint of Israelites as they wandered in the desert and waxed nostalgic over the conditions of their lives in Egypt. See Numbers 11:5. The citation is in Hebrew in the text.
8. The Jewish section of the Communist Party, which carried out repressive policy among the Jews.

not on Yom Kippur.[9] And I asked one of the worshippers: "How come so many Jews are in synagogue for Simchas Toyre?" He replied simply: "A great cantor was leading the service there today."

After everything I saw and heard during my brief stay in Soviet Russia, I did not conclude — as I have often heard in Poland and in the Land of Israel at various assemblies — that the Jews of Russia are lost to us. I said back then that a community of a few million Jews couldn't and wouldn't disappear, even in Soviet Russia. Just as it did not disappear in Babylon, where the Jewish collectivity even created the Babylonian Talmud. Nor did I doubt for one moment that when the three million Russian Jews were concentrated in one place, we would surely have an autonomous Jewish republic in the Soviet Union.

I spent three whole months in Moscow, and it was hard for me to be idle so long. Looking at the pace and enthusiasm at which people there were working, achieving, creating, and building a new world, I occasionally felt jealous that I simply couldn't find a place for myself. I went to the passport office, extended my stay for three months, and decided to go to Novorossiysk to see my youngest sister and her family; on the way back, I wanted to get off in Rostov to see a close friend from Warsaw, and from there to go to the Crimea to visit the Jewish colony.

In the passport office, I ran into a student of mine from Warsaw, who couldn't believe her eyes when she saw me in Moscow. (And now, unfortunately, I have to write about my trip back to Novorossiysk in 1928 — that is, fourteen years ago — now that it is early September 1942, and Hitler's bestial armies stand before the gates of that port city on the Black Sea.) I went from Moscow to Novorossiysk on an express train in two-and-a-half days. Only when you travel through the endless expanses of that gigantic land do you understand the "broad nature" of the Russian people and the epic character of Russian literature.

My youngest sister, once one of the most beautiful girls in Bialystok and a teacher in a Jewish gymnasium, had married a certain Bomash, a nephew of the Duma Deputy Dr. Bomash, a chemist by profession. In 1906, she went off with him to Petersburg, where he got a job in a chemical factory and she enrolled at a pedagogical institute. In 1909, they moved to Novorossiysk, where he was appointed manager of a mill named "Cement" — the same mill about which Gladkov later wrote his famous book, also called *Cement*. My brother-in-law was not only a good professional, but also one of the most popular educated chemists in general. Economically, they were doing well. They lived like real

9. That is, on a festival that was less central than the Day of Atonement.

bourgeois in a seven-room flat, richly furnished, with modern appliances, etc. Neither of them was a party member; and they had no interest in politics at all.

When I arrived in Novorossiysk in August 1928, eleven years after the Revolution, I was surprised to find my sister's family in the same seven-room flat, with two servants and the same bourgeois conditions that they had lived in earlier. My amazement increased when I saw that, one floor below them, lived seven workers' families. My sister did not live in Novorossiysk itself, but outside the city, near the cement works that had added the ending "Proletarian" to its name and where two thousand workers were employed. My sister and her family went into the city either by bus or by ferry.

There were five persons in my sister's family, for they had three children. My sister was teaching the two older children at home because their father did not want to send them to school with the workers' children. He felt this way for two reasons: First, the children wouldn't find a teacher who was as good as my sister; and second, he didn't want his children to study with the workers' children. My sister didn't like that arrangement. She thought they should adjust to the new regime. But he, as they say in Soviet Russia, was still stuck in the "engineering caste" from head to foot. My sister asked me to try to persuade him to let her send the children to the factory school. I told him purely and simply that he had no right to destroy his children, who weren't to blame for the fact that he couldn't change his attitude. They were born under the new order, felt comfortable with it, and wanted to be friendly with the workers' children. The whole atmosphere was stronger than his resistance, and in the end he created a horrible abyss between himself and his children. It wasn't easy for me. But he gave in and the children went off to the factory school for the new school year.

When I came back from Novorossiysk, I spent a week with my old friend from Warsaw and then went to see the Jewish colonies in the Crimea. On the way, I had the good fortune to meet a cousin of Chaim Weizmann and her husband, who were both working as engineers and on their vacation were traveling to the Jewish colony. We therefore traveled the entire way together. The Jewish colonies, known as the kolkhozn [collective farms], were located mostly on the steppe around Feodosia and Evfatoria, which once had been rich estates where no Jew could ever have set foot. But now, large areas were empty and vacant because, back in the time of Catherine, hundreds of thousands of Tatars had emigrated from there.

Nothing special was demanded from those who wanted to emigrate to the colony. The government gave the land for free, and you didn't need to drain any swamps or dig wells.[10] The "Joint"[11] built very comfortable houses with the most modern appliances, and the villages made an extraordinary impression. Grammar schools, clinics, and cooperatives were set up by the government. The people only had to work, transform themselves [into agricultural laborers], and adjust to the new collective life. People in the Jewish villages didn't complain of "anti-religious" agitation. In many villages, there were kosher slaughterers and *minyanim*[12] for worship. But for former shopkeepers, brokers, and merchants, mostly from the provinces, the transformation was hard.

When I asked how their lives were under the new conditions as Jewish farm laborers, I often got this reply: "We're not bad off, but if 'they' allowed a little trading, at least during the winter, for example, when work in the field is hard, things would be very good." Like our citrus grove owners in the Land of Israel, the Jewish colonists in the Crimea didn't want their children to become farm workers, and they sent them to study in the city. But soon, aside from general studies, there were compulsory studies of agriculture in all schools, coupled with practical farm work.

From my trip to Novorossiysk and the Jewish colonies in the Crimea, I returned to Moscow in a good mood, firmly convinced that antisemitism in the Soviet Union had been destroyed and that the issue of women was resolved, in the fullest sense of the word. But soon after, when I started talking about going back to Poland, my son grew very depressed. Externally, he remained calm, but I felt how hard it was for him to part from me. It wasn't easy for me either.

One evening, when we were at home alone, we talked sincerely and seriously. "Tell me, Mama," my son began, "why don't you want to stay with us? What is really pulling you back to antisemitic, fascist Poland? Your work? I'm convinced you have already given it up. Poor for almost forty years and suffering emotionally, maybe you have worked enough. I know that would be hard for you. I have mentioned your energy and ability to work as an example for our young female comrades. But there is a broad field of work for you in the culture here, and you can still achieve a lot and also find intellectual and emotional satisfaction. I have many concrete suggestions for you: Edit a Jewish journal that would be published by the carpenters' cooperative; teach Hebrew at the

---

10. A reference to the work facing pioneers in the Yishuv in Palestine.
11. Popular name for the American Joint Distribution Committee, an international aid organization, established in 1914.
12. The quorum of males necessary, in traditional Judaism, for public prayer.

university in the Oriental department; translate. In addition, you could get a pension in return for your twenty-five years as a Russian teacher in Poland. It doesn't make sense to me that you don't want to stay with us because of our new social order. If you see bad sides, you certainly understand as well as I do that ten years is a very short period of time for such upheavals, and that this is merely 'Communism on the way.' We are steeped in a rock-hard belief in the final victory of our reconstruction and liberation. As for your personal and family matters, I consider Soviet Russia more suitable for Comrade Birnbaum than fascist Poland. Sarah is doing well in Romania, and in time, when she and her husband become convinced that the dark, ultra-antisemitic Romania is no place for them, I will bring them here. I feel close to my dead sister's children. But Arye-Shmuel is in the Land of Israel, a great idealist, I hear, and has found his way and is probably satisfied. Shoshana is finishing gymnasium and going to France to study agronomy. I like that idea very much. I want to see her support herself, and later we'll try to bring her here, where there are precious few agronomists. I don't see anything to keep you from moving here."

"I have listened very carefully to what you say, my child," I replied. "It is just as hard for me to part from you as it is for you to part from me. But what can we do, since our ways part? In fact, we aren't political opponents, because I am just as much a sworn Socialist or Communist — the word *Communist* doesn't scare me at all — as you. But our work leads us (in your opinion) in opposite directions. I believe, however, that this is only temporary, a mere misunderstanding, that must finally be cleared up. The guilt for that lies with our 'Yevsektsia,' the former Bundists, who persuaded you that Zionism is a 'bourgeois' movement, whose mission is to drive the Arabs out of the Land of Israel with English weapons so that we can grab the Land for ourselves.

"That statement of the 'Yevsektsia' is wrong, from top to bottom. For me and the work force of the Land of Israel and the entire working Land of Israel in general, Zionism is as revolutionary a liberation movement as your socialist reconstruction, a movement striving to build its old-new home in the Land of Israel on just national and social bases, to make the Jewish people productive in the Diaspora and prepare them for a better life in their national home. For that ideal, as you know, my son, I have given almost forty years of work, and you don't trade a life-ideal overnight. In truth, all my life I have been a revolutionary, a socialist — even when I didn't fully understand those words because no one had prepared me for them or explained them to me. I came to them on my own through simple intuition. From my childhood on, my sympathies have always been on the side of the suffering and the oppressed. And aside from my Jewish upbringing, Zionism brought the awareness that, because they do not have their own land, our persecuted and tortured Jewish people are the most wretched of the wretched. For that I must devote all my energy and all my abilities, not to others but to our own Jewish liberation movement. *For a free and socialist Land of Israel.* It is not personal affairs or family matters that are making me return to Poland. My whole life, as you know, my son, I have been a social and political person, as they say. I have constantly been in public life; and now, at a time when my oppressed people are striving for national and political equality in the Diaspora, and for the reconstruction of their national home in the Land of Israel, shall I run away from the arena because I have a good chance to better myself? I am sure that as my son, you wouldn't think that to be right. I have always been an avowed supporter of a just socialist order throughout the world, not just in the Soviet Union, but also in the Land of Israel. But my highest wish is that the future socialist brotherhood of peoples will not only recognize the right of the Jewish people to its national home in the Land of Israel, but, in word and deed, will help realize our thousand-year-old ideal. As for your last question about the bad side I have noticed in your country, I will allow myself to say that there is one aspect, not of your program, but of your tactics, that is completely incomprehensible to me: the Communist treatment of those who think differently, and even of your own party members who have a different understanding, even only in terms of nuances, of your future revolutionary work."

After my son tried to justify those tactics with the excuse that Russia was surrounded by enemies on all sides and therefore had to be 100 percent hard on all external and internal opponents, we both tried, as much as possible, to control our feelings about having to part. Of course, I didn't know that two years later, in 1930, I would happen to translate Trotsky's memoirs, *My Life*, into Yiddish and lose forever the possibility of seeing my son again.

Shortly before my departure, my son came up with a pleasant surprise: "You will leave here as a pensioner," he said to me jokingly. "The Comintern is allowed to send eight thousand dollars of support abroad every month for close relatives. So I can send you twenty-five dollars every month, officially, through a bank in Warsaw. Just as you decided to send Shoshana to France to study agronomy, I at least want to relieve you of the burden of caring for her." For four years, from 1928 to 1932, I regularly got the promised pension from my son, until sending money out of the Soviet Union was forbidden.

Ten

Aliyah

I returned to Warsaw at the end of October and immediately went back to work in the secretariat of the Jewish women's association. How petty and insignificant did that activity now seem to me in comparison to the grandiose work of building socialism in the Soviet Union. I was gripped by a horrible envy, and was constantly tormented with the thought of the bitter fate of our landless people. The world is big, I thought, but for us there is no place on it.

Materially, I wasn't badly off. In May 1929, my granddaughter Shoshana completed middle school and at the end of August left for Nancy to study agronomy. Naturally, it wasn't easy for me to part from her. But I had no choice because no Jews were allowed to study at the agronomic institute in Warsaw. At that time, I was living in a room with my younger sister, the dentist. Both of us would leave in the morning for work, not returning until evening. I would usually get home very late, only to sleep, because my own apartment was the site of the Y.F.A. women's association.

During the six months I was in the Soviet Union, I was completely cut off from events in Jewish society in Poland in general, and from the Zionist world in particular. Now and then my son brought me the bulletins he got from the PKP (Palestine Communist Party), but they were hardly satisfying. I soon caught up, however, with what was going on in Warsaw in various areas.

Meanwhile, in the Land of Israel, winds were starting to blow. Between 1927 and 1929 the economic situation in the Land improved fundamentally, unemployment almost disappeared, people started getting certificates again as pioneers, after having suffered terribly when aliyah was prohibited. Aside from the national settlement, private enterprises also increased sharply. The economic depression and the crisis were over, and hopeful prospects for the near future emerged. The new hard-tested Land of Israel had withstood the assault and had shown its ability to resist. Encouraged and heartened, a sufficiently large group of delegates went to the Sixteenth Congress in Zurich between July 28 and August 14, 1929. That Congress, which instituted the expanded Jewish Agency, was in general well attended.[1]

How did the political and economic situation of the Jews in Poland look in 1929–1930, four years after Pilsudski's May upheaval,[2] which we had hoped would grant our just demands? In fact, nothing changed. There was the same Sejm with its rightist majority, an "Endeks"[3] spirit, its parliamentary shortsightedness, and its total impotence. With regard to less important issues, the situation supposedly improved. The futile and disturbing persecution did stop; but we were told to be patient and wait, which was the same thing we had heard for years. But when we showed signs of dissatisfaction, we were immediately declared enemies of the state, just as before the upheaval.

The economic situation of the Jews had not improved at all. At first glance, it seemed as though economic antisemitism would be destroyed, and that the special tax thumbscrews for the Jews would be canceled. That's what the merchants hoped, especially the prosperous ones, right after the upheaval. Initially the big merchants and industrialists were treated differently, but this situation did not last for long. The Jewish masses still suffered under the heavy burden of ever-increasing taxes, under the burden of ruinous etatism. The struggle against the hooliganish, openly antisemitic Endeks, along with the supposedly more humanistic treatment of Jews by other authorities, could not alleviate the bitterness of the unemployed people who had no livelihood and who had been maliciously pushed out of their economic positions. The new rulers did just as little to satisfy the needs of the impoverished masses as their predecessors. Indeed, they complained about those who reminded them of their duty. They felt offended that people didn't rely

---

1. The Jewish Agency was expanded in 1929 to include non-Zionists who supported the Jewish presence in Palestine.
2. Jozef Pilsudski (1867–1935), Polish political leader, who seized power in independent Poland in 1926.
3. A reference to the Endecja, a right-wing nationalist and anti-Semitic party established in 1897, familiarly referred to as the "Endeks."

on their mercy and couldn't wait until governmental leaders regulated their governmental affairs and had time for the demands of the national minorities. Those who could not and would not wait were considered enemies of the government. Thus they frightened the masses and tried to corrupt them by undermining their belief in their leaders, who went into the opposition as soon as they realized the transparent intentions of those who won in the May upheaval.

My personal situation had entirely stabilized during those few years. I now lived solely for my duties, and the only worthwhile content of my life was my work. Before 1929–1930, our Y.F.A. association had increased greatly in membership. The number of women's organizations, not only in Congress Poland but also in the eastern areas, had constantly increased. Because of the government subsidy, our institutions in Warsaw developed so much that we had to expand the office and move to a big building with modern furnishings, where we concentrated all our cultural and educational institutions.

For years, our Y.F.A. organization — aside from Y.A.F., the women's section of the Bund — was the only large Jewish national women's organization in Poland. Our association had joined WIZO right after it was established, in 1920, participated actively in all its campaigns, attended its international conferences, and helped in its propaganda work in Yiddish-speaking countries. Therefore, there was no official WIZO section in Poland. Not until 1930 did Dr. Salome Levitte, after a visit to the Land of Israel, establish a WIZO association in Warsaw, which carried out its activity exclusively among rich Jewish women.

After almost two years of hard work, I took a vacation in June 1930 and went to Bucharest to see my daughter and her family. My granddaughter Shoshana, studying in Nancy, also came along, and we spent a few weeks in Moldavia, in a Romanian village called Korka, near the city of Piotra-Niametz, where Zvi had built a bridge over the Bistritsa River, near Zahorne. A Jewish family still ran the grocery store in that village. Like many areas in Romania, the place was enchanting. The village was in a valley, surrounded on all sides by enormous mountains that were covered with thick primeval forests. When it was very hot down in the valley, in the wooded mountains you forgot it was summer, and the air there, just as in the town of Meron,[4] felt delightful.

In September, right after the vacation, my granddaughter went back to school in Nancy. Parting was again hard for both of us. As usual,

---

4. A village in the hills of the Galilee, associated with the Talmudic Rabbi Simeon bar Yohai. It is a pilgrimage site.

I tried hard to control myself; but my Shoshana couldn't. More than once, she asked me with tears in her eyes: "Why, Bobbe, don't I have a home like all my friends? I almost didn't know my mother, and my father is like a stranger. In Warsaw, back then, with you, I didn't feel how miserable I was; abroad, it is simply unbearable. So I want to finish school as fast as possible and then the two of us will go to the Land of Israel. Arye-Shmuel is also there, and we'll be together again. We'll work, Bobbe, and you can rest."

That summer in Bucharest with my daughter and her husband, I noticed how the environment can have an influence, especially on a child. Neither of the adults belonged to any political party. Their friends were Romanian engineers, his colleagues and bosses, and the Jewish haute-bourgeoisie, manufacturers and industrialists, who came to do "business," and whom they had met at the house of Zvi's uncle, the industrialist. The uncle had died in the meantime, and Zvi's mother had gone back to Lódz. That whole group had practically no interest in the Jewish liberation movement; at most they contributed to the National Fund. For them, Romania was the Promised Land. Since they lived in a country that was only three days away from the Land of Israel, they traveled there for pleasure, but didn't buy a single dunam of land or make even the most minimal investment there. It never occurred to them that a time might come when they would have to flee from the Romanian "Paradise."

Looking at the lifestyle of those Jews, I kept regretting that my daughter had gotten into that dark, antisemitic Romania, where the environment was devouring her. The worst thing for me was that their four-year-old daughter Hemdah, who for two years couldn't fall asleep except to the Hebrew song "Come here, my little girl" — now told me that she was not a Jewish child. I responded very seriously: "If you are not a Jewish child, you are not my granddaughter and I am not your grandma. We are all Jews: I, your mother, your father, and you too." I simply asked my daughter: "How could your environment have devoured you so much in such a short time?"

I stayed in Bucharest through the holidays and in early October, on my return to Warsaw, once again plunged into the work of the Y.F.A. secretariat. A short time before, I had received the opportunity to translate Trotsky's memoirs, My Life. The work was urgent and I did it in six weeks, receiving a fee of 1,250 Polish zlotys for the translation. I was so steeped in that work that I felt as if I personally had gone through all his experiences. But despite the great intellectual satisfaction, I would have given it all up if I thought for one moment that it would prevent me from seeing my only son again. It is common sense that, as a professional translator, unaffiliated with the Communist movement, I had no intention of promoting Trotsky. I could just as easily have translated a book by Stalin. But no arguments helped, and the fact could not be changed.

In late April 1932, I decided to take a long leave to spend the summer vacation with my daughter in Romania, and then go to Moscow to see my son. In early May, just before I left for Romania, I requested an entry visa to Moscow at the Soviet consulate. It usually took about two months to get an answer, precisely the time I would be spending with my daughter. In 1932, my daughter wasn't living in Bucharest, but in Kishinev, where her husband had gotten a major government contract. I was very happy to spend the summer in a city with a large Jewish population, most of them Zionists, and where people spoke Russian.

Eighty thousand Jews lived in Kishinev, out of a total population of about 120,000. The other 40,000 were Moldavans, Russians, Armenians, and a few Romanians. The great majority favored the Soviet Union and were waiting for a plebiscite to solve the Bessarabian issue.[5] The Zionist Organization in Kishinev was very active, both politically and culturally, and worked vigorously for the Jewish National Fund. The movement was led by popular veteran Zionists. There was also an energetic WIZO chapter led by my first student, Masha Berger, now one of the Zionist activists in Tel Aviv.

When I came to Kishinev, my daughter's family was automatically drawn into the Zionist milieu. By chance, my younger sister Dina Shapiro came from Haifa to see me. She loved the Land of Israel so much that she tried to persuade not only her friends and relatives, but also everyone she met, to come there.

My daughter's six-year-old child attended a Romanian school, but in the summer we went to Bugatz, a spa on the shores of the Black Sea, quite close to the Russian border, where we lived with a Russian family. In the evening, we would see the illuminated village houses on the other side of the border. The main occupation of the Bugatz population was fishing, but they also had big vineyards. Not far from Bugatz was the famous spa of Shavo, where people suffering from lung ailments were sent for a special grape-cure. The population of Shavo consisted of German- and French-speaking Swiss. Bessarabia is an unusually fertile

---

5. To which state the territory of Bessarabia, located between Romania and the USSR should belong. The USSR held sovereignty until 1940.

land; not only rich in produce, but blessed with an abundance of vegetables, fruit, and dairy products. At that time, there really was a flood of food. Even our Jewish group became more sated there in food than in learning. There wasn't even a piece of black bread there. When we were amazed by this, the people joked: "Here, we eat Challah all week long . . . " But that wasn't all. Bessarabia, like Egypt in the Bible, also had the big "flesh pot" and the right "fish." I still recall one incident in the sea spa of Bugatz: One fine morning, the whole seashore for miles was covered with a mountain of all kinds of fish, making it impossible to walk on the beach. The local residents told us that this happened frequently. The strong tides, driven by the wind, cast enormous masses of fish of all sizes, from small pilchards to ten-kilo flounders, onto the shore. Hundreds of carts came from the nearby city of Ackerman and they worked until late in the evening to clear the beach of the flood of fish.

When I returned from Bugatz to Kishinev, I found a categorical refusal from the Soviet consulate, forwarded by my sister from Warsaw. I would not receive an entry visa to Moscow. No reasons were given. A second request could not be submitted prior to one year. Meanwhile, my sister from Haifa went to Warsaw and Bialystok for the holidays, to see our other sister and brother. After the Moscow refusal, my daughter and her husband wouldn't let me go so I stayed in Kishinev.

My little granddaughter, seven-year-old Hemdah, went back to the Romanian school. But at home, she was now not only in a Jewish milieu, but even a Zionist one. At that time, Dr. Emanuel Elshvanger visited Kishinev on behalf of the Jewish National Fund, and was a frequent guest in our home. At the same time, Ze'ev Jabotinsky of blessed memory also came to Kishinev, so the city was lively, with people going from one meeting to another. Heated discussions were conducted in houses; some of our friends were Revisionists. Hemdah listened to the discussions in our home, and once said to me: "You know, Bobbe, I can already be a Revisionist, I can already fight." That was how, simply and coherently, she comprehended the essence of Revisionism.

One day she came home from school excited, whispered with her mother in another room, and didn't say anything to me. Later my daughter told me that Hemdah asked her not to tell Bobbe that she had attended a class on religion. The teacher was a Russian priest who made the children kneel, and they didn't want to go back to that class again. The next day, my daughter went to the school, said that they were Jews, and asked that her child be released from the religion class. Because of that, the other Jewish children were also released from the Christian religious classes they had all been forced to attend.

Since I was staying in Kishinev for the winter, I started teaching little Hemdah Hebrew. My daughter didn't object, but my son-in-law argued that Hemdah had a mishmash of four European languages in her childish head, and he didn't think I should confuse her with a fifth, especially not an Oriental tongue. I replied that I wouldn't advise him about his building, and he shouldn't advise me in pedagogical matters. To tell the truth, I was quite satisfied with the result of my experiment. The four languages Hemdah already spoke — Russian, Polish, Romanian, and German — had absolutely nothing to do with Hebrew. But remarkably, from the very first lesson, the child was so interested and studied so diligently and so easily that she could hardly wait until the next lesson. During the winter, she became a real scholar; but she especially loved the language itself. Naturally, you can learn Hebrew only in connection with the Land of Israel, and it wasn't long before she started developing a strong love for the Land of Israel as well, and was constantly fantasizing about it.

The sudden catastrophe in 1933 that struck the Jews of Germany like a thunderclap and knocked out their generations-long illusions of emancipation and assimilation resonated among the Jews of many other countries. A special terror fell on the Jews of Romania. If such horrors could take place in cultured Germany, what could you expect from dark Romania? And that terror was not in vain, as the foreign citizens soon felt. Exiles and persecutions increased, and more foreigners were deported every day. At the end of winter, shortly before I returned to Warsaw, my children also felt uneasy. People weren't sure of what the next day would bring. To tell the truth, I was also impatient for them to get out of "kindly" Romania. Foreigners would clearly be the first to leave, and it was only a question of time, of how long they could stay there.

Right after Pesach, I left Kishinev. Before I left, a Hebrew teacher was hired to take Hemdah and another little girl for walks for two hours, in addition to their lessons, so they could practice the Hebrew language together. I left with a heavy heart, and my children felt the same.

Fortunately, from 1933 to 1935 our movement increased greatly, and immigration to the Land of Israel grew by more than 100,000 Jews, including 27,000 from Germany alone. As for the Warsaw Palestine Office, the phrase "renew our days as of old"[6] came true. The work

---

6. From the liturgy, recited when the Torah is returned to the ark.

proceeded at a fast pace. Once again, the office occupied both floors in one of the biggest buildings on Krolewska Street, and once again seventy-five clerks were employed. As soon as I got off the train, I went back to my job, plunging into work, and I naturally didn't imagine that a few new harsh blows were in store for me.

In early 1934, my children were still in Bucharest. As I said, they were ready to leave, but they couldn't decide where to go. The Land of Israel was the issue, and for a year, all our correspondence dealt with that matter. My closest friends in Warsaw, both on the left and on the right, all warned me: "Puah, don't give any advice. Don't assume such a responsibility. Let them go where they want to." This was said by popular leaders of the movement, when the Land of Israel was flourishing, and a building engineer with many years of experience was in demand.

It was hard for me. As an honest person, I had advice for them. This is what I wrote to them: "If I were a thirty-six-year-old engineer who didn't belong to any political movement and was only looking for work as a 'specialist,' I would go to the Soviet Union, simply because there is a lot of work there for any capable, able-bodied professional. But since you are three days away from the Land of Israel, here is my advice. I think that Zvi should go there alone as a tourist, and there he will see if he prefers to stay or not." They took my advice. Zvi took leave for six weeks and, in early February 1934, he went to the Land of Israel as a tourist. Later he admitted to me that his eight-year-old Hemdah influenced his decision to go there, because she kept pestering him and claiming that she wouldn't go to any other country.

Shortly before he left, Hemdah became ill, but he didn't want to postpone his trip, and my daughter remained alone with the sick child. All those close to me in Warsaw knew this; the secret was kept only from me. It later turned out that the Kishinev professor had made a wrong diagnosis and that she had nothing more than whooping cough.

On the ship, Zvi met an old building engineer from Galicia and before they even saw the Land of Israel, the two of them decided not to look for any job, but to open a building company together. Zvi landed in Haifa, where my sister Dina Shapiro and her family lived. Her earlier visit to Kishinev was another one of the positive factors in his decision to go to the Land of Israel.

In the Palestine Office, I learned that Zvi's partner was an honest man. That experiment failed, however, and cost my son-in-law a lot of money. But they were neither the first not the last to fail. It was our administration at the time that was to blame for such failures. For years there was not a single information office in the Land of Israel to give the new immigrants from all classes correct information about labor conditions and industrial possibilities. Even now, people who have been in the country for years say that fifteen or twenty years ago, money was lying around in the streets. You could buy big tracts of land for nothing, and now these are built up as city centers. But as I said, there was no office to instruct the new immigrants and show them what they had to do.

When his first experiment failed, Zvi got a job in Haifa with a respectable building company; and my brother-in-law, Zerah Birnbaum of Petah Tikvah, helped him get his legal papers. He moved into a room at my sister Dina's flat, and submitted a request to bring his wife and child. But the doctor in Kishinev advised my daughter not to travel to the Land of Israel with the child during the summer. We rented an apartment in Otwock, and Sarah and Hemdah came to Poland in early May. Zvi's mother also came from Lódz to spend the summer with us. Hemdah improved and soon started studying Hebrew with a teacher friend of mine, who lived in Otwock and was about to leave for the Land of Israel with his family. At seven in the morning, I would go to work in the office, and at five in the afternoon would come back to Otwock. At the end of the summer, my companion Birnbaum also decided to visit his brother in Petah Tikvah, on a tourist visa. Naturally, none of imagined that fate was preparing another sad surprise for us, a harsh and bitter blow.

One Saturday afternoon, Birnbaum said he didn't feel well and wanted to go to the doctor in Warsaw who had been treating him for a long time. From there, he was taken to a private clinic of one of the best Warsaw specialists, Dr. Indelman, who decided that he had to have an operation, even though his heart was weak. He had the operation. For a few weeks, he suffered horrible torments, and he died of a heart embolism on August 15, 1934. Our daughter, who never left his bedside the whole three weeks, was shattered by that blow, like all of us. She stayed in Otwock through Sukes. In October, she got the necessary papers from her husband and left for the Land of Israel, where she lived in two rooms in my sister's flat in Haifa. Sarah soon got a job in city hall, and nine-year-old Hemdah was in the fifth grade of grammar school. She attended that school for only a short time because they sent her to boarding school in Mishmar Ha-Emek. My older granddaughter, Shoshana Elshvanger, had finished her course in agronomy in Nancy, and had immigrated to the Land of Israel in early summer 1933, a year before our daughter and son-in-law.

After a year, I submitted my second request to the Soviet consulate for an entry visa to Moscow, and at the end of June, was turned down, with no explanation. Then I wrote my son to find out what sin I had committed to be denied a chance to see him once in five years. Yud-Ber answered at once, sneaking into a Russian letter a few words in Yiddish — this is because of "Leybele's translation."[7] He also wrote that he was now so busy that he had to interrupt our correspondence and would talk to me twice a month by telephone. I understood that because of my "great sin," he was not comfortable writing to me. Every two weeks, I was informed by the Warsaw Central Telephone Office that at ten in the evening, I would receive a phone call from Moscow. And from 1933 to 1935, two years in all, we didn't correspond in writing, but now and then, I got personal regards from him.

I was so busy, especially in the Palestine Office in those years of the great immigration, 1933–1935, that there weren't enough hours in the day. But in spite of everything, I decided that now was the time for me to go to the Land of Israel. Neither of my individualist grandchildren, Arye-Shmuel and Shoshana, could adjust to collective life and were suffering there. I was still able-bodied, I thought, and could get a job and they would have a home once again. Unfortunately, my trip was delayed. Perhaps if I had gone earlier, I might have warded off the dreadful blow that cruel fate had in store for me.

One morning, in early April 1935, one of my close friends, Mrs. Shek, came into the Palestine Office, to the room where I was sitting at my desk. She waved at me from afar and sat down at my colleague's desk. Before she left, she came to me, took my hand, and said: "My sympathies for your misfortune in the Land of Israel." Terrified, I jumped out of my chair. I didn't know what else had happened to me. They took me into the doctor's room, comforted me, and so on. I found out that my grandson Arye-Shmuel had died in Hadassah hospital in Jerusalem after two days of pneumonia. He had become sick during his last job at the Dead Sea, worked until the last minute, with a temperature of 104 degrees, until he passed out. He was taken to Hadassah Hospital, where he expired the next morning. He had come to the Land of Israel at the age of sixteen and a half, he drained the swamps for eleven years, and at the age of twenty-seven, he died.

And I survived that. I stayed on the sofa in the doctor's room for a while. I got up and went back to work. Everybody in the office had known about it, but had hidden the newspapers. My whole family knew it, too. My sister had torn out the announcement from the newspaper in

---

7. Leybele was the Yiddish diminutive of Leon, Trotsky's first name.

our home. As usual, I was the last to know. Before we went to sleep that night, I said to my sister: "Tsirel, don't be afraid if you have to take me to a lunatic asylum tomorrow morning." I remained alive, even sane, and in the morning, I went to work as usual. I asked comrade Kashtan to write to the Jewish Agency in Jerusalem to send me an immigration permit from my son-in-law Zvi Cohen. I soon received permission to immigrate, and on the eve of Passover, April 17, 1935, I was in Haifa, in the home of my children and my sister Dina Shapiro.

When I learned of my misfortune, I wrote my son in Moscow that I was going to the Land of Israel and two years later, I got a letter from him saying: "I am glad and offended at the same time that you are going to Palestine. I am glad that you are going to the land for which you have given your life. I am offended because here with us, you would have lived a quieter and more interesting life."

Since then, from 1935 to 1942, for the seven and a half years that I have been in the Land, I have not received another letter from him. But a few times, I have had written regards from him, not directly, but through my brother's son, the writer Mark Rakovsky, and recently also from my brother's daughter, who is now in Oltaiski Krai, in the city of Bisk. She said that my son was now in the capital of Oltaiski Krai in Korneul — Siberia — and that she would try to find him and send me his address.

When I started preparing for my trip to the Land of Israel, it never occurred to me that I wouldn't get any work in the Land. The only person who doubted that was the director of the Palestine Office, Comrade Shafar. But he didn't tell me this directly, only in general, to prevent me from immigrating: "Why are you running, Comrade Rakovsky?" he argued with me. "We need you here, you have a good job, you'll manage." When I talked to Comrade Grünbaum about a job in Jerusalem, he told me: "For you, Comrade Rakovsky, I will do all I can." Shortly before my departure, Comrade Barlas was also in Warsaw and he told me: "Don't worry about work, I have prepared a very suitable job for you in the archives of the Zionist organization. Your work there is a continuation of your work here in Warsaw. You haven't been rejected. You are leaving because you are immigrating to the Land of Israel, and you haven't lost your right to work there."

It was very hard for me to leave my younger sister Tsirel, who had resigned from the Bund after the Russian Revolution. She, too, took my departure very hard. Even though we had been avowed political opponents for years, my sister had lived in my home from 1898 to 1905. Later, from 1927 to 1935, we lived in the same room for eight years. In general, we were so close intellectually, understood each other so well, and experienced so much together that there was nothing we wouldn't do for each other. A dentist by profession, my sister Tsirel was very successful, beautiful, smart, capable, unusually energetic, and exciting. But her tragic family life had a strong impact on her, and it broke her spirit. In April 1935, when I left Poland for the Land of Israel, she stayed behind in Warsaw, waiting for her two grown daughters to take her to Paris.

During the years 1935–1939, that is, up to the outbreak of the war, I often got letters from my sister. In November 1939, I got another letter from her, not from Warsaw, but from Bialystok. She wrote that she had managed to flee to Bialystok a few days before the German invasion. For the time being, she was with our brother and already had found work as a dentist. Throughout 1940, we corresponded almost regularly. In late summer 1941, I got the last letter from my sister asking me to find out if her children were still in Paris, because she had now been cut off from them completely. I wrote to an old address and got an answer from her older daughter that they had stayed where they were. I immediately forwarded that letter to her at my brother's address in Bialystok. But to this day, I have not gotten any letters from Tsirel. Of course, I imagine the worst because I can't conceive of any other reason why she wouldn't write to me.

On April 17, 1935, on the eve of Passover — as I said — after fifteen years, I arrived in the Land of Israel for the second time. My nerves were shattered by my personal tragedies and I felt that, as always, I had to find consolation only in my work.

On the first day after the beginning of the Passover holiday, I went off to Jerusalem, where I hoped to get a job. Naturally, I went first to my old friends from Warsaw who had assured me that I would find work. But my disappointment and bitterness grew not by the day, but by the hour, as soon as I started knocking on the doors of our leaders and power brokers. Even my most devoted friends didn't treat me properly as before. They merely told me that I wasn't hired because I had been born too soon. That is, because of my age.

I had no idea that what prevailed in the highest institutions of our new national home was not the Jewish ethic, but benighted bureaucracy; that our spokesmen were still stuck in the period of the Giving-of-the-Torah,[8] when old people were flung off high cliffs. It was hard for me to imagine that a healthy, energetic, able-bodied person who could

---

8. That is, in the ancient past.

still be useful wouldn't be given work merely because, as an older person, he might be sick in half a year and need a pension; such "logical" reasons simply cannot be grasped by flesh and blood. And the decision not to give me a job for the *eight* pounds a month I was to get, was made by one single person.

After many futile interventions by my friends — both on the right and on the left — I appealed directly to the person himself. He listened to me and answered officiously that I should wait patiently until after the Congress (that was right before the Nineteenth Congress in Lucerne). As a veteran teacher, I naturally didn't lack patience. I waited. Some time after the Congress, when I went back to his office, he informed me tersely that he had to watch the budget, given the present financial situation of the Jewish Agency, and could not hire any new officials. How could he burden the budget of the Jewish Agency with *eight* whole pounds a month?

After the failure in the Jewish Agency, I went to Tel Aviv to my old comrades, who had been former Zeirei Zion party members in Poland. I didn't have to sit in the corridor at the door of their offices for an hour before I got an interview. Here was the same bureaucracy, but with a green background. But with them, I could at least talk as with friends, and demanded work in one of the Mapai or Histadrut institutions, where they had recently hired several young comrades, who had worked with me in the Palestine Office.

That I, the "grandma" in the Zionist movement and the initiator of the Zionist women's movement in Poland — despite my good health, my energy, and my ability to work — should not be able to get a job in the Land of Israel solely because of the "sin" of my age, is not merely a bankruptcy of my personal life of work and struggle, but also a bankruptcy of all the collaboration of Jewish women in our national and social liberation movement. All negotiations were futile. I didn't get a job.

More than my own personal situation, I worried about the condition of my lonely granddaughter, Shoshana Elshvanger. After she had adjusted to the climate, she returned to Haifa from Jerusalem. Despite all my cares, I couldn't persuade her to go to a kibbutz, where she would have the surest chances of working as an agronomist. She thought she should work until noon as a maid and seamstress. I considered the futility of such employment and made her the following proposal: "I am willing to support you to study either clerical work or dressmaking, decide which you prefer. I won't pressure you, but I want you to have a profession, because economic independence is the most important fac-

tor for the liberation of women. You devoted almost four years to studying agronomy, the most suitable thing for the Land of Israel. And right
after the first, by chance unsuccessful, experience in that field, you
decided to throw that profession away. So you have to start all over
again and learn another profession."

It wasn't easy for me to persuade her, but she finally gave in and
trained as a seamstress in one of the finest stores of Haifa. With a
diploma in agronomy, she now sewed clothes for the ladies in the Jewish
city of Tel Aviv. Maybe she is right . . .

After I arranged things for her, I went back to Jerusalem, where I
had lived during the year of my first stay in the Land of Israel, and to
which I was also now drawn. By chance, my younger brother also lives
in Jerusalem, the one who had lived in Berlin for a few years and had
managed to get to the Land of Israel, along with his wife, in early 1933.
Both of them have good professions: He is a pharmacist and she is a
beautician. In Jerusalem, they opened a chemical laboratory and a
beauty salon and, as they say in America, they make a living. And as we
know, all cosmetics come from the Orient and were always in demand
among Jewish women, even at the time of the Prophet Isaiah.

I got a temporary roof over my head in 1935 with my brother, and
that is the main thing. And according to the latest theories of modern
medicine, old people shouldn't eat much; they should leave the table
not fully sated. Fortunately, I still had some money. I lived like that for
the year during which I was completely unemployed. And, as I said, I
also helped my granddaughter learn a new trade. I was bitter and upset
at human injustice. But these factors had little impact on my general
mood; frequently in a life that has been so rich in suffering, I have been
poor and have always reacted to that coolly, never losing heart.

One day, my old friend from Warsaw, the Hebrew writer Mrs. Dvora
Lochover, brought me an article from the Jewish National Fund to
translate from Hebrew to Yiddish. She told me: "Last night, I told
Comrade N. Bistritski that you have been here in the Land for more
than half a year and still don't have a job, even though they promised
you in Warsaw that you could continue working as an official in the
Palestine Office. Comrade Bistritski was very much offended by that
and remarked that it was not only unfair, but was also foolish not to use
the abilities of Comrade Puah Rakovsky as a translator of our propaganda into Yiddish for the Diaspora. Give her this article and tell
Comade Rakovsky, in my name, that I guarantee her all the translation
work from our Jewish National Fund propaganda into Yiddish."

Saying a blessing[9] over my first Yiddish translation in the Land of Israel, I delivered the article to Comrade Bistritski and got my first fee — I was paid not by the article, but by the line — and only then did I realize that if I hadn't been so honest, I could have avoided the struggle for a job as a "clerk" and gotten work immediately as a translator. Why hadn't I done that from the beginning? I didn't do it simply because there were chauvinistic anti-Yiddishists in the Land of Israel who knew of my outspoken positive position on our popular language, and I didn't want to give them an opportunity to say that Comrade Puah Rakovsky came to the Land of Israel to spread the Yiddish language.

Encouraged by Comrade Bistritski, I went to the Keren Hayesod office, to see Comrade Leyb Yaffe. He had already heard of the whole discussion about my position and naturally was very upset. He replied immediately to my request for Yiddish translations: "With pleasure, Comrade Rakovsky, will I give you all the Yiddish translations of the National Fund, and will make sure you get work for the Jewish Agency, too." And he gave me several articles to translate. A few days later, I got a letter from Dr. Leyterbukh asking me to come to the propaganda department of the Jewish Agency; in short, I regularly got work from all three institutions. My personal issue was thus solved, both economically and emotionally.

After a few months, since they were pleased with my work and especially impressed by my precision, I proposed to Comrade Grünbaum that all three institutions together should give me a regular position as a translator, with a fixed monthly salary.

I was soon informed that the chairmen of all three institutions agreed to appoint me as a translator with a salary of seven pounds a month.

Under those conditions, I have worked intensively for five years. There was always too much work to do in all three institutions. But at the outbreak of the war in 1939, that written propaganda for the Diaspora, of the Jewish Agency and the two Funds, ceased almost completely.

But I was not dismissed.

---

9. The blessing is the "sheheheyanu," "who has kept us alive to see this day."

INDEX

Paula E. Hyman is the Lucy Moses Professor of Modern Jewish History at Yale University. Among her many publications are *The Jewish Woman in America* (with co-authors Sonya Michel and Charlotte Baum) and *Gender and Assimilation in Modern Jewish History*. She is co-editor (with Deborah Dash Moore) of *Jewish Women in America: An Historical Encyclopedia*, which won the Dartmouth Medal of the American Librarians Association.

❖

Barbara Harshav's translations include *A Surplus of Memory* by Yitzhak Zuckerman, *Memoirs of a Warsaw Ghetto Fighter* by Simha Rotem, and *Only Yesterday* by S. Y. Agnon.

❖